# THE CUSTODY REVOLUTION

## THE FATHER FACTOR AND THE MOTHERHOOD MYSTIQUE

**RICHARD A. WARSHAK, Ph.D.**

POSEIDON PRESS

New York London Toronto Sydney Tokyo Singapore

**Poseidon Press**
Simon & Schuster Building
Rockefeller Center
1230 Avenue of the Americas
New York, New York 10020

Designed by Pei Loi Koay
Manufactured in the United States of America

1 3 5 7 9 10 8 6 4 2

Library of Congress Cataloging-in-Publication Data

Warshak, Richard Ades, date.
The custody revolution : the father factor and the motherhood
mystique / Richard A. Warshak.
p.   cm.
Includes bibliographical references (p. 253) and index.
1. Divorce—United States—Psychological aspects.   2. Custody of
children—United States—Psychological aspects.   3. Children of
divorced parents—United States—Psychology.   4. Parent and child—
United States.   5. Fatherhood—United States—Psychological
aspects.   6. Motherhood—United States—Psychological aspects.
I. Title.
HQ834.W38   1992
306.89—dc20                                                92-19468
                                                               CIP

ISBN: 0-671-74694-4

*In loving memory of my father,*
*Henry L. Warshak*

*and to my mother,*
*Raye Ades Warshak*

*and my wife,*
*Sandra L. Warshak*

# ACKNOWLEDGMENTS

I am grateful to the many families—those who participated in research projects and those who sought my professional assistance over the years—for all that they have taught me about the impact of divorce. I hope they will be gratified to know that what has been learned through their struggles may help others traverse the "psychological minefields" of divorce with minimal injury. Some of their stories are told in these pages. To preserve privacy I have changed names and certain identifying details, while retaining the essence of their experiences.

Ethel Weiss-Shed, Ph.D., and Gertrude Schmeidler, Ph.D., instilled in me a respect for, and commitment to, methodologically rigorous psychological research. Equally important, their warmth, personal interest, and vote of confidence, as I embarked on my graduate education, were and are deeply appreciated. One of the goals of this book is to offer the reader advice that is backed up by scientific research. This would not be possible without the dedicated work of a cadre of researchers, many of whom are listed in the reference notes. Their investigations continue to provide answers to the questions addressed in these pages.

The specific direction of my own studies in child custody was set by John Santrock, Ph.D. Mentor, collaborator, and now colleague, Dr. Santrock insisted on the highest research standards and state-of-the-art techniques. As a result, our research has received the respect of the professional and scientific community. The Hogg Foundation of Texas recognized the importance of studying child custody and awarded a grant to get our project started. They are not, however, responsible for the opinions expressed in this book.

William Tooley, M.D., deserves special thanks for computer assistance and years of friendship. He gave generously of his time and expertise to resurrect portions of the manuscript that seemed to have been erased from

# ACKNOWLEDGMENTS

existence by a temperamental computer, and to ensure that such a catastrophe never recurs. I am grateful to Sandra Woodford, who, through her dedicated and competent management of myriad administrative details, has allowed me more time and energy for my writing. For Sunday sustenance and consultation as an on-call grammarian I am indebted to my mother-in-law, Allie Brock. Many other relatives and friends provided ongoing encouragement during the long gestation of this work. I do not want to try to list every one, for fear of forgetting one or two. But they know who they are and I would like to thank them for their interest and support over the years.

Susan Ginsburg was instrumental in helping me translate a dream into reality. She believed in the book's value and in my potential to bring it to fruition. Susan's suggestions for improving the manuscript and her guidance in navigating the seas of the publishing world—always offered with authority and sensitivity—have earned her my respect and affection.

Publisher Ann Patty's enthusiasm for the book and her quick understanding of what I was trying to accomplish are deeply appreciated. Robert Withers made exquisitely intelligent and perceptive editorial suggestions, which resulted in a better final product. In addition to diligent copy editing, Terry Zaroff directed my attention to important issues that required clarification. Also, I appreciate the extraordinary patience of Lydia Buechler and Connie Morrill in the face of the author's anxiety.

My final thanks go to the people whose names appear on the dedication page. My parents provided a secure and loving home, enabling me to avoid much of the suffering that is detailed in these pages. Notwithstanding the support of all of the above, I doubt that this book would have been completed without the support of my wife, front-line editor, colleague, and soul mate, Sandra Warshak. Through the many years (too many) between my first mention of the idea for the book and its actual publication, she has been unflagging in her support and enthusiasm. More than anything, it was her confidence that allowed me to risk thinking of myself as an author. She provided the "essential background" (and the desk) that made it possible for me to give the manuscript the attention it required. Her active involvement in her own professional and horticultural pursuits allowed me to devote time to the book without having to feel that I was robbing our relationship. For all this, and much more, I am forever grateful.

*What shall we do with the child*

*Who's got your eyes my hair your smile*

*Reminding me that we fell in love*

*but just for a little while.*

**—Kate Reifsnyder, Nick Holmes,
and Carly Simon**

# C O N T E N T S

# CONTENTS

# PREFACE

In 1912, when my father was only two years old, his father was struck by a runaway horse and cart and was killed instantly. I suppose this book had its origins in that incident, because I have always wondered what it was like for my dad to be raised without his dad. How did it feel to be deprived of a father? How would his life have been different if his father had survived the accident? When, as an adult, I came to understand and appreciate the extent of my dad's contribution to my life, it saddened me to think about all that he missed out on with the loss of his father.

Until 1977, these thoughts were, for the most part, occasional and muted. Then I began a psychology internship at the Dallas Child Guidance Clinic. The first three children I was assigned to treat were all boys from divorced homes. Was this just a coincidence, I wondered, or did their parents' divorces make growing up that much more difficult for these boys? The answer I found in the psychology journals was that, indeed, children from divorced homes, particularly boys, were more likely than other children to need professional help to cope with emotional and behavioral problems. In psychology parlance, these children were "at risk."

In the same year, I had the good fortune to participate in a graduate seminar on parent-child relations led by Professor John Santrock. Dr. Santrock had already earned an outstanding reputation among his peers for his scientifically sophisticated studies of boys who grew up without fathers in the home. When he learned of my interest in children of divorce, and it came time to select a topic for my doctoral dissertation, Dr. Santrock suggested we collaborate on a study that he had been planning.

Almost all previous research on divorce focused on families in which the mother had custody of the children. The limited information available about children in father-custody families came solely from interviews with their fathers. Although this was helpful, we could not rule out the possibility of bias in such reports.

Dr. Santrock proposed that we study mother-custody *and* father-custody families and observe the children ourselves rather than rely on third-hand reports about how they were doing. I wanted to include certain psychological tests that would help us better understand the deeper thoughts and feelings of children from divorced homes. We both understood the importance of using precise, state-of-the-art scientific safeguards to ensure the accuracy of our results. Through carefully designed research we would explore not only how children were doing, but the factors that helped or hindered their ability to cope with the breakup of their family and the absence of one parent from the home.

Here was an opportunity to learn more about what we could do to prevent the problems that were showing up in my clinic cases. It was also an opportunity to get closer to understanding my father's experiences as a father-absent child, though I wasn't consciously aware of this motivation until years later. I accepted Dr. Santrock's invitation. We joined forces and launched the Texas Custody Research Project.

Nine months after I completed my dissertation, *Time* magazine wrote about the study. This brought a flurry of media interviews, followed by a storm of inquiries from desperate fathers fearful of losing meaningful contact with their children. Distraught grandparents also wrote, asking if there was anything I could do to help them stay in touch with their grandchildren.

These people helped me see, in very human terms, the magnitude of suffering caused by our current custody policies—policies that have little to do with the actual needs of children. For the past seventy years, custody decisions have been ruled by a cultural myth, a myth that I came to call "the motherhood mystique."

The motherhood mystique is the belief that mothers, not fathers, are uniquely suited to raise children.

In the past quarter-century, the women's movement has made great strides in removing the cultural straitjacket of rigid sex-role prescriptions and expanding the range of what is considered "appropriate behavior" for women and men. But this progress has not extended to the realm of parenting, and particularly not to parenting after divorce. This one area has been stubbornly resistant to change, even among many feminists.

And so, in nine out of ten divorced families, women are charged with sole responsibility for the daily care of their children and for all major decisions regarding them. In some of these homes the children see their father four days per month; in all too many homes the children see their father fewer than ten days per year, or never.

The motherhood mystique is deeply embedded in our national psyche and will not yield its grip easily. Nevertheless, we must give it our best effort. For too long this myth has scarred the lives of divorced families. It has left millions of children sadly longing for a deeper relationship with their fathers, millions of mothers overburdened with the job of raising children alone, and millions of fathers alienated from their offspring.

The situation is appalling and getting worse; our record-high divorce rate creates new victims daily, but no new solutions. And the worst battle scars are borne by the children. Mental-health experts agree: One of the leading causes of emotional problems in children of divorce is the diminished contact with their fathers.

A major goal of my professional life has been to learn what we could do to help children avert these problems. Fifteen years of research and clinical investigation, along with the findings of other leading divorce researchers, point to one inescapable conclusion: *If we are to prevent much of the suffering of divorced families, what we need is nothing short of a revolution in the way we think about and handle child-custody decisions.*

This book describes such a revolution and the reasons why it is our only hope. This book is not about fathers' rights or mothers' rights. It is about what, together, parents can do to help their offspring weather what is probably the gravest crisis of their youth.

Parents and grandparents will find practical suggestions on how to improve their children's chances of coping with divorce. Lawmakers, attorneys, and judges will find proposals for modifying the current system of resolving custody disputes. Mental-health professionals will find information to help them guide parents down safer roads following divorce.

But more than practical advice, this book offers the hope that the drama of divorce can be performed in a civilized manner, on a stage illuminated by wisdom and compassion for our children.

## Introduction

# CUSTODY CASUALTIES

**D**ivorce has become a familiar scene on our national landscape. Most people have had their sense of security shaken by a divorce or the prospect of one—if not their own, then a relative's.

When a couple decide to divorce, they face many subsequent decisions. The most important decisions—often the most painful—concern the children. Where should the children live? Who should be responsible for them? In legal terms, who should have custody? The answers to these questions form the core of this book.

Given a matter as crucial as custody, you might think that most divorcing parents would agonize over the decision, that they would carefully weigh the possible alternatives and the potential effect of these on their children and themselves. Or you might think that many parents would consult psychologists who specialize in divorce to assist them with this difficult decision, just as they consult attorneys to help them with other aspects of the divorce. Or you might think that most parents, unable to reach an agreement on their own, would take their case to court to let a judge or jury decide the fate of their children.

Actually, only a very small minority of divorcing parents travel any of these paths. Instead, astounding as it may sound, most divorcing couples spend less time and energy deciding the custody of their children than they do deciding the custody of their books and furniture. These parents love their children. But when it comes to child custody, most couples blindly follow a cultural prescription that relieves them of the need to

17

make an independent judgment. This cultural prescription dictates the same custodial arrangements for all children: After divorce, children should live with, and be the sole responsibility of, their mothers.

Supporting this prescription are two related assumptions: (1) Women, by nature, make better parents than men, and (2) mothers are more important to children than are fathers. I refer to these two beliefs, collectively, as the motherhood mystique—"mystique" because there is no basis in reason for it. Part one of this book shows that such beliefs cannot be justified by appeals to instinct, historical imperative, psychological theory, or research. *Raising children should not be the exclusive prerogative of women any more than work outside the home should be the exclusive domain of men.*

Abner Camp sat opposite me and covered his face with his large hands. If he were an actor, I thought, he would surely be typecast as the tough army drill sergeant. But today he was not tough. He was in tears.

Abner was beginning to face the truth that he was waging a battle for his son that he could not win. The tears were his recognition of defeat, of the fact that he might never see his child again. Abner had just been drafted into a legion whose ranks grow daily—the legion of divorced fathers shut out from meaningful involvement with their children. They are shut out by a judicial system that enforces a cultural myth and a social stereotype.

Theresa Rothstein was tired and enraged. Like most single mothers, she was feeling overwhelmed by the combined demands of her job, housework, and children. Her words were delivered with venom reserved for her worst enemy. "Right after the separation, he came around often, maybe too often. Then he started complaining that he didn't know what to do with the children during their visits. The kids began to see less and less of him. It's been three months since their last visit. I realize now, doctor, that he doesn't give a damn for his kids. He probably never really did. If I thought I was going to have to do this job all alone, I never would have had children." Theresa was another victim—of the same system and the same myth—the motherhood mystique.

As we see in the next chapter, the motherhood mystique originated at a time when women traditionally held little status in society. For centuries, women saw their own and their families' destiny controlled by men.

Against this background, the idea of a mother's unique importance to her children brought women more power and prerogatives and thus was probably welcomed by most mothers.

But the motherhood mystique may also have allowed men to continue their age-old domination over women. Certainly the idea that a woman's place is in the home cut down on competition in the workplace and kept positions of overt influence and power closed to women. With rare exceptions, such as Ayn Rand's portrait of railroad tycoon Dagny Taggart in *Atlas Shrugged*, for seventeen years following World War II our culture celebrated an ideal of femininity that encouraged women to search for fulfillment exclusively as housewives and mothers.

Then, in 1963, Betty Friedan wrote the influential book that is generally credited with inaugurating a rebirth of feminism. *The Feminine Mystique* focused attention on some problems with the traditional division of roles between man/breadwinner and woman/nurturer. Friedan exposed the frustrations, boredom, and lack of fulfillment felt by many women who tried to compress their lives within the boundaries of the socially sanctioned roles of housewife and mother. She called for a "drastic reshaping" of the conventional image of women to include roles beyond those of wife, housekeeper, and mother.

Nearly thirty years later, our culture has clearly answered Friedan's call by opening many doors previously closed to women. Women can now do a lot more. But, for too many women, *can* has become *must*.

Wives who choose to study or work outside the home find that their husbands do not take up the slack at home. Instead, men expect their wives to cope with the demands of a job outside the home in addition to, and not in place of, their more traditional responsibilities. The result is what has often been described as the plight of the "superwoman."

If the problem is manageable in the intact family, where the husband is around to lend some assistance, however limited, it becomes insurmountable in a divorced family. Every major study of divorce has reported that divorced mothers feel overburdened with the responsibilities that accompany sole custody. All but the most wealthy single mothers walk a spirit-sapping treadmill that leaves them little time or energy to attend to personal needs or pursue interests in life other than their children and their jobs.

What may have begun, seventy years ago, as a welcome addition to women's prerogatives—the opportunity to play the central role in their children's lives—has now become a burden that limits the divorced mother's chances of leading a satisfying and fulfilling life. At the same time, it deprives the divorced father of meaningful access to his offspring.

The motherhood mystique is so entrenched in our culture that most courts will grant custody to a father only if the mother grossly neglects or abuses her children. Popular interest in father custody has increased, but the proportion of children who live with their single fathers has not changed substantially over the past twenty years. It remains about one in ten.

Clearly, our society regards divorced fathers as second-class parents. We need no more vivid symbol of this than the prevailing practice of restricting a divorced father's contact with his children to every other weekend—what our courts call "regular visiting privileges." This practice uproots the father-child relationship from the fertile soil of natural, daily interaction and transplants it to the artificial turf of weekends crowded with entertainment and gifts. But two weeks does not easily compress into two days. In most cases, the relationship suffers.

If a divorced father attempts to see his children more often than the divorce decree allows, he can be thrown in jail. It is worth considering that the only other circumstance in which the state forcibly separates parent and child is when the parent is suspected or convicted of child abuse. But four days per month is what our society considers sufficient for a divorced father to take his rightful place in the life of his children!

Ask children what *they* think and we get a very different picture. For them, the current system of deciding custody leaves much to be desired. The casualties are numerous, and have been well documented by two decades of social-science research, work that is discussed in chapter 3. But most of the popular accounts of this research commit a crucial error. Problems endemic to traditional mother-custody families are described as inevitable consequences of divorce.

The experts' sobering portrait of life after divorce, the one we read about in magazine articles and books, does not fit the experience of a substantial minority of families—families in which the children see their fathers more than four days per month. The parents in these families, some with joint custody, some with sole father custody, recognize the importance of what we can call "the father factor." They reject the motherhood mystique and choose to defy convention for what they perceive as the best interests of their children.

Are they correct? Can a divorced father competently manage the day-to-day responsibilities of child custody? Or is it better for children to live with their mothers after divorce? It is now possible to answer such questions without relying on tradition, stereotypes, and myths.

Drawing on systematic research and clinical experience, parts two and three of this book provide the first comprehensive account of father-custody families, their joys and sorrows, their triumphs and hardships.

- Which children do best in father-custody homes and which ones are most likely to suffer when living away from their mothers?
- Are the problems that boys experience in mother-custody homes avoided or compounded in father-custody homes?
- Are daughters more difficult for single fathers to raise than sons?
- If a mother agrees to father custody or joint custody, will she regret her decision later on? What impact will her decision have on her relationship with her children?

In answering questions such as these, my intent is to provide authoritative guidance to parents, attorneys, and judges and enable them to individualize their custody decisions rather than pigeonhole every child into the same living arrangement.

I have found that many mothers with sole custody would prefer to try alternative custody arrangements that involve more participation by the father. But two issues stand in their way. First, in our culture any woman who does not maintain sole custody of her children is stigmatized. Society assumes that this woman could not possibly love her children "enough." For many women, this is too high a price to pay. Second, mothers are reluctant to allow their children more contact with their fathers because they are uncertain about how this will affect the children. Reliable research concerning the effects of father custody and joint custody on children can help parents make more informed decisions. By presenting the case for increased father involvement from the point of view of the children's best interests, I hope to initiate personal and cultural attitude changes that will permit the mother who declines sole custody to live without shame.

Several million divorced mothers now live without their children. Some have voluntarily relinquished custody; others have lost custody in bitter court battles. These women are social outcasts; they endure a constant barrage of accusations and disapproval from family, friends, and even strangers. Because they are largely "in the closet" (they dread being asked about their children's living arrangements), they do not have the opportunity to compare experiences with others in similar situations. Books on divorce rarely address issues from their point of view. Chapter 5 redresses this imbalance by speaking to the concerns of such "maverick mothers" and helping them come to terms with their unconventional parental role.

Not every parent will embrace the messages of this book. Some divorced fathers have no interest in meeting their parental obligations and maintaining contact with their children. Hence my discussion of why children need an involved father will be an unwelcome interference with the rationalizations such men use to justify their absence. Perhaps, though, the arguments in these pages will inspire some of them to rethink their position and reconnect with their children.

Then there are some divorced mothers who would do everything possible to keep their ex-husbands away from the children. Often the motive is a wish to punish the father by denying him access to his children. In some instances, the mother may fear for her children's safety—for example, when the father is likely to abuse or kidnap the children. But in many cases, the divorced woman's own hurt or anger clouds her assessment of her ex-husband's worth to the children.

Even when a mother favors the father's having contact with his children, she may request sole custody in order to regulate this contact at her discretion. The policy of lodging so much power in the hands of the mother has been supported by a spectrum of thinkers ranging from traditional Freudian analysts (for example, Sigmund Freud's daughter, Anna) to certain factions of the feminist movement. This may come as a surprise to the reader (it did to me), considering feminism's traditional opposition to arbitrary sex-based distributions of power. Nevertheless, as one feminist scholar puts it, feminists are now "reinstitutionalizing motherhood" for themselves.

Writing in *Ms.* magazine, Ann Snitow describes the dilemma facing feminists:

> *How special do we want mothering to be? My reading makes more obvious than ever that feminists completely disagree on this point—or rather that there are many feminisms, different particularly on this point. And here's another viper's nest: Do feminists want men to become mothers, too; that is, to have primary child care responsibilities? Again, the feminist work on this point veers wildly, is murky. Women ask, for example, "Can men really nurture?" And behind that doubt, or that insult, hides our knowledge of what psychological power mothers have. Why give that up, we may well ask. . . .*

Although Snitow favors "gender-blind" custody, she is ambivalent about endorsing this policy. "We give up something, a special privilege wound up in the culture-laden word 'mother.' . . . Giving up the exclusivity of motherhood is bound to feel to many like loss. Only a fool gives up something present for something intangible and speculative."

Apparently the motherhood mystique is so strong that it stops many feminists in their theoretical tracks. Yes, women should assume roles traditionally held by men. And, yes, married men should do more housework and more nurturing of the children. But after divorce, to protect women's power base, we should revert to the traditional division of labor.

Although I would like to see women, particularly single mothers, treated better in our society, I do not think that being saddled with the responsibility of sole custody represents a step down the path of liberation. *But even if it did,* your children's lives should not become the battleground on which to strike a blow for women's liberation. Children should not be sacrificed on the altar of gender politics.

And so this is my response to those who ask, "Why give up power for 'something intangible and speculative'?": The likelihood of gain is more definite than speculative. Throughout this book we will see over and over again how, and why, children benefit by retaining solid relationships with *two* parents. And helping your children cope better with a crisis that, after all, was not of their making, is, to my way of thinking, a far stronger and morally superior expression of power.

Part four presents a blueprint for radical change in our custody practices. The custody revolution will be fought on two fronts. First, we need to expand the divorced father's role in the life of his children. I believe joint custody (chapter 9), notwithstanding its challenges, is the best vehicle by which to accomplish this goal. Second, we need to make fundamental changes in the way custody decisions are handled. At least as important as *what* parents decide about custody is *how, when,* and *why* they make their decision.

In chapter 10 I exhort parents to avoid custody battles at all costs and I illustrate how parents can use professional consultation and mediation to reach mutually agreeable custody decisions. This chapter also provides guidelines to help parents create custom-tailored living arrangements that accommodate their own circumstances and abilities and suit the current and future needs of their children. Included are such topics as the role children should play in custody decisions and how to prepare children for the changes in their living arrangements.

*The Custody Revolution* addresses a wide audience. Primarily it is for the over two million parents who divorce each year, as well as the millions more who are already divorced.

Over twenty million adults were themselves raised in mother-custody homes. Most have wondered what their childhood would have been like if they had lived with their fathers. Here they will find the answer.

This book is also addressed to two groups of professionals: those in the fields of mental health and law. Both are in a position either to promulgate myths regarding divorce and custody or to provide accurate information to guide effectively those who seek their counsel. Until now, the results of research on father custody and joint custody have been scattered throughout several dozen professional articles. Here I pull together this research and present it in what I hope is a clear and balanced manner.

A nontechnical account of current knowledge regarding the effects of different custody dispositions on children should interest judges and family-law attorneys. It is my hope that *The Custody Revolution* will contribute to legal changes in custody procedures, either through our legislatures or in the courts.

Grandparents are the forgotten victims of modern divorces. Too often, the father's parents lose all contact with their beloved grandchildren. Much of my mail is from grandparents who are desperate for information about how they can retain meaningful involvement with their grandchildren after a divorce. They will find such guidance in this volume.

Desperation is the emotional chord most evident when custody is the topic of discussion. Everyone admits that there is something drastically wrong with current custody policies. Custody litigation is on the rise. Divorced fathers are angry, mothers are overburdened, and children from divorced homes are crowding our mental-health facilities and juvenile-detention homes in record numbers. Reports of homicides and kidnapping by frustrated parents in bitter custody battles are becoming common. We cannot expect the situation to improve until the underlying problems are recognized and rectified.

*The Custody Revolution* offers, not a panacea, but a prescription for alleviating much of the suffering of divorced families. It offers a new vision of divorce in America, one in which the needs of the children are given a priority they have not previously received.

I expect, and hope, that *The Custody Revolution* will shake our consciousness, not only because it asks us to rethink long-held views on child custody, but because it challenges our deepest assumptions about motherhood and fatherhood.

# PART 1
## THE MOTHERHOOD MYSTIQUE

# 1

## THE BIRTH OF THE
## MOTHERHOOD MYSTIQUE

*New opinions are always suspected
and usually opposed, for no other
reason than because they are not
already common.*
**—John Locke**

**J**oseph Young was alarmed when his two-year-old son arrived for his visit. The child was emaciated. He looked as if he hadn't eaten in days. Joe tried to stay calm. Perhaps he was mistaken. He sought his father's advice, and Joe's father agreed that the boy was starving. They rushed him to the hospital, which notified juvenile authorities. A pediatrician and a psychologist examined the child and concluded that the boy was virtually starved while in his mother's care.

Joe knew that he would have to take over the primary responsibility for his son's care. He went to court repeatedly, pleading with the judge to overturn the divorce decree giving custody to his former wife. Each attempt was unsuccessful. Having exhausted his legal remedies, Joe was now desperate. Seeing no alternative, Joe took his son and hid from the authorities. Warrants were issued for the boy and his father. Three years later, the FBI caught up with Joe, arrested him, and took away his son.

I do not know what became of the boy; with this start in life, the odds are certainly not in his favor. He and his dad are among the many victims of the motherhood mystique—a myth that is relied upon in contemporary custody decisions. I will present strong evidence demonstrating that this myth makes no sense in the light of our current knowledge of children's needs. As Joe Young learned, though, the myth does not topple easily.

Sometimes we cling to old views because they "feel" right, and dismiss without a hearing facts of reality that do not conform to our beliefs. So it is with the motherhood mystique. The idea that children in divorced families belong with their mothers and not their fathers has been with us for so long that many people, judges included, take it for granted. It is accepted uncritically, as though it were naturally ordained. And when people do question the assumption that mothers should be solely responsible for their children, they are apt to hear the response "There must be a good reason, because it has always been that way." Of course this answer begs the question; this answer is also wrong.

Mother custody is a social custom that developed relatively recently in history. It is not a biological imperative. In order to gain a better perspective, and demystify the motherhood mystique, let us take a look at how our ancestors dealt with custody decisions.

## AN EARLY PREFERENCE FOR FATHERS

In the days of ancient Rome, fathers had total control over their children; they could sell their children into slavery or even kill them. Mothers' rights were virtually nonexistent. In the event of divorce, therefore, child custody was automatically lodged with the father. His right to custody was essentially equivalent to a property right.

The tradition of paternal supremacy was perpetuated through British common law. In 1776, Abigail Adams wrote to her husband, John Adams, hoping he would use his influence in the new government to change the legal status of married women. "I desire you to remember the ladies," she wrote, "and be more generous to them than your ancestors. Do not put such unlimited power in the hands of husbands. Remember, all men would be tyrants if they could." At that time, women had no political rights and were forbidden to enter most occupations. As the legal authority William Blackstone put it, "The husband and wife are one person in law; that is, the very being or legal existence of the woman is suspended during the marriage."

Abigail Adams did not get her wish. The founding fathers did not upgrade women's legal status. A married woman could not sign contracts, testify in court, or own property. Even the wages she might earn belonged to her husband. Society considered the father the natural guardian of his children, in accordance with the laws of God. It was a father's job to prepare his children to live in the world outside the home. Mothers could not perform this task, according to eighteenth-century beliefs, because they were too insulated from society and themselves required the protection of men.

Since the father was deemed the children's natural protector, and only he had the financial means to support them, American judges believed that the children's best interests would be served by assigning custody to the father. The notion of making child-support payments to an ex-spouse had not yet been invented. In fact, the courts ruled that a father's financial support of his children was given in exchange for their labor. When a father was deprived of custody, a rare event in those days, he was no longer obligated to support his children.

## CUSTODY GUIDELINES IN TRANSITION

In the nineteenth century, courts gradually began to place limits on the father's near-absolute right to custody, as in the case of the famous poet Percy Shelley. In 1817, Shelley, married to the creator of *Frankenstein*, Mary Shelley, lost custody of the children from his first marriage because of his "vicious and immoral" atheistic beliefs. Even when a father was not "morally unfit," courts sometimes awarded custody to the mother if her child was still nursing.

Increasingly throughout the nineteenth century, young children came to be regarded as having special needs, needs that mothers were better suited to meet. This sentiment prevailed in custody cases and came to be known as the "tender-years presumption." The Talfourd Act of 1839 formalized this presumption by giving courts the authority to award custody of children under seven to the mother.

At first, the tender-years presumption was invoked to give mothers *temporary* custody of infant children. When the children reached the age of four or five, they were returned to the custody of their fathers. This guideline was unique in the history of child-custody decisions. For the first and only time in history, the law specified that custody decisions should routinely take into account another factor in addition to the sex of the parent. Also, the new guideline introduced the idea that the optimal custody arrangement may not be a permanent one, but one that is subject to change over time as the needs of the child change.

Regrettably, these ideas were left behind with the nineteenth century and have yet to be rediscovered by our legal system. This is unfortunate because now we know that such ideas have much merit. The best custody decisions are carefully thought out, take into account several factors, and are flexible enough to accommodate future changes. What might have been the start of a trend in the direction of more individualized custody decisions led instead to a new stereotype to replace the old; a wholesale preference for mothers replaced the former preference for fathers.

## THE RISE OF MOTHER CUSTODY

Over time, the age of "tender years" was extended upward, and eventually the tender-years presumption became the rationale for awarding custody of children of all ages to the mother on a *permanent* basis. Toward the end of the nineteenth century and in the early twentieth century, the legal pendulum swung away from fathers; by the 1920s, the preference for mothers was firmly established. As with so many cultural transformations, the reasons for this radical change are unclear. Scholars have identified several trends that accompanied this change, but no one knows for sure how these trends interacted and which were most responsible for the revolutionary change in custody practices.

By most accounts, the Industrial Revolution figures prominently as a catalyst for this change. With men leaving the farms for work in the city, the structure of family life changed radically. Children were no longer needed as field hands, and space was at a premium in the cities where jobs were located. As a consequence, children became less of an economic asset. They could still contribute to the support of the family by working in mines and factories, and children as young as five did so. But such employment was outlawed in the beginning of the twentieth century with the passage of legislation regulating child labor. Children thus became even more of a financial liability, and men became more willing to relinquish custody to their ex-wives. Probably this contributed to the change in attitudes regarding financial support of children after divorce. In the early 1900s, for the first time, courts held the father responsible for child support even when the children were not in his custody. By removing the financial constraints from mothers who received custody, child-support decrees were instrumental in fueling the shift toward a preference for mother custody.

Accompanying these economic changes were changes in the way society thought about families. Instead of being viewed as an entity that prepared children for participation in society, the family came to be seen as a place where children were nurtured and protected from the dangers of the outside world, dangers that were dramatized in the nineteenth-century novels of Charles Dickens. Fathers were increasingly employed away from home. And mothers could no longer participate in the material support of the family while staying at home, as in preindustrial times. Thus became established the now familiar division of roles between mother as nurturer and father as breadwinner.

In the twentieth century, the popularization of Sigmund Freud's psychoanalytic theories further supported the growing preference for maternal custody. Psychoanalysis emphasized the mother's unique contribution to her child's psychological well-being and provided a scientific sanction for society's changing attitudes.

Reverence for motherhood, conveyed in unabashedly sentimental rhetoric, began appearing in court decisions. A 1916 opinion reads: "Mother love is a dominant trait in even the weakest of women, and as a general thing, surpasses the paternal affection for the common offspring, and moreover, a child needs a mother's care even more than a father's. For these reasons, courts are loath to deprive the mother of custody of her children." Two years later, a North Dakota judge wrote the following: "It is not for a court to rend the most sacred ties of nature which bind a mother to her children, except in extreme cases." Another judge wrote in 1921: "The mother is God's own institution for the rearing and upbringing of the child." The same year, a different judge delivered this opinion:

> For a boy of such tender years nothing can be an adequate substitute for mother love—for that constant ministration required during the period of nurture that only a mother can give because in her alone is duty swallowed up in desire; in her alone is service expressed in terms of love. She alone has the patience and sympathy required to mold and soothe the infant mind in its adjustment to its environment. The difference between fatherhood and motherhood in this respect is fundamental.

The tender-years presumption reached its most lyrical extreme in this 1938 opinion: "There is but a twilight zone between a mother's love and the atmosphere of heaven."

In time, a guideline known as the "best-interests-of-the-child" standard replaced the tender-years presumption. Courts rely on this standard in contemporary child-custody cases throughout the country. Anyone involved in a custody dispute is certain to hear the phrase "best interests of the child" invoked repeatedly.

Theoretically, the best-interests standard focuses attention on the needs of the child rather than attributes of the parents. Opponents of the best-interests standard, however, point to the wide latitude that this vague label gives judges. It is left to the discretion of each judge to decide the best interests of a child in any particular case. The legacy of the tender-years presumption has continued to influence custody decisions, so that the best-interests standard, despite its literal meaning, has come to be interpreted primarily as a justification for the mother's preferential claim in custody disputes. In most parts of the country, only if the mother is grossly negligent or abusive does the father have a chance of keeping custody. Even then, the cards of the family court system are stacked against him.

Several years ago, an attorney from a small Southern town sought my assistance with a rather bizarre case. The attorney's client was a distraught father who wanted custody of his four-year-old son. The father had found over a dozen pornographic photographs showing his boy nude with ribbons and stickers on his erect penis.

In her interview with a court-appointed psychiatrist, the mother admitted taking the photographs. During this interview, the boy sucked and fondled his mother's breasts for about a half-hour. The psychiatrist concluded that both the boy and his mother were seriously disturbed, as was their relationship. A Duke University professor told the attorney that the photographs strongly suggested a form of witchcraft in which young boys figured prominently in the rituals. The district attorney wanted to prosecute the mother for sexual abuse of her son.

Even more bizarre than the mother's satanic-pornographic practices was the psychiatrist's recommendation that the mother be awarded custody (until the boy was twelve, at which time he "might do better with the father")! The psychiatrist, a recent mother herself, defended her position by appealing to a theory about the primary importance of the "mother-child bond." Her interpretation of this theory was none other than the motherhood mystique in modern garb. Actually, the doctor had only a superficial and inadequate understanding of the theory she cited. Moreover, she was ignoring two entire branches of psychological research that emphasized the importance of the father-child bond and the devastating, personality-warping effects of sexual abuse.

Sadly, the court followed the psychiatrist's recommendation. The father, his hopes dashed and his funds depleted, admitted defeat, stopped pursuing custody, and left his son in the care of a woman who might very well be a "witch."

From the point of view of children's welfare, the evolution of child-custody decisions leaves much to be desired. There has never been a genuine attempt to understand how children are affected by different custody arrangements. Instead, stereotypes about the nature of men, women, and children have dictated custody decisions throughout history. In earlier times, it was assumed that men, by nature, are better suited to protect and provide for children. Since 1920, it has been assumed that women, by nature, are better suited to love and care for children.

These assumptions, which so powerfully affect so many children's lives, are based on nothing more than folklore and sexual stereotypes. So why do parents and judges continue to rely on these formulas? One reason is that such generalizations simplify what otherwise would be complex and difficult decisions. The simplest solution, though, is not always the best. When we automatically pigeonhole every child into the same custody arrangement, we lose the opportunity to tailor custody to the needs of the individual family. Every family does not fit the same mold. What works for the family across the street may not be best for yours.

As guidelines for custody dispositions, folklore, sentiment, and stereotypes are poor substitutes for factual information. In the last two decades,

---

## LESSONS FROM HISTORY

**1.** Reliance on stereotypes about men, women, and children provides a poor basis for custody decisions. Children's true needs are bypassed; and inadequate, psychologically harmful, and sometimes dangerous and bizarre living arrangements are sanctioned by the courts.

**2.** Generalizations about custody, while simplifying difficult decisions, force families with different needs into the same mold.

**3.** Our society is long overdue for a revolution in the way child-custody decisions are made. Custody decisions need to be informed by an understanding, based on scientific research, of how children are affected by different custody arrangements.

---

social scientists have examined different custody arrangements and their effects on children's development. If this information is ignored, and we continue to allow myth and sentiment to rule custody decisions, we short-change our children and we short-change ourselves.

# 2

# THE FATHER
# FACTOR

The motherhood mystique might not have retained its influence throughout the twentieth century without an intellectual foundation. In 1940, Sigmund Freud provided this foundation. In his last book, Freud championed the mother's role as "unique, without parallel, established unalterably for a whole lifetime as the first and strongest love-object and as the prototype of all later love-relations." Freud based this claim on his interpretations of his patients' histories.

A decade later, systematic research data seemed to confirm Freud's theory. In the aftermath of World War II, a large number of European children were orphaned, inadvertently separated from their parents, or intentionally removed from their parents in attempts to spare them the horrors of war. These children were housed in orphanages designed to provide adequate physical care to large numbers of children. Although operated with the best of intentions, the orphanages produced unexpectedly tragic results. Physical and medical needs were met in most of these institutions, but the children showed signs of serious psychological problems. The most frequently noted problems were inability to develop caring feelings for others and aggressive, antisocial behavior.

Alarmed by the growing number of reports on the harmful effects of what was called "maternal deprivation," the World Health Organization commissioned a study by John Bowlby, an eminent psychoanalyst. In his 1951 report, Dr. Bowlby declared his belief that "the child's relation to his mother . . . is without doubt in ordinary circumstances, by far his most important relationship." Bowlby concluded that "prolonged deprivation of the young child of maternal care may have grave and far-reaching effects on his character."

Bowlby's pronouncement was itself to have "far-reaching effects." Largely as a result of his study, child-care institutions made sweeping reforms in order to better meet the child's emotional need for a stable relationship with a parental figure. But for children from divorced homes, the effects of Bowlby's conclusions were not so positive. By attributing the serious problems of institutionalized children to the separation from their mothers, Bowlby gave scientific credence to the motherhood mystique. The mother's preferred status in custody cases was reinforced, just as we stood poised for a dramatic rise in divorce rates. To help children avoid the "separation anxiety" described by Bowlby, psychologists discouraged overnight visits between toddlers and divorced fathers, thus severely restricting the scope of the single father's access to his young children—a practice that persists to this day.

Bowlby's conclusions were accepted uncritically because they confirmed social prejudices. But today child-development specialists agree that the conclusions drawn from the maternal-deprivation studies were unwarranted. The term "maternal deprivation" is itself a misnomer—these studies described children who were deprived of contact with their mothers *and* their fathers. If this had been recognized in the 1950s, custody policy might have evolved to protect the child's relationship with *both* parents. In his later years, even Bowlby acknowledged the enduring attachment bond between father and child. Indeed, as the ink was drying on Bowlby's manuscript, reports of the harmful effects of *paternal* deprivation began accumulating. Unfortunately, the revised interpretation of Bowlby's findings has not penetrated to the popular culture, and thus has yet to influence custody policy.

## FORGOTTEN FATHERS

For two decades, the motherhood mystique dominated the work of child psychologists. Their theories ignored the father's influence on his children. Fathers were not invited into the university research laboratory, and they were not invited into the clinician's consultation room when their children were being treated for emotional problems.

By 1975, the situation was so extreme that a young Yale psychologist working in Bowlby's footsteps, Michael Lamb, wrote an influential article in which he dubbed fathers the "forgotten contributors to child development." Dr. Lamb's article was the seed that bore fruit throughout the late seventies and the eighties as child-development experts were galvanized into exploring the father's impact on the life of his children. The result is a collection of books, articles, and conferences with titles such as *The Nurturing Father, The Role of the Father in Child Development, Fatherhood and Family Policy, Fatherhood Today,* and simply *Fathers.*

Fifteen years of research have revolutionized the way psychologists think about the relative contributions of fathers and mothers. It turns out that fathers make a difference, not just as children grow older, but even in the early years.

## BABIES AND DADDIES

Much of the earlier work in infant development concerned the "bonding" between mother and child. Under the influence of the motherhood mystique, we had always assumed that these bonds were the exclusive province of mothers and children. We were wrong. Numerous studies have established beyond a doubt that infants form close attachment bonds with their fathers and that this occurs at about the same time that they form attachments to their mothers. Although father and mother usually play different roles in their child's life, "different" does not mean more or less important.

Another myth is that, by nature, men are less competent than women in taking care of infants. Psychologists Ross Parke, of the University of Illinois, and Douglas Sawin, of the University of Texas, decided to test this belief scientifically.

First they had to find an appropriate measure of "parental competence." One aspect of being a competent parent is to be able to "read" your baby's signals correctly and respond sensitively. For instance, think about the feeding situation. The aim of the parent is to make sure the baby receives enough milk. By coughing or spitting up, babies indicate that some adjustment is needed. Therefore, one way to measure how capable parents are as feeders is to examine the degree to which they modify their behavior in response to their baby's distress signals.

Parke and Sawin carefully observed fathers and mothers bottle-feeding their newborns. They found that fathers were as sensitive as mothers to their baby's signals. Fathers, like mothers, responded to their infant's cues by stopping the feeding for a moment, talking to the baby, and looking more closely to see what was wrong. Moreover, the amount of milk consumed by the infants with their mothers and fathers was nearly identical.

Another series of studies has found that men—even bachelor college students—are as sensitive as women in discriminating among different crying patterns of infants. Whether or not we want to attribute these findings to a "paternal instinct," these, and many similar studies conducted at universities throughout the world, have established beyond a doubt that women have no monopoly on child-care skills.

Bill Gale is one of more than a hundred volunteer "baby holders" in a hospital in New York City. He cuddles, talks to, feeds, and diapers babies born to drug-addicted mothers who are unable to care for their infants. As people pass by the nursery and see Gale cradling a baby, they do double-takes and give puzzled looks. "For all the talk of the emergence of a new, sensitized American man," Gale writes, "the sight of one happily and capably caring for a baby is something akin to culture shock. Men are supposed to relate more to objects; women are more sensitive to people. Or so goes the moss-covered myth."

Yale University psychiatrist Kyle Pruett has studied fathers who stay home to raise their children, men he calls "primary nurturing fathers." With strong conviction, Dr. Pruett summarizes his understanding of the consensus of father-infant research: "We know for certain that men can be competent, capable, creative caretakers of newborns. This is all the more remarkable given that most men are typically raised with an understanding that they are destined through some natural law to be ineffective nurturers. . . . The research on the subject, some of it now decades old, says this assumption is *just not so*. And it says it over and over again, in data from many different disciplines."

Nevertheless, what our professional baby-watchers "know for certain," the average American finds hard to believe. The motherhood mystique is a vigilant sentry blocking the scientific data from reaching public consciousness. And so the legacy passes down to future generations: By our example, we teach our sons that the father's role does not encompass tenderness and sensitivity with his young children. We are making a big, big mistake.

Not only *can* fathers competently care for their children, but the more

38

they do so, the more their children are likely to benefit. Warm, involved, caring fathers provide their children with advantages in several areas of psychological development.

## INTELLIGENCE, ACADEMIC ACHIEVEMENT, AND MOTIVATION

What determines a child's IQ? Why do some children progress well in school while others underachieve? Why do some children strive to go far in school and choose challenging occupations while others seem to give up early in the game? Nature certainly plays a role, but most experts emphasize the contributions of the environment to children's intellectual functioning. As part of the environment, fathers have a critical influence on their children's mental development. In some cases, the father's impact is positive; in other cases, it is negative.

Jim is in business for himself as a plumber. He is good at what he does and his business has grown since he began it three years ago. One of the advantages that Jim offers his customers is his willingness to work in the evenings and on weekends, even to make routine repairs. But this doesn't leave him much time for his four-year-old son, Peter. One Saturday, he took Peter to his shop, but Peter wanted to touch everything and look in every drawer. Jim decided that he could not get enough work done with Peter underfoot, and that was the last Peter saw of his dad's workplace.

Jim was not treated with much patience when he was growing up, and in turn he has little patience for his own boy. When he tells Peter to do something, he expects instant compliance. Most of the time when Jim speaks to Peter, it is for the purpose of scolding him or restricting his activities. Occasionally Jim tries to have a more positive involvement with Peter by offering to help with something Peter is working on, such as a jigsaw puzzle. But when Peter makes a mistake, Jim gets frustrated and ends up doing the puzzle himself.

Cameron lives across the street from Jim. He is a subcontractor who does the framing for new houses. He, too, works on Saturdays, inspecting the various work sites and checking to make sure the correct supplies have been delivered to each site. But often Cameron takes his son, Howie, with him to the job site. The pace is more leisurely on Saturday, and this allows

Cameron time to answer Howie's many questions. Cameron enjoys teaching his son about the building trade. He is proud of how quickly Howie grasps and remembers what he is told.

Howie treasures this time with his dad. Cameron enjoys the time, too, but he doesn't realize how important it is. Howie doesn't yet realize its importance either. But years from now, Howie will look back on these Saturday excursions with fondness and he will appreciate their significance. It is no mere coincidence that Howie wants to be an architect when he grows up. His interest in building grows out of his identification with his father; his aspiration to be a designer of buildings is nurtured by his dad's attitudes and encouragement. Cameron projects high expectations for his son, confidence in Howie's abilities, and praise for his achievements.

Henry Biller is one of our country's leading authorities on the father's role in child development. He conducted pioneering studies in the late 1960s and early '70s, during the time when fathers were still largely ignored by psychologists. In fact, when I met Biller at a Chicago conference in 1986, he was much younger than I had expected. Evidently he got an early start in his field.

According to Biller and Margery Salter, "There is a great deal of data indicating that strong father-child relationships, even in infancy, can facilitate the child's intellectual competence." One research team discovered that a father's impact on mental development begins as early as five to six months of age. Frank Pedersen, Judy Rubinstein, and Leon Yarrow found that baby boys who have more frequent contact with their fathers have more precocious mental skills and curiosity than those who have less contact. Baby girls at this young age do not seem to derive such benefit from contact with their fathers. Fathers do influence their daughters' intellectual development, but this occurs a little later.

How do fathers promote cognitive growth in their children? Kathleen Alison Clarke-Stewart, of the University of California, observed fifteen-to-thirty-month-old children and found that the process is different for boys and girls. A boy's intellectual development is enhanced if his father is a good playmate—able to keep the boy interested in his games (such as peek-a-boo) and providing a lot of physically stimulating play. In contrast, a girl's mental development is facilitated if her father provides much verbal stimulation, such as talking and praising, and if he responds to her overtures for social interaction.

The father's influence on his child's intellectual attainments extends beyond infancy. University of Michigan professor Norma Radin interviewed fathers at home and observed how they handled interruptions by their four-year-old children. Later she tested the children's intelligence and vocabulary. She found that boys who scored higher on the tests had fathers who were more receptive to their approaches. These fathers praised their children and welcomed the opportunity to be helpful. Lower test scores were earned by boys whose fathers were more likely to scold and restrict their sons, or to react to their approaches by being cool and aloof.

Fathers can interfere with intellectual growth by overly restricting children's freedom to explore their environment. This is the mistake Jim made with Peter, and it is likely that Peter's curiosity and intellectual self-confidence will be hampered as a result. As in Pedersen's study, Dr. Radin found fewer links between a father's behavior and his daughter's intelligence.

Robert Blanchard and Henry Biller studied boys in the third grade to see what impact, if any, their fathers' availability had on their academic performance. Academic performance was measured by classroom grades and scores on the Stanford Achievement Test, the computer-scored test that public-school children take every year. They found that boys whose fathers spent the most time with them earned far superior test scores and grades and performed above third-grade level. Boys whose fathers worked long hours, like Peter's dad, or were often out of town on business, or were just uninterested in spending much time with their sons, performed somewhat below grade level.

Dr. Biller believes that a highly available father helps his son reach his intellectual potential in school by serving as an example of a male who functions successfully outside the home. No matter how successful the father, however, if he is not around enough he will not have the same impact on his son's intellectual development. Although Jim was very successful in his plumbing business, he did not give Peter enough opportunity to observe, imitate, and identify with him.

The studies by Radin, Blanchard, and Biller allow us to predict that the difference in the quantity and quality of their fathers' involvement will work to Howie's advantage in school and to Peter's disadvantage. That we can make such a prediction underscores the critical contribution that a father makes to his son's cognitive status.

Other studies have demonstrated the impact that fathers have on their daughters' intellectual development and achievements. A team of researchers found that second-, third-, and fourth-grade girls who were accomplished in both reading and mathematics had fathers who consistently supported and praised their academic efforts. Also, outstanding female mathematicians and college women with strong analytical ability are more likely to have close and positive identifications with their fathers.

According to Biller and Salter, "Data from a number of studies when taken together indicate that high paternal expectations derived from a context of a warm father-daughter relationship are conducive to the development of autonomy, independence, achievement, and creativity among females."

A number of well-known women confirm this conclusion by crediting their fathers with inspiring their achievements. Among these are Prime Ministers Margaret Thatcher and Indira Gandhi, anthropologist Margaret Mead, Congresswoman Shirley Chisholm, opera diva Beverly Sills, and psychoanalyst Anna Freud.

Just as a father can encourage his daughter's achievement, so he can hinder it by neglecting or abusing her. Such mistreatment is pernicious and will undermine her school achievement.

The bottom line is that the father plays a central role in his children's intellectual and academic performance. His impact may be positive or negative. But it is not insignificant.

Nor is it just the realm of the intellect in which a father makes his presence felt. A child's personality also owes a lot to the father's contribution.

## LEAVING THE NEST

Fathers play an important role in helping their children make the essential transition from immediate family to the outside world. The father's influence is evident beginning in infancy. Pedersen and his associates observed the reactions of five-month-old infants to an unfamiliar but friendly examiner. Even at this young age, boys who had more contact with their fathers were more "sociable" with the examiner. They showed more willingness to be picked up, vocalized more, and enjoyed active play more than baby boys who had less involved fathers.

In a series of studies with older infants in Boston, Milton Kotelchuck found a similar pattern. Children whose fathers were very involved in their care were better able to handle the stress of being left alone with a stranger. It may be that, through the repeated process of having the mother leave and the father take over, children whose parents share child care become accustomed to being apart from either parent and thus have less anxiety over separations.

Studies of older children suggest that fathers affect how well their sons get along with peers. When fathers are away for long periods of time, as in the case of sailors at sea, their boys are less popular with classmates and do not enjoy friendships as much as do boys who have more contact with their fathers.

Boys who have missed out on extensive contact with their fathers in their preschool years are generally less assertive and more dependent on their peers by the time they reach elementary school. They are more likely to shy away from physical and competitive activities, eschewing contact sports such as soccer. Although some might regard this life style as preferable to engaging in stereotypical "masculine" activities, it does set these boys apart from their peers and contributes to their unhappiness, loneliness, and sense of alienation.

Several years ago, I treated one such boy. Bruce was a frail-looking youngster with low self-esteem and a high IQ. He was able to engage comfortably in conversations with adults, but he was at a loss when it came to dealing with boys his own age. If he had to be around other children, he preferred the company of girls or younger boys, which worked out okay because they were the only children who would have anything to do with Bruce. But his peer problems were not the reason Bruce's mother brought him to see me.

She first contacted me because Bruce was having trouble leaving the nest—literally. Each morning, when it came time to leave for school, Bruce developed terrible stomach pains or headaches that kept him from leaving home. His pediatrician could find no physical reason for Bruce's pains, and so, as a last resort, Bruce was referred to me.

My evaluation revealed that Bruce's pains were associated with extreme anxiety at the thought of leaving the security of his home and his mother's side. He had no trouble accompanying his mother on errands, but he hated to go outside on his own. Each morning, Bruce's pains subsided as soon as he was reassured that he did not have to attend school that day. But then the process began all over again the next morning— except on the weekends.

Bruce resisted going to school, in part because it required a separation from his mother, and in part because he felt so uncomfortable around his peers. Despite his intelligence, Bruce earned poor grades in school, as a result of missing so many exams. The situation had become so desperate that a truant officer threatened Bruce's mother with legal action if she didn't get Bruce to school. This forced her to seek help for him.

It took years of individual and group therapy to help Bruce overcome his anxieties and develop age-appropriate and rewarding friendships. Although several situations contributed to his problems, a key factor was the relatively little contact Bruce had had with his father since infancy. This left him insufficient opportunity to identify with his father, which would have helped Bruce become more independent of his mother and feel more secure away from her. As with the toddlers in Dr. Kotelchuck's study, the lack of interaction with his father left Bruce more vulnerable to separation anxiety. As he grew older, Bruce felt unsure of how to behave around boys. He was intimidated by the usual roughhousing, since he had never experienced this with his own father. Bruce's situation demonstrated, by its absence, the importance of a father's contribution to his son's social development.

A central psychological task of adolescence and young adulthood is the development of relationships with the opposite sex. A father's interest, support, and availability give his son a distinct advantage in dealing with females. When a man has grown up enjoying a warm and close relationship with his father and has observed a harmonious relationship between his parents, his own marriage has a better chance of succeeding.

A father's contribution to his daughter's social development becomes most apparent in adolescence, when relationships with boys begin to occupy center stage. The father's impact can be positive or negative. In general, girls who have a warm relationship with their fathers and feel accepted by them are more likely to feel comfortable and confident when relating to the opposite sex. Biller and Salter, drawing on the results of several studies, conclude: "A woman's ability to have a successful marriage relationship is increased when she has experienced a warm, affectionate relationship with a father." Also, the best-adjusted females have grown up observing a positive relationship between their fathers and mothers.

During the teen years, and later, a girl who has not had a rewarding relationship with her father is apt to feel insecure around males. She may feel unattractive as a woman, doubt that any man could love her for herself, and distrust men in general. These attitudes make it difficult to establish a gratifying heterosexual relationship. Research has shown that girls raised solely by their divorced mothers are more likely to have their own marriages end in divorce. Even problems reaching orgasm during marriage have been traced to the absence of a father in early childhood.

The mere presence of a father in the home, however, does not guarantee that he is an adequate father or that his influence will be positive. Some fathers are so destructive to their daughters' mental health that the children might be better off being raised without them.

I am thinking of situations in which the father is guilty of physically or sexually abusing his daughter, what psychiatrist Leonard Shengold calls "soul murder." The devastating trauma of incest, which we now realize is all too common in our culture, has been well documented by Shengold, Alice Miller, and Judith Herman, among others. A father's sexual abuse leaves his daughter at a higher risk for severe depression, suicidal behavior, substance abuse, low self-esteem, and a tendency to re-enact her trauma by becoming involved in abusive relationships.

So, as with the earlier discussion of intellectual development, my point is not that a father always makes a positive contribution. Rather, my point is that he makes a difference. He is not, as the motherhood mystique would have us believe, a peripheral figure.

## MORAL DEVELOPMENT
## AND SELF-CONTROL

> Our mothers all are junkies,
> Our fathers all are drunks,
>
> Golly Moses—natcherly we're punks!

In *West Side Story*, the Jets' gang members enjoy their lampoon of Officer Krupke. But of course there is truth in what they sing. Parents *do* shape the moral development of their children, and fathers play a large role.

## Empathy and Caring

One of the most socially desirable personality traits is empathy, the ability to put yourself in someone else's emotional shoes, to experience another person's feelings vicariously. Empathy is an essential trait of a caring person. It is what psychopaths lack for their victims and what good psychotherapists possess in abundance. Indeed, many psychologists believe that empathy is the cornerstone of effective psychotherapy. So a recent study that looked at the factors that help shape empathy is of more than just passing interest.

Richard Koestner, of McGill University, tracked seventy-five men and women who, as five-year olds, had participated in a study at Yale University in the 1950s. He was interested in identifying the circumstances in childhood that are linked to empathy in adulthood. His was the first study of empathy that had available this type of longitudinal data.

Dr. Koestner concluded that the best way to predict who will become an empathic adult is to measure the amount of time spent with the father while growing up. Of all the factors studied, and there were many, this was the most powerful predictor.

It is not clear why the link exists. It may be that fathers who spend more time with their children have more opportunity to model empathy for them. Or those fathers who spend more time with their children may be more empathic to begin with. Dr. Lamb suggests an alternative explanation: Perhaps households in which fathers are more involved with their children are more harmonious, and this is what contributes to the development of empathy. Marian Radke-Yarrow, laboratory chief of the child-development section at the National Institute of Mental Health, agrees: "It's probably not time with the father in itself that is so important for empathy, but what it reflects: a family where there is a joint commitment by parents to their children." Nevertheless, the fact remains that fathers play a major role in helping their children become caring adults. And the world certainly needs more caring people.

## Right and Wrong

In addition to empathy, parents want their children to develop a strong conscience, personal standards of right and wrong that guide behavior. Again, fathers figure prominently in the development of a conscience.

My close colleague John Santrock asked elementary-school teachers to rate the moral maturity of boys in their classes. Then he compared the ratings of boys who had fathers at home with those who were father-absent. He found that boys with fathers present were consistently rated as having a higher level of moral maturity.

Martin Hoffman, psychology professor at New York University, studied seventh-grade boys and girls. He was interested in determining if there was any relationship between the absence of a father and the development of conscience. The aspects of conscience that Hoffman looked at were guilt following transgressions, acceptance of blame for wrongdoing, compliance with rules, and internalized moral standards. He found that boys who came from homes in which the father was absent received lower scores on each measure of moral development. Also, these boys were rated by their teachers as being more aggressive than boys whose fathers were present. There were no such differences for girls.

In another study, Dr. Hoffman asked seventh-graders whom they most admired, whom they felt most similar to, and whom they most wanted to emulate when they grew up. He found that boys whose responses indicated strong identifications with their fathers scored higher on measures of internal moral principles and conformity to rules than boys with weak identifications with their fathers. Again, there was no similar link between father identification and moral development in girls.

## Responsibility versus Impotence

Children differ in how much responsibility they take for their own actions. Some are more likely to see themselves as the master of their fate, accepting the credit when things go well (such as earning a high test grade), and taking the blame when things don't. Other children are more likely to believe that external circumstances rule their lives. When they get a high grade, they say that the test was easy; when things go wrong, they blame others or "bad luck."

Biller has found that children whose fathers are very involved with them, who show their love by giving lots of affection and setting appropriate limits, are much more likely to develop a sense of their own potency. These children do not tend to see themselves as at the mercy of forces beyond their control. They not only accept responsibility for their behavior; they are more likely to behave responsibly. These children emulate the responsible behavior they observe in their fathers. Other studies support Biller's observations by showing that warm, involved, caring fathers tend to foster highly moral children and adolescents.

## Delinquency

In every large city in the United States, newspapers trumpet a daily, familiar, and wearisome account of drive-by shootings, vandalism, gang fights, and worse. Much of this crime is committed by adolescents. In Dallas, for example, it is no longer unusual for guns and knives to make an appearance at teenage gatherings. I suspect it is the same in cities throughout the country.

We would all like to do something about the problem. But what can we do? Our public schools' response is to conduct routine locker searches, launch antidrug campaigns, and prohibit the wearing of gang "colors" and apparel on school grounds. In my opinion, such actions have about as much likelihood of being effective as trying to stop a shark with a butterfly net.

Instead of focusing all our attention on the unfortunate manifestations of problems, we would do better to learn more about the causes of such pervasive and destructive antisocial behavior. Of course, the roots are many and the solutions complex. Here I would like to look at just one aspect of the problem.

Since the late 1950s, psychologists have known about the link between inadequate father-son relationships and juvenile delinquency. The typical delinquent has a poor or nonexistent relationship with his father. Even when the father is living at home, he gives his son scant praise during the formative years, but much hostility, rejection, and punishment—usually physical, often violent. If you want to raise an angry boy, a boy with little tolerance for frustration and weak self-control, a boy prone to impulsive and aggressive behavior, there is no better way. By his example this father teaches his son, in the early, impressionable years, how to behave aggressively, irrationally, and without restraint. Unfortunately, all too many boys learn these lessons all too well.

Proportionately far more delinquents come from homes in which the father is absent. Not only is there a strong association between father absence and delinquency in males, but among delinquents those who were father-absent before the age of six have higher rates of recidivism than those whose fathers were present in the home while they were growing up.

The connection between antisocial behavior and inadequate fathering certainly does not mean that all poor father-son relationships are going to lead inevitably to delinquency, or that having a positive relationship with a father guarantees that a child will avoid antisocial behavior. Many other factors come into play, including economic circumstances and the quality of the boy's relationship with his mother. But a warm, involved, caring father does militate against antisocial behavior, and an inadequate father does increase the probability of delinquency.

As in the case of intellectual development and social development, a father can be a predominantly positive or negative influence with regard to his children's moral development. But he is an important influence. And this runs counter to our cultural prejudice, which consistently devalues the father's contribution to his children's psychological development.

I should mention that in this chapter I have discussed only a father's *direct* influence on his children. As Professors Michael Lewis and Marsha Weinraub point out, through his emotional and economic support of the mother, and in myriad other ways, a father also contributes to his children's development indirectly. But this would take us too far afield. I hope my discussion of research documenting the father's direct impact has been sufficient to make the case for the father's overriding value to his children.

As I conclude this chapter, which is filled with references to objective scientific studies, I am struck by a more immediate example of a father's love and devotion, importance and meaning to his child. And this example, more than all the studies, leaves me appalled at how unfair and unreal is the popular conception of the father's role.

For the past three weeks, my friend's seven-year-old son has been in a hospital intensive-care unit with a rare illness that has left him temporarily incapable of speaking or moving his muscles voluntarily. The boy's parents have been taking turns sitting with him throughout this terrible ordeal. His distraught father, obviously suffering along with his wife and son, has not returned to his office since the hospitalization. Imagine what an affront it would be to tell this man that he is only marginally important to his son.

Watch a father's reaction to the birth of his child. Then watch a child's reaction to the death of his father. Witnessing only these two events makes it difficult to understand how anyone could fail to appreciate the central importance of the child's relationship with his father. But for the better part of this century, our society and its institutions have overlooked all but the father's economic contributions to his children.

If a married father wants to devote more time to his family and less time to his work, he will quickly learn that his opportunities for advancement in most careers are curtailed. Most corporate structures frown upon such involvement and assume that a man who seeks it is less committed to his work and thus less valuable to the company than the man who places job above family.

If a divorced father wants to see his children more than four to six days per month, he will quickly learn that the odds of being allowed to do so are very slim. His lawyer, his ex-wife, his boss, his peers, and perhaps even his psychotherapist will discourage him from trying. The divorced father's second class status as a parent is firmly entrenched and accepted without question.

Chapter 1 demonstrates that the preference for mother custody is not a historical imperative and did not arise in response to well-established theories or scientific research, but in response to economic pressures and social prejudices. The present chapter reveals that there has never been a scientific justification for the motherhood mystique. The consensus of research findings, far from validating the mystique, underscores the importance of both parents.

*The evidence is overwhelming and demands that we re-examine the wisdom of conventional custody.* Unless you believe that a father's value to his children diminishes after divorce, it is hard to justify a custody policy that routinely and automatically disrupts the divorced father's relationship with his children. The notion that only mothers are important to their children is false; it is time to jettison it from custody policy.

Two other themes emerge from our survey of psychological research. First is the specific benefit to children of having a warm relationship with a father who is more than minimally involved with them. Second is the father's greater impact on boys than girls in certain spheres of development and at certain ages (although it is clear that fathers make major contributions to their daughters' development as well); I will return to this theme in my discussions of mother-custody and father-custody families. Both themes should affect how parents and courts handle custody decisions; the latter theme has some surprising and revolutionary implications.

With the father having such a major impact on his family, you would expect that his absence from the home would compromise his children's psychological development in some fairly substantial ways. It does. And you would expect that he would be sorely missed by his children. He is. Next we see how, and why.

# 3

## CONVENTIONAL
## CUSTODY

*We did not encounter a victimless divorce.*
**—University of Virginia study of mother-custody families**

**T**en-year-old David hated when his parents argued. Sometimes he tried to intervene and persuade them to stop. He was always unsuccessful. Most of the time, he retreated to his room and listened to Bruce Springsteen, volume turned up, headphones securely in place.

When his parents announced their decision to get a divorce, they were surprised by David's reaction. They figured he would be as relieved as they were to see an end to the hostilities. He was, but he was also mad, scared, and embarrassed. This last feeling his parents would never have predicted. Eight of the fourteen boys in his scout troop came from divorced homes. David was aware of this, but he was ashamed that *his* parents were not living together.

Every loving parent on the verge of divorce wonders, "How will my children react?" Those who anticipate some initial negative response worry, "Will the children ever 'get over it' or will they be irreparably harmed?" Over the past fifteen years, divorce researchers have discovered some valuable answers to these questions. This chapter explores the plight of children growing up in conventional mother-custody homes. Even when the term "divorce" is not qualified, the reader should assume that I am referring to mother custody. Subsequent chapters will address alternative types of custody and how they compare with conventional approaches.

For all children in the custody of their mothers, the rupture of the family is a sad and distressing experience. In the early weeks and months following their parents' separation and their fathers' departure from home, virtually all children show some negative reactions.

Not every child reacts in the same manner, but certain symptoms of stress do occur most frequently. In response to their parents' separation, children feel angry, confused, and worried. We see children demanding more attention from their parents and teachers, and crying more frequently and with less provocation.

Older children may complain of physical ailments, such as headaches and stomachaches, for which no medical basis can be found. Often these (very real) pains disguise underlying anger or hunger for more loving attention. One of my patients was so distraught by his father's departure that he developed swelling, stiffening, and severe pain in his muscle joints that lasted for six weeks. His pain was so incapacitating that his mother had to carry him to bed.

Young children often undergo what psychologists call a "regression" in response to the stress of separation and divorce. This means that their behavior becomes less mature as the children struggle to come to terms with the upheaval in the family. For example, bed-wetting or thumbsucking may reappear. It is as though the youngsters wish to return to an earlier time in their lives, when they felt more secure.

In my practice, I see a fair number of children who have suffered some horrible trauma. One preschool girl had her lips ripped apart by a dog, a second-grade boy witnessed the murder of his parents, another boy witnessed the accidental electrocution of his father, one boy got his hand caught in an escalator, and another partially severed three fingers when he became fascinated by the rotating chain of an exercise bicycle.

Terrible things happen to children. And when they do, I have noticed an interesting reaction on the part of the parents. Almost without exception, parents overlook or underestimate the extent, severity, and duration of the trauma's impact on the child. This denial occurs even when it means passing up lucrative insurance benefits that could be awarded for the "mental anguish" the child has suffered. No matter how awful the trauma, loving parents much prefer to believe that their children have not suffered much anguish and that any reactions they see are only transient. The almost universal impulse is to "put it all behind us" as soon as possible, even when this means ignoring the reality of psychological scars.

Divorced parents do the same thing. Most parents prefer to think of their divorce as a one-time event that causes, at worst, some brief negative reactions in their children. This is especially true of parents who sought the divorce and want to assuage their guilt by minimizing their children's distress. Most parents believe the popular notion that children are so resilient that they can easily bounce back from any crisis, including divorce. This is not so.

Even those children of divorce who manage to escape long-term problems take about two years to regain their psychological equilibrium. In the meantime, they face a series of changes which, like the ever-widening ripple of waves around a stone dropped in water, expand to encompass many aspects of life.

As the months went by, David and his family went through many of these changes. David's mother increased her hours at work and David had to take the bus to day care every day after school. He missed riding his bike home from school. He missed the time he used to spend building models at his special worktable in the corner of his bedroom. Most of all, he missed his mother's being around in the afternoon and his father's coming home in the evening. He missed the conversation at dinnertime, when his parents discussed their day at the office. The names of their co-workers and bosses had become so familiar that he had constructed mental images of them. He missed his father's kiss good night. He missed the "essential background" events of daily life that capture our attention only by their absence.

Friday night, in preparation for the weekend visit with his father, David packed his clothes and his video games in the special backpack his grandmother had given him on his last birthday. Sometimes he forgot his homework or his pajamas or his baseball mitt. He no longer had to remember his toothbrush; his father had finally bought him a second one. David didn't know why, but he always had butterflies in his stomach just before his father came to get him. After he was with his dad for an hour or so, he felt better, and he usually had a good time. But before the visits, his stomach felt funny.

His father lived in a pretty small apartment which David thought was really neat, at first. Now he wished his dad lived in a house with a backyard and a place to keep a bicycle. And he wished he had a bicycle at his dad's. His father had said he'd buy a rack to carry David's bike on the car, but that was two months ago and he still had not bought it.

David liked going to Dad's office on Saturday mornings and then having pizza for lunch. This reminded him of "the good old days." The worst part of the visit was at the end, when he had to say goodbye to his dad. Even Dad was sad at these times.

When David returned to his mother on Sunday evening, the butterflies returned to his stomach. Somehow he and his mom always argued about something on those nights. Mom didn't seem very interested in hearing about the neat things he did with Dad, and David could not bring himself to do the things she asked, like take a bath and clean up his room. Dad didn't make him do those things. Each time David and his mom argued, he vowed that next time his dad brought him home he would be good. But then the next time came and so did the arguing. David was beginning to think the Sunday-night fights were inevitable.

His parents said things would be better for everyone after the divorce. Maybe it worked like that in other families, but not in his. As far as David was concerned, he would choose "the good old days" any time.

Millions of children share David's sentiments. Over one-half the children interviewed in a California study of mother-custody families thought that their families were no better off after the divorce. According to the researchers, "Many of these youngsters, some of whom were doing well, would have preferred to turn back the clock and return to the predivorce family, despite its remembered failings."

Even more children, about four out of five, cling to the hope that their parents will reunite. No wonder. Although divorce offers parents a second chance at life's brass ring, for most children divorce sets in motion a sequence of unwelcome changes that present obstacles to their happiness.

Dad moves out of the house. Mom is less available as she devotes more time to earning a living. Money is in short supply. You move away from your familiar home and neighborhood to smaller living quarters in a worse section of town. Mom and Dad cry more, and fight more, than you've ever noticed before.

What leaves the deepest impression—although it is usually unspoken—is the shocking awareness that *love does not last forever.* Parents don't stay around forever. The one certainty that children count on—as much as we adults count on the sun to rise—is the consistent presence, and protection, of their parents. Divorce takes away this certainty. And it leaves a legacy of distrust in the permanence of love, which handicaps children later in life, when they set out to forge their own relationships.

Considering the problems associated with growing up in a mother-custody household, parents in a troubled marriage may wonder if they should stay together merely "for the sake of the children." On the one hand, I believe they ought to do everything possible to heal their marriage and spare themselves and their children the pain of divorce. The risks to their children's welfare should be an additional deterrent to divorce. On the other hand, children who live in the sole custody of their mothers are not necessarily worse off than those who remain in a conflict-ridden, chronically tense and miserable two-parent home. In fact, divorce can bring positive changes for such children. Certainly for those chronically abused by their fathers, mother custody represents an escape from "soul murder." And for as many as 50 to 70 percent of children, divorce leaves no obvious permanent imprint on psychological development. I use the word "obvious" because it is well known that the psychological measures used by divorce researchers cannot capture all of the nuances of a child's developing personality.

We know that trauma victims can sometimes function quite well in areas unrelated to the trauma. Similarly, children of divorce can excel in a number of areas while harboring subtle encapsulated problems with self-esteem and interpersonal relationships that may remain hidden for many years.

Even if we discount these subtle problems for the moment, this still leaves 30 to 50 percent of children who suffer obvious long-term harm directly traceable to their parents' divorce. This means that *every year* one-third to one-half million children are added to the casualty list.

## LONG-TERM PROBLEMS OF CHILDREN IN MOTHER-CUSTODY HOMES

The psychological injuries suffered by children growing up in mother-custody homes take different forms: insecure gender identity, impaired capacity for intimate relationships, depression, anxiety, poor self-control, and—accompanying nearly all emotional and behavioral problems—low self-esteem.

### Self-Esteem

Of all the psychological traits studied by divorce researchers, the one that has received the most attention is self-esteem. Self-esteem is the degree to which one has an inner sense of being a capable and worthy person—what one psychologist has called the reputation we have with ourselves. Because self-esteem affects our ability to enjoy all aspects of life, child-development specialists have been most concerned about the self-esteem problems identified in mother-custody children.

When we consider the conditions that most favor the development of healthy self-esteem, it is easy to understand why children from divorced homes suffer in this respect. Self-esteem flourishes when parents relate to their children with warmth, understanding, and positive attention. For parents who are going through a divorce, though, these commodities are in short supply.

Preoccupied with their own worries, sadness, and anger, divorced parents, at least for a time, are severely taxed in their capacity to respond optimally to their children. In the aftermath of divorce, single mothers are more apt to nag, disapprove, and punish their children. The more depressed the mother feels, the more difficulty she will have being positively involved with her children. She will withdraw from the children, in some cases immersing herself in a whirlwind of activities outside the home in an effort to distract herself from her painful inner state.

Children, especially younger ones, do not understand adult depression. When a mother seems inattentive, lukewarm, and unaffectionate, her children may assume that they have done something to alienate her. "Perhaps, if I behaved better, Mommy would be nicer to me." In the same way, children personalize their fathers' absence. "If I was a good girl, maybe Daddy would not have left."

Naturally, the sooner the mother regains her emotional balance, and the more physically and emotionally available she is, the better off her children will be. And the father can complicate or alleviate his children's suffering by the manner in which he conducts his relationship with them. If he sees them often, is reliable and consistent with them, and maintains a close and caring relationship, his children will be reassured that the loss of love in their family does not extend to them.

If, on the other hand, the father has limited contact with his children, or disappoints them repeatedly by being late to pick them up or canceling planned times together, his children will conclude that their father no longer values them very much. From there it is a short step to self-deprecation: Rather than believe their fathers are deficient as parents, most children assume the deficiency lies within themselves.

Dressed in her best clothes, her hair fixed up specially, eleven-year-old Diana kept looking out the window with the excited anticipation of a child walking into Disneyland. She hadn't seen her father for several months, even though he lived less than one hour away. He had a history of disappointing her. Broken promises, last-minute changes, postponed activities, no-shows at dance recitals. But this time things would be different. Diana had earned straight A's on her report card with no bad marks in conduct. As a reward, Daddy had promised to take her to dinner at a fancy restaurant.

He was supposed to pick her up at six o'clock; Diana was ready at five. By six-fifteen, he hadn't arrived. By six-thirty, Diana stopped looking out the window. By seven, still no sign of him. To make a sad story short, he finally showed up at seven-thirty. He had already eaten dinner and figured that she had, too. When he learned that she hadn't, he took her, not to the special restaurant, but to get a quick slice of pizza.

Diana's mother told me this story while doing her best to keep her anger and disapproval out of her voice. She knew it only made things harder on Diana to hear her mother criticize her father. When her mother was finished, Diana rose to her father's defense: She didn't really mind skipping the fancy restaurant; she'd had a good time with her daddy; anyway, she loved pizza.

Diana could not acknowledge the hurt and anger she felt toward her father. Instead, she tried to preserve her image of a loving father. Each time he disappointed her, she made excuses for him: "He really wanted to come." "It wasn't that important anyway." "Next time will be even better." But ultimately these rationalizations were unconvincing. Each disappointment chipped away at Diana's self-esteem. What she really thought was, "If Daddy doesn't show me more love, I must not be that lovable."

And, sad to say, Diana's experience is typical of what thousands of mother-custody children go through every day.

Experts tell parents to emphasize to their children that divorce is a grown-up thing between Mommy and Daddy, that the children are not getting divorced and they are still loved. Excellent advice. But should we expect our children to believe this when the divorce results in a significant reduction in the quantity and quality of their contact with their fathers?

Low self-esteem also results from the shame attached to divorce. Recall David's embarrassment when his parents separated. To him this meant his family was not as good as an intact family. And, by extension, he was not as good. The prevalence of father absence among his peers did little to "normalize" the experience, because David was reacting to more than just a sense of being different and flawed. He was identifying with his parents' own shame.

Divorce is a public announcement of failure. The knowledge that many have failed before us does little to assuage the inevitable shame. No matter how many people have already slipped on a banana peel, we still feel embarrassed when it is our time to hit the ground. A sense of personal failure and loss of social status almost universally accompany divorce. You should expect your children, despite reassurances, to resonate with this discomfort.

## Masculinity

A child's self-esteem is closely tied to his or her sense of being an adequate male or female. As discussed in the preceding chapter, boys who are deprived of contact with their fathers are more likely to feel handicapped in this regard. In particular, when the divorce occurred in the child's preschool years, the average mother-custody boy feels and acts less masculine than a boy whose parents have not divorced. When asked about what activities, toys, and future vocations he prefers, his choices have less in common with those of other little boys and more in common with those of little girls. And it is not just his thoughts that are different. He actually does play more with girls and younger children than do boys whose fathers live at home. Also, he is more likely to play the types of games and activities that little girls enjoy.

If this were merely a rejection of conventional stereotypic masculine behavior, it would be of less concern, and perhaps something to be welcomed. After all, the central message of this volume is the imperative need for men to become more involved in nurturing their children despite conventional proscriptions that reserve this role for women.

But mother-custody boys who avoid traditional masculine behavior are not consciously choosing a liberated life style. Quite the opposite. These boys would like to be different, but they either don't know how or are too insecure and feel too inadequate to try. Like my patient Bruce, discussed in the preceding chapter, they generally depend too much on their mothers, are unsure of how to deal with male peers, and are often intimidated by them. Even when they try to play with other boys, they get ignored or rejected. Boys like Bruce are not just unconventional; they are unhappy.

Let me emphasize that the differences between boys in mother-custody homes and those with two parents at home represent averages. Whether or not any individual boy achieves a secure masculine identification depends in large measure on his parents.

A mother with custody can help by encouraging and rewarding her son's independent and exploratory behavior. It is also important that she support her son's relationship with his father by expressing positive attitudes about the father and facilitating the boy's contact with his dad.

Unfortunately, many mothers with custody discourage, inhibit, and restrict their sons' independent behavior. They become apprehensive when their boys engage in adventurous or boisterous activities. And they openly criticize their ex-husbands' worth as fathers. When a mother is fearful and restricts her son's active and assertive behavior, and openly denigrates the father, her boy is more likely to be timid, to be overly dependent, and to feel inadequate as a male.

A noncustodial father can help by seeing his son frequently and by maintaining a warm and close relationship with him. This increases the likelihood that his son will identify with him. The research is very clear on this point: Boys who miss out on frequent contact with their fathers are more likely to be uncertain about their masculinity.

The greater risk of insecure masculine identity in mother-custody boys can be traced to more than just the fathers' absence. Other factors are involved, such as the mothers' attitudes and behavior. We take up this issue again in chapter 8, exploring in greater depth how and why problems with gender identity develop and what parents can do to protect their children from these hazards. But for now it is sufficient to point out that boys in mother-custody households are more likely to develop these problems. Try as she might to be both mother and father to her children, there are some things a single mother finds difficult to give her sons; a strong masculine identity is one.

## Intimate Relationships

Interpersonal relationships are the litmus tests of personality development. Success in love requires several ingredients. These include the capacity to: believe in our intrinsic value as partners; trust in the love of another; separate adequately from our parents so that we are psychologically available for an intimate relationship with another adult; and cope effectively with the inevitable differences that arise in close relationships.

If single mothers find it difficult to give their boys masculine self-confidence, they find it nearly impossible to raise girls who possess a deep trust in their appeal to males. This is, in large measure, the father's role. And if—by attitude, behavior, or lack of involvement with his daughter—

he performs poorly, his daughter is more likely to suffer anxiety and doubts about her attractiveness as a female. And she is less likely to find satisfaction in love.

About twenty years ago, one of the world's leading authorities on divorce, Dr. E. Mavis Hetherington, compared teenage girls from mother-custody homes with a group of girls whose parents had not divorced. The two groups were similar in many respects, but those who were raised without a father in the home had much more difficulty interacting comfortably with boys and men. They spent more time and effort seeking the attention of males. During their free time, they could usually be found hanging out where the boys were: carpentry shop, basketball court, etc. At dances they spent more time at the boys' end of the hall than the other girls. They began dating at an earlier age and were more sexually active. With adult male interviewers they were more receptive than other girls in the study: they sat closer, spoke more, smiled more, made more eye contact, and in general had more open body language. (There were no such differences with female interviewers.)

It might be argued that the mother-custody girls were precocious, self-assured, and assertive with men. But their behavior did not result in their being any more popular with the boys. And rather than confidence, they reported feeling insecure around boys and men. This was evident in their frequent nervous mannerisms while being interviewed by a male: they bit their nails, twirled their hair, and pulled at their lips and clothing.

The strongest evidence of their difficulties in relating to the opposite sex comes from Dr. Hetherington's follow-up study of the girls years later. It turned out that the nervous, attention-seeking behavior of adolescent girls in mother-custody homes foreshadowed later troubles with heterosexual relationships.

They married at an earlier age than girls from intact families, and were more likely to be pregnant at the time of marriage. They also were less satisfied with their husbands and their sexual lives. The men they married were less educated, less successful in their work, and less emotionally mature. They had more negative feelings toward their wives and infants, lost their tempers more frequently, and got in more trouble with the law than did the husbands of women raised with fathers at home.

The difficulties with intimate relationships experienced by women raised in mother-custody homes have been recently confirmed by the well-known California Children of Divorce Study initiated twenty-one years ago by Drs. Judith Wallerstein and Joan Kelly. Ten years after their parents' separation, adolescents and young adults raised in mother-custody homes expressed fears of being hurt, abandoned, and betrayed by men. As a result, they felt more apprehension and less satisfaction in their heterosexual relationships.

The message is clear: When a girl feels rejected by the first man in her life—her father—all future encounters with men are seen through a lens clouded by fear and suspicion. Good relationships with other men—a caring stepfather, older brother, grandfather, uncle, teacher, or psychotherapist—can wipe the lens clean, fostering confidence and trust. But too often streaks of fear remain.

The California study also looked at the intimate relationships of young men who were raised in mother-custody homes, a subject about which less is known. Like their female counterparts, this group had difficulty achieving fulfillment in heterosexual relationships. Ten years after their parents' divorce, almost half of the young men were lonely and had experienced few, if any, lasting relationships with the opposite sex. Their fear of rejection held them back. Playing "hard to get" would not be an effective strategy with these men, because they would not reach out; they would pull back at the slightest sign of disinterest.

Their dilemma is described by New York psychoanalyst Dr. Ethel Person: "Falling in love is, by its nature, predicated on risk-taking. . . . One must gamble on opening up psychically to achieve real intimacy and mutuality. But by revealing oneself to the Other, one becomes vulnerable. Therefore, falling in love—and the ultimate achievement of genuine love—requires an ability to trust oneself as well as the Other, to reveal one's weaknesses and foibles and risk becoming the object of fear and hatred, of condescension, humiliation, or rejection." It is precisely this type of trust that is so difficult for many adults who grew up in divorced families. They are afraid to gamble on love, perhaps because they remember their parents' pain when the wheel came up against them.

"Unlike the women who are worried about betrayal," Dr. Wallerstein writes, "the men seem worried that they won't find true love." It seems that both men and women from divorced homes expect and fear failure in their own love life. And with good reason. Statistics indicate that children whose parents divorced, especially those from mother-custody homes, are more likely to have their own marriages fail. Divorce, then, may leave a sad legacy that is passed down from generation to generation.

I must point out that the conclusions of the California study have been questioned. Because there was no comparison group of children raised in nondivorced families, we cannot be certain that the problems with intimacy found in males were a result of being raised in mother-custody homes. It may be that men from intact families are just as likely to have identical problems. A definitive answer will have to await future research. However, one piece of evidence suggests Dr. Wallerstein is on the right track. A group of men who, prior to the age of twelve, suffered the death of their fathers were more likely than those who lost their fathers later in life to avoid closeness and intimacy and to be dissatisfied with their marriages.

The father plays a key role in helping his offspring develop the skills necessary for healthy interpersonal relationships. It makes sense to assume that his absence will have an impact on his children's future relationships.

Madlyn was in the midst of reciting a familiar adolescent litany of complaints about her mother when she stopped suddenly, looked into my eyes, and said, "Of course you know that if anything ever happened to my mother that would be the end of me." I asked her what she meant. "You know how most children divide their love between their mother and father? Well, I put all mine into my mother, since my father has nothing to do with me. So I'm more dependent on her." If I didn't know better, I would have sworn that Madlyn had been reading the professional literature on adolescent daughters of divorce.

Overdependence on the mother contributes substantially to the problems with intimate relationships experienced by children raised in mother-custody homes. By offering his children a safe relationship independent of the mother, and by providing a buffer between mother and children, the father is instrumental in helping his children psychologically separate from their mother. Without the father's presence, children have more difficulty achieving a comfortable sense of independence. Instead of gradually separating, they either avoid this central task of adolescence by clinging to the safety and security of home, or declare their independence in a dramatic, often premature manner. This sometimes involves transferring dependency from the mother to a boyfriend or girlfriend. Without a genuine sense of psychological separateness, though, their efforts to establish mature interpersonal relationships are doomed to failure.

One hallmark of a healthy and viable intimate relationship is the couple's ability to resolve successfully the differences that inevitably arise.

Children pay close attention to how their parents deal with conflict. Years later, they draw on these early lessons when faced with their own marital conflicts. In fact, this may be one reason why children from divorced homes are more likely to seek divorce as an answer to their own marital problems. Divorce deprives children of the opportunity to observe close-up how two adults cope successfully with conflict.

I am reminded of the following story of something that took place in a nondivorced family, and which illustrates some of what children lose when both parents no longer live under the same roof.

Nicole was twelve years old, beginning junior high, and ready for her own private telephone. Or so she believed. Her father had a different opinion. He thought she shouldn't have a phone in her room until she was in high school. They argued about it, to no avail. Nicole's mother was not sure at first, but gradually came to agree with her daughter. The topic came up several times over a period of three weeks, with the mother raising arguments in favor of the new phone and the father raising arguments against it.

Eventually Nicole's father relented and agreed to the phone. The parents kept their decision a secret, and one day, while Nicole was out, her father wired a telephone jack in her room. The night before her birthday, Nicole's parents slipped into her room while she was asleep and plugged in the new phone. They arranged for a friend to call the next morning, and Nicole awoke to the ringing of her new phone.

This sort of parental teamwork is something that Nicole will always remember. The absence of parental harmony is something that children from divorced homes will never forget, and will never stop regretting.

Years from now, Nicole's family will talk about this episode as the story of how Nicole got her phone. But Nicole really got much more than a phone. She received a lesson about how a couple can manage conflict without letting it tear them apart. The phone was a minor issue, to be sure. But multiply this episode by several hundred in the course of a childhood—Should Andrew take guitar lessons? Is John ready for camp? Should the family move to a new neighborhood?—and you begin to get some idea of what is lost with divorce.

All other things being equal, if Nicole's parents had been divorced, Nicole would have got the phone if she lived with her mom, and done without it if she lived with her dad. Period. End of discussion. She would have missed out on the negotiating, the persuading, the struggling with different opinions, all of which are part of the essential background of an intact family. And the phone would not have nearly the value and meaning to her that it acquired through its fitful birth.

It is observing repeated negotiations like this that sows the seeds for children's future success in interpersonal relationships. Although children whose parents are divorced do not witness such negotiations on a daily basis, the opportunity for parents to model the successful resolution of conflict does not vanish after divorce. As long as the father has any contact with the children, the parents will need to cooperate with each other, at least minimally. Times and places to pick up the children must be arranged, medicines must be transferred, special events must be discussed.

Unfortunately, in some families divorce does not end parental hostilities. In these families, every contact between parents, whether by phone or in person, leads to an angry confrontation and unresolved conflict. Sometimes the warring parents try to pull the children into the battles, enlisting them as spies or messengers. Several studies have demonstrated beyond a doubt that such unremitting anger makes it all the harder for children to adjust to their parents' divorce. Though we don't know all the long-term effects, it is safe to say that children in such families see a seamier side of love, which is apt to leave them with an even more jaundiced and pessimistic view of intimate relationships than those whose divorced parents are able to avoid excessive bitterness.

## Mood

Children lose a lot in a divorce. Besides losing daily contact with their fathers, they usually see less of their mothers, who devote more time to earning a living. Sometimes they cease contact entirely with certain relatives, such as paternal grandparents. And they may lose their familiar homes, neighborhoods, schools, friends, and even pets.

It is not generally recognized that, in families with more than one child, conventional approaches to custody deprive siblings of the chance to spend time alone with each parent. Siblings visit their father, together, and then return to their mother as a group.

Children lose their sense of the family unit as they have known it. I asked one mother if her teenage son, Joey, still talked about his parents' divorce, which had occurred eight years earlier. "He understands why his father and I couldn't stay together," she told me, "but he says he would like to have known what it was like to have parents who are married. What it would have felt like. He's curious about it."

Especially distressing, divorce shatters the comforting assumption, taken for granted by most children, that parents stay around forever.

Many children, after the initial turmoil of the divorce, recover their equilibrium and live a fairly normal childhood. Despite their regrets, they come to accept their losses, make peace with the reality of divorce, and adjust to the reorganization of the family under two roofs with possibly more adults in their life.

Some children, though, do not make this adjustment. In some children, the divorce leaves psychological wounds that resist healing despite the passage of time. One indication of such wounds, a warning signal to parents, is a disturbance in the youngster's mood. This may take the form of pervasive sadness and depression, excessive worry and general anxiety, or extreme fluctuations in mood.

Many circumstances affect whether or not a particular child will become depressed. But, other things being equal, the greater a child's loss, the more susceptible he or she is to depression, either in childhood or later in life.

Joey could express a curiosity about growing up in an intact family without its becoming an overwhelming preoccupation. Other children, though, find themselves obsessed with the loss of their family unit. They sadly cling to the dream of an intact family. This is not the normal child's occasional fantasy of living in an idyllic television family where all conflicts are solved with love in thirty minutes. Children from divorced homes would be happy to settle for much less. What would thrill them is just to be part of an ordinary family in which the mommy and daddy live together under the same roof. Parents underestimate how important this is to children, how much their children took it for granted before the divorce, and how much they miss it when it is gone. To cope with this loss, children sometimes make desperate attempts to get their parents back together.

Conventional approaches to custody appear to compensate children for the loss of the father by allowing intermittent contact with him— usually a maximum of every other weekend. I use the word "appear" because I believe that this tradition reflects an adult sense of time and shows an appalling lack of understanding of the way a child experiences time. The older we get, the faster time flies. For anyone over thirty, two weeks zip by in a flash. For preadolescent children, though, two weeks take a lot longer, particularly when the children are eagerly anticipating something. Making children wait thirteen days before seeing one of their parents, and repeating this ordeal twice a month for the duration of their childhood, is, to my way of thinking, cruel.

We do not recognize the cruelty, perhaps because we have taken traditional practices for granted without careful scrutiny. Or perhaps we know of no better alternatives. Or perhaps we cannot bear to accept and own the harm we are inflicting on our children. Nevertheless, the harm exists. In study after study, children have been letting us know just how difficult is the loss of a parent, even when this loss is mitigated by four days of contact per month.

Perhaps the most unnecessary loss inflicted by divorce—and one frequently overlooked—is the disruption in the relationship between children and their paternal grandparents. In her wish to distance herself from her ex-husband, a woman may deny his parents access to their grandchildren. When this occurs, it is a most unfortunate byproduct of conventional custody. Grandparents can make a precious contribution to divorced families.

In the aftermath of a breakup, parents are often too preoccupied with their own troubles to respond with pleasure to anything, including their children. This deprives children of a major source of self-esteem—the ability to see themselves as a source of joy to their parents. Grandparents who take obvious delight in their grandchildren offer a priceless antidote to such deprivation. Also, grandparents who remain available to the children provide a safe haven from parental hostilities and a valuable sense of stability. Especially if the grandparents' own marriage is a good one, children reap the benefit of witnessing a successful long-term relationship. Later in life, this may help offset some of the fear of intimate relationships to which children of divorce are prone.

I am convinced that the love, attention, and concern of grandparents can help steer children through the stormy seas of the immediate aftermath of the breakup as well as inoculate them against some of the longer-term hazards we have been discussing. From a child's perspective: "In their house things go on just as they always have. We eat dinner at the same time. Grandma wants us to drink milk. Grandpa sings his silly songs. It's nice to know that, no matter what, they will always be there. Same house, same garden, even the same car. They're always happy to see us. It kind of makes me feel good inside." One boy described his grandmother as simply "the most important person in the world to me."

Many children reared in divorced families suffer not just depression but a high level of *anxiety* as well. In common with other childhood traumas,

# ATTENTION: GRANDPARENTS

Grandparents can offer children a safe harbor from the turmoil of divorce. In order to be most effective, grandparents should conduct themselves in a sensitive and judicious manner.

**1.** Do not take sides in the divorce. This cannot possibly benefit you or your grandchildren. If either parent presses for allegiance, explain that you can help best by supporting your grandchildren. Since your relationship with the grandchildren has the best chance of being effective when both parents value your contribution, it is crucial not to alienate either parent. This does not mean that you withhold sympathy and care for your grown child who is going through the pain of divorce. But it will help no one for you to choose sides in a battle. Your most honorable role will be to serve as the Red Cross, taking care of the wounded while maintaining political neutrality.

**2.** Avoid criticizing either parent in front of the children. Most children have a strong sense of loyalty to both parents and are confused and upset when one adult whom they love encourages them to turn against another adult whom they love. If you put down one of their parents, your grandchildren are likely to resent you secretly for this, and your relationship with them will certainly suffer. The one important exception is when a parent has abused a child. In this case, it is incumbent upon any adult who discusses the issue with the child to reassure the child that the abuser's behavior was wrong. Not to acknowledge this in clear and definite terms conveys the impression either that you are not interested in discussing the abuse or that you do not acknowledge the horror of being abused.

**3.** Support and encourage the children's relationships with their other set of grandparents, stepparents, and stepgrandparents. There is no such thing as too many loving adults in a child's life.

**4.** If you can spend more time with the children in the weeks and months immediately following the separation, this can help the entire family as they struggle to adjust to the many challenges that lie before them. Parents whose own emotional state may be depleted will welcome the relief from child-care responsibilities. And the children will benefit from high-quality involvement in a familiar, stable, and nonconflictual atmosphere.

**5.** If you live too far away for regular, frequent contact, reassure the children of your love and interest through letters and telephone calls.

**6.** When the children are with you, relax your expectations somewhat. Although there are advantages to firm limits and a "business-as-usual" policy, the reality is that business is not as usual. In the aftermath of their family's collapse, be prepared for more problem behaviors in children.

**7.** Remind your grandchildren about how happy both parents were when the children were born. At a time when their parents' love for each other has died, children need a lot of reassurance that they will continue to be loved. Explain that divorce is something that happens only between grown-ups and that parents never stop loving their children.

divorce changes permanently the way children think about the world and their lives. Even in homes where the children have witnessed much open warfare between their parents, the news of a divorce usually takes the children by surprise. That their parents will be around forever is such a given that most children give it no thought. Once a parent leaves the home, however, many children never regain the sense of security they felt before the divorce. If you can't count on your parents—your bedrock of security—you can't count on anything. Life is no longer so safe, so predictable, so secure.

Anxiety may find expression in psychosomatic symptoms such as frequent aches and pains for which no medical reason exists. It may take the form of "nervous habits" such as chewing on pencils, biting fingernails, and suffering tics. Or it may take the form of specific fears. Some children develop excessive separation anxiety. They are afraid to be left alone or apart from parents. They may worry about being abandoned by a parent, or being kidnapped, or having something harmful happening to a parent.

In some situations, such as extremely hostile custody battles, these fears may not be unrealistic. Parents sometimes *are* violent to each other, or *do* kidnap their children. But these are the exceptions. In most cases, children's anxiety can be eased if parents handle their divorce in a mature and civilized manner. One of the surest ways to do this is for divorcing partners to work through, reduce, or contain their conflicts. Numerous studies reveal that, the greater the cooperation and the fewer the conflicts between divorced parents, the better chance their children have of coping successfully.

Unfortunately, in many families conflict does not diminish after the separation. Children reared in such families are the ones most likely to suffer long-term psychological problems and to look back on childhood as an unhappy journey. When parents are busy arguing, demeaning, or fighting one another, they are often oblivious to the pain this causes their children. Yet, of all the findings of child psychology research, one of the most solidly established is the harmful impact of excessive parental conflict on children. Dr. Neil Kalter, in his book *Growing Up with Divorce*, says it well: "Missiles aimed at an ex-spouse will more readily lodge in the heart of the children, wounding and frightening them."

Imagine that you are with a group of tourists on an expedition in an African jungle. You have two guides on whom your survival depends. All of a sudden, the guides stop walking and begin arguing.

Guide 1: "We should veer to the left. Although it is a more treacherous path, tourists can manage it. We will meet cannibals if we go in the other direction."

Guide 2: "You don't know what you are talking about. You haven't spent enough time in the jungle to understand the terrain. And you have a poor understanding of tourists' abilities. If only you would cooperate, the expedition would be a lot easier and safer. Your judgment is probably impaired because of your drinking problem. Don't you know that there are crocodile-infested swamps to the left?"

Guide 1: "You underestimate the abilities of the tourists. They need to build more skills. You're just being disagreeable because of the full moon. Your judgment can't be trusted."

I don't know about you, but I would be beside myself with anxiety at this point. You need to rely on the direction of a guide, but each one undermines your trust in the other. I believe this is somewhat akin to what goes on in the mind of a child whose parents are locked in bitter battle.

When parents undercut each other, children are not sure whom to identify with, whom to respect, whom to believe. When parents show that they can work with each other in raising their children, even if they can't live with each other, their children feel a sense of protection that enables them to continue to identify with both parents.

## Self-Control

Our heart goes out to depressed and worried children. Their pain is directed inward and we wish we could do something to relieve it. Often, though, troubled children direct their problems outward in the form of difficult behavior. When this occurs, it is not so easy to respond with patience and understanding.

Shortly after divorce, children become more negative, impulsive, aggressive, and disobedient. This occurs at home and in school. In a landmark project at the University of Virginia, Dr. Hetherington, Dr. Martha Cox, and Dr. Roger Cox studied a large group of preschoolers for several years after their parents' divorce. All the children lived in the custody of their mother. Results indicated that both sons and daughters acted up more in the immediate aftermath of the divorce. But the boys' problems were more severe and enduring. Two years after the divorce, the average girl's problems had virtually disappeared; her behavior resembled that of girls in nondivorced families. In the same time period, although the average boy's behavior improved a great deal, many continued to have significant behavior problems. And these problems persisted even six years after divorce. Similarly, in a nationwide study of 699 elementary-school children, boys in mother-custody homes, when evaluated four and six years after the divorce, had far more behavior problems than did girls. Finally, we learned in the preceding chapter that many studies have demonstrated a strong link between father absence and juvenile delinquency in boys.

Several factors contribute to the behavior problems of boys and girls from divorced homes. As discussed earlier, divorce takes many things away from children, and many children are consequently depressed, frustrated, and angry. When they feel bad, many children are prone to act "bad," especially when they sense that their parents are less able to control them. In the average American family, the father's prohibitions carry more weight with his children than the mother's. Our culture reinforces this—wrongly, I believe—by vesting more power and authority in men. (Just look at television cartoons for evidence.) Often, when the father is absent from the home, his children feel a weakening of the power structure. Most children feel they can get away with more around their mothers.

In some cases, a child's misbehavior mirrors the misbehavior of the parents. Divorcing spouses often become enraged with each other and lose their temper. It is not unusual for angry confrontations to be accompanied by physical violence. When parents demonstrate such poor control over their own behavior, how can they effectively set limits on children's explosive behavior? A mother once told me that her six-year-old boy began hitting her violently the night after he witnessed his father striking her. Somehow, witnessing this episode had weakened her son's control over his own violent temper.

Children with behavior problems that are brought on by divorce do best with parents and teachers who maintain consistent rules and routines, are warm and nurturing, and are firmly in control. The Virginia study found that, when custodial mothers learned more effective discipline techniques, children's behavior improved dramatically.

Two additional factors are important, particularly for boys. First, problems with self-control are least likely to occur when parents support each other's relationship with the children by communicating well, avoiding mutual denigration, and agreeing on child-rearing practices. In effect, these parents continue to function as a parental team in behalf of their children, despite the differences that ended their marriage. Second, boys who frequently see their fathers have the most self-control.

So we see that, whether we consider such factors as self-esteem, mood, or behavior, parents play a large role in how well their children cope with divorce.

## CHILDREN WHO COPE AND CHILDREN WHO DON'T

Other factors in addition to parents' behaviors influence how an individual child responds to his parents' divorce. The child's age, basic temperament, predivorce personality, and the economic circumstances and geographical stability of the family all play a role. For example, all other things being equal, we can predict that a child with severe psychological problems or learning disabilities before the divorce, who has always had difficulty adapting to changes and adversity, and whose mother has to work long hours and move to a high-crime neighborhood because the father reneges on child support, will be a lot harder hit by the divorce than a child who had been well adjusted before the divorce, who continues to live in the same house and attend the same school, and whose mother is not preoccupied with financial worries.

## Boys versus Girls

One other factor stands out as critical in predicting the probability of a child's making a good adjustment to divorce. At least before adolescence, girls in mother-custody homes do far better than boys—at home, in school, and with peers. Boys are more vulnerable in several respects. They are more likely to be unhappy, depressed, and withdrawn. They get along worse with their parents, teachers, and peers. They are more likely to get in trouble with the law. They are more insecure about their gender identity. And they don't concentrate as well or work as hard in school.

These findings are, perhaps, not surprising when we recall the research reviewed in the preceding chapter that indicated that, before adolescence, fathers play a more salient role in the psychological development of sons than daughters. Several theories have been advanced to account for the greater suffering of boys than girls in mother-custody homes. Traditionally it has been attributed to girls' being more resilient and to boys' being more negatively affected by parental conflict. If this were accurate, then we would expect to find the same difference in father-custody homes. But we don't. The implications of gender differences in response to divorce are so important that they deserve a full and separate treatment, which I provide in chapters 7 and 8.

Children are not the only ones who experience problems in mother-custody families. Mothers with custody and fathers without custody find this life style difficult, but for different reasons.

## ONE PARENT DOING THE JOB OF TWO

The job description of a typical single mother reads something like this. She is, of course, solely responsible for all aspects of her children's upbringing. Unless her children are teenagers, she must supervise the morning routines, prepare breakfast, make and pack a lunch (or remember to provide lunch money), arrange for after-school day care (or worry about having a latchkey child), read and respond to papers brought home from school, supervise the completion of homework, set and enforce limits, give her children dinner, make sure they bathe adequately and often enough, put them to bed . . . and much more.

If they wake in the night, she gets them back to sleep. If they become ill, she takes their temperature and gives them aspirin, cough medicine, etc., and if the problem persists she makes and keeps the appointment with the pediatrician. If they are hurt or sad, she soothes them. If there is trouble at school, she visits with the teacher, counselor, or principal. If there is trouble with a peer, she talks with the other child's parents.

The mother with custody arranges medical and dental checkups, carpools, birthday parties, overnights with friends, registration for soccer, baseball, basketball, football, gymnastics, ballet, scouts, and camp . . . and much more.

She does the laundry, cleans the house, makes or buys costumes for Halloween and school plays, keeps track of food on hand, shops for groceries, household supplies, school supplies, clothes, gifts . . . and much more.

She chauffeurs her children: to school if they are late, home from day care, to and from music and dance lessons, sports practices and games, scouts, friends' homes, parties, movies, doctors, dentist . . . and much more.

On top of all this, the typical single mother works full-time outside the home and would like to find time to pursue a social life and to be alone. Single parenthood is an exhausting life style. Its competing demands for time and attention keep the single mother running on a treadmill that stops only twice a month—and then only for a short while—when the children visit their father. When they return, the treadmill starts up again, often in a higher gear: The emotional wear-and-tear of parting with their father for two weeks can result in moody behavior that taxes a mother's patience.

One mother gave this comparison between home life before and after the divorce: "Before we split, Richard's father took him to scout meetings every Monday night, soccer practice on Thursday night, and the soccer game Saturday morning. I used to look forward to these times. This was when I could do the laundry and talk to friends without being interrupted. Even more valuable was the opportunity to have time just for myself. I might catch up on my reading or just relax and enjoy the peace and quiet. Now it is my job to drive Richard to his activities or else take the time to make arrangements for him to go with a friend. His father still takes him to the games during his visits every other weekend, but that still leaves a lot more work for me. The laundry doesn't get done as often as I would prefer. And I don't cook a whole meal as often as I used to. We are more likely to have fast-food Styrofoam boxes on our kitchen table than dinner plates. As for my reading? Surely you jest. By the time Richard is in bed, I'm too exhausted to do anything. I hate to admit it, but sometimes I fall asleep before Richard."

And this mother speaks for the more fortunate families in which the father lives in close geographical proximity and meets his commitment to see the children every other weekend. In an estimated 3.2 million families, 40 percent of all mother-custody households, the children rarely see their father, and so the mother rarely gets time off from parenting. In many other families, the father lives out of town and sees the children only on holidays and for two weeks in the summer.

It is not just the work load that weighs heavily on the single mother. She must also contend with financial worries and a lower standard of living. Another significant burden for the mother with custody is the responsibility for making all the child-rearing decisions on her own. As one mother puts it, "I never thought much about this until Arthur left, but it was always comforting to discuss things with someone else who cared as much about Pauline's welfare as I do. Like the time we moved Pauline from her crib to a regular bed. Arthur and I decided that together. Now I'm more afraid of making a mistake or overlooking something important. If I'm too preoccupied with my own worries—which happens a lot more lately— and I forget to do something, it just doesn't get done. I miss the backup that Arthur provided." Another mother tells about several friends who rushed into second marriages to escape the wearisome feeling of always being responsible.

Not only does the mother with sole custody take on the job of two parents, she does so when her capacity to be a good parent is at an all-time low. The end of a marriage, regardless of who initiates it, is a time of crisis. It tears asunder much of the familiar fabric of everyday existence that gives our life meaning and comfort—the "essential background" of daily routine and family interaction that we take for granted until it is taken from us. Without this emotional anchor, we remain adrift at sea, disoriented until we find our bearings. Even when the separation brings relief from painful daily hostilities, it results in fundamental changes that throw us off balance. The process of emotional realignment takes time and a good deal of energy. During this period, it is understandable that parents will be preoccupied with their own worries and less available to their children.

74

This often leads to the type of domestic disorganization and disruption of routines described by Richard's mother. Household chores go undone. Children are more likely to have erratic meals and bedtimes and to arrive late at school. Their mothers are less likely to have the time, energy, or frame of mind to play with them during bathtime or read to them before going to bed. As Wallerstein and Blakeslee observe: "Divorce is associated with a diminished capacity to parent in almost all dimensions—discipline, playtime, physical care, and emotional support. Divorcing parents spend less time with their children and are less sensitive to their children's needs."

One professional, a competent and hardworking woman, described her conflict upon returning home in the evening after a busy day at the office. After helping people all day long, more than anything she wanted time for herself. She felt depleted. Her five-year-old son, on the other hand, had different ideas about what his mother should do at home. He demanded instant attention, and lots of it. She recognized the legitimacy of his demands and did her best to meet them, yet she was exhausted.

For a brief unexpected moment during our consultation, this mother gave full expression to the depth of her frustration. She began sobbing and asked, "When do I get *my* turn? Why do I have to keep giving and giving when no one is there for me? I know I don't have the patience I should for Scott. And I know it sounds selfish, but sometimes, just once in a while, *I* want to be the one taken care of, treated special, comforted."

Moreover, the single mother's "diminished capacity to parent" comes at a time when the children themselves are in a crisis and demand more emotional support than usual. As Drs. Mavis Hetherington, Martha Cox, and Roger Cox of the Virginia divorce study observe: "The divorced mother is harassed by her children, particularly her sons. . . . They nag and whine, make more dependency demands, and are more likely to ignore her. . . . Some divorced mothers described their relationship with their child one year after divorce as 'declared war,' a 'struggle for survival,' 'the old Chinese water torture' or 'like getting bitten to death by ducks.' " All too often, the single mother is the target of all her children's anger while the infrequently seen father is treated only with benevolence.

This was a big complaint of Diana's mother. Whenever Diana's father disappointed her, Diana pretended that she wasn't upset. But her anger didn't disappear. It spilled out in the wrong places—at school and at home. Her mother was a primary target. Each time Diana felt rejected by her dad, she became negative and moody with her mother. Refusals to comply with simple requests, like taking a bath or going to bed, invariably culminated in prolonged, exhausting tantrums which left both Diana and her mother emotionally depleted. In a very real sense, her mother was paying for the sins of Diana's father. Not a very fair arrangement, but unfortunately all too common in mother-custody families across the country.

And because this is so common, it would be a mistake to let our analysis rest at the level of blaming all the "lousy fathers" who default on their commitment to their children. We need to search deeper to identify the root causes of the problem. Why do so many divorced fathers renege on their parental responsibilities? What happens to the father-child relationship after divorce? And what can we do to improve the situation?

## WHERE HAVE ALL THE FATHERS GONE?

Conventional custody throws father-child relationships into a tailspin from which relatively few recover. Many—all too many—crash. Consider the evidence. *One-third of all children who live with their single mothers never see their fathers.* Their fathers give up on them entirely. One-quarter see their fathers less than once per month. One-fifth have monthly contact. A little fewer than one-fifth see their father weekly. Even phone contact between children and their divorced fathers is very limited. Only about one of every four children talks to his or her father weekly. Overall, the relationship between children and their noncustodial fathers is so limited that less than a third view their fathers' households as their own homes. In a very real sense, many single fathers have partially or completely abandoned their children.

### Why Men Fail to Visit Their Children

Why aren't divorced fathers more involved with their children? Probably, in large measure, because many men have been raised with a deficient appreciation of the value of strong emotional bonds between fathers and their offspring. The motherhood mystique has written the script, and many fathers have accepted their assigned role. Divorced fathers who aspire to break free of society's formula meet formidable legal obstacles. Our courts have institutionalized their second-class status by allowing them only minimal contact with, and authority over, their children.

But this does not explain why so many fathers fail to exercise even the limited "visiting privileges" that the court has awarded them. Some of these men were very involved with their children during the marriage. But soon after the separation, contact begins to dwindle and fathers drift away from their children. Why?

Mothers, children, and courts often assume that such fathers don't love their children. Though this is true for some men, it grossly oversimplifies the situation for most. Experts are more likely to place the blame on the inherent difficulties in maintaining a "visiting" relationship.

The intact family provides a framework that facilitates a father's meaningful presence in his children's lives. He has one or two meals a day with them. He helps with homework. He quizzes them on their spelling words. He signs their report cards. He drives them to soccer games. He works on projects with them. He reminds them to do their regular chores. He listens to them recite their lines for the school play. He enforces the rules of the house. He watches television with them. He takes them to the video-rental shop. He plays with them. He gives good-night kisses.

All this is lost when a father lives apart from his children. From the children's point of view, what is gone is what Dr. Kalter calls "the atmosphere of father-presence." As an occasional "visitor" with his children, the noncustodial father finds it difficult to retain the same depth and diversity of parental involvement. Because their time together is so limited, the father tries to maximize the "good times" by planning an event-filled visit. He becomes, in essence, a recreational director coordinating a tight schedule of activities. Homework and chores are no longer his concern. His children no longer accompany him on routine errands to the dry cleaner and grocery store. Nor do the children want to "spoil" the precious hours they have together; like Diana, they are reluctant to express negative feelings to their father. They also fear that, if they get angry with their father, he may abandon them totally. "After all," they reason, "if he walked out on Mom, he can walk out on us."

Despite the pleasure of the trips to the mall, park, movies, and fast-food places, the Disneyland Daddy relationship eventually wears thin. Something essential is clearly lost. The father-child relationship is no longer as rich, or as comfortable, or as meaningful as before the divorce. And it is no longer as gratifying. One man compared the role of the noncustodial father to that of an ice-cream man "coming around the corner and stopping to give out all sorts of delights, then disappearing just as quickly around another corner."

Contained within the question "Why do men fail to visit with their children?" is a clue to its own answer. By labeling a father's contact with his offspring as a "visit," we implicitly undermine the father's status. Children "live" with their parents. They don't "visit" them. Cast in the peripheral role of a visitor, some men fail to appreciate their importance to their children, and thus gradually drift out of their lives. They are aided in this by society's devaluation of their role, as in the case of the judge who ruled that a father could not see his children on Christmas "because children belong with their families at Christmas."

For some fathers, the limitations of the visiting relationship are too much to surmount. Aside from the logistical problem of scheduling fun-filled activities (the problem is multiplied when there are two or more children who differ widely in age or interests), each visit is a painful reminder of what has been lost. Many fathers find four days per month insufficient contact to sustain a sense of deep connection to their children. Also, the repetitive separations and reunions create an emotional strain that takes a toll on both children and fathers. Parting at the end of the visit is especially sad for both. To avoid the pain, some fathers find it easier to forgo the visits altogether, or at least reduce their frequency.

Other fathers avoid contact with their children in order to distance themselves from feelings associated with the divorce. These men are so preoccupied with their guilt, anger, shame, or depression that they cannot bear to face a potent reminder of the failed marriage. The father of one boy I worked with was so insistent on cutting off all contact with his former wife that he refused to see his son or even talk with him on the phone. Any contact with his boy aroused irrational fears of being somehow controlled by or linked to his ex-wife. The excuse he gave his son was that it just "wasn't the right time." In two years, the "right time" never came. As far as I know, this father has yet to resume contact with his son. On Father's Day, my patient was in a quandary about whether or not to send his father a card. He couldn't see the point in acknowledging the existence of a father who couldn't acknowledge the existence of his son.

## Involuntary Child-Absence Syndrome

The decline in contact between father and child is not all within the father's control. The mother may play a significant role. She may seek through legal means to curtail the father's access to his children. Or she may undermine the visits in a more indirect manner—for example, by scheduling the children for a fun activity at the same time that they are supposed to be with their father. One mother registered her children for a museum class that met every Saturday for four hours. This effectively cut the father's time with his children in half. When the father objected, the mother made him out to look like the "bad guy" for depriving his children of such an opportunity.

Some mothers make visits more difficult for the fathers by criticizing them when they pick the children up or drop them off. Not having the children physically or emotionally ready for the visits is another way in which a mother can frustrate and discourage her former husband's wish to maintain his commitment to the children. One mother's strategy was to begin an exciting game just before the father was due to pick up his children. When he arrived, the children were so engrossed in the game that they greeted their father without enthusiasm. The father's feelings were hurt, and the visits got off to a poor start.

Then there are some mothers who simply disallow the visit. A recent study found that between one-fourth and one-third of custodial mothers have, at least on one occasion, denied the father access to his children.

When a loving father is denied access to his children, or is merely threatened with the complete or partial loss of contact, he is liable to suffer significant psychological disturbance. Dr. John Jacobs calls this "involuntary child absence syndrome." The syndrome is characterized by high levels of anxiety, outrage, and depression in reaction to the rupture of the parent-child relationship. I note in passing that these symptoms are not unlike many children's reactions to being abandoned by their fathers.

Mothers have various reasons for interfering in their children's relationship with their fathers. Some mothers have genuine concerns for the children's safety. I have consulted with several women who were worried that their ex-husbands might get drunk while the children were in his care. Other mothers interpret their children's uneasiness at the beginning and end of visits as an indication that the visits are psychologically harmful. They may even begin to suspect that their children are being physically or sexually abused during the visits. In such a case, it is incumbent upon the mother to seek an evaluation by a qualified mental-health professional with substantial expertise in child development, psychological testing, and psychotherapy with children.

Just as a father may avoid seeing his children in order to distance himself from feelings about the divorce, so a mother may try to erase a father from her children's lives in order to avoid facing the reality of her failed marriage. It is as though she can pretend the marriage never existed if she has no contact with her ex-husband. Such a mother may quickly attach herself to another man and expect her children to call this new man "Daddy." In my experience, this is virtually guaranteed to threaten and enrage the father.

Some mothers are so angry with their ex-husbands that they cannot acknowledge his importance to the children. Or their wish to punish the ex-husbands blinds them to the harm they are causing their children by depriving them of their fathers' company. Ultimately, these women may find that their opposition to the father-child relationship backfires. When a mother succeeds in preventing her children from seeing their father, they are apt to worry about what else she might take away from them. Their trust in her is weakened; in later years, they may come to blame her for their father's absence. In the end, the mother's own relationship with her children suffers, and this makes growing up that much more difficult for her children.

In this chapter, we have seen that all is not well with the mother-custody family. Mothers are overburdened, fathers are reduced to a superficial presence in their children's lives, and children experience a deterioration in their relationships with both parents.

This predictable deterioration must be given weight in any custody decision. The married woman who stays at home and devotes a lot of attention to her well-behaved children gives way to the woman who works more outside the home, has less time and energy for her children, and finds her children's behavior, particularly her sons', unmanageable. The relatively uninvolved father, who finds his parental identity threatened, may regard the divorce as a second chance to develop a more meaningful commitment to his children. Or he may take flight and abandon his offspring. One cannot easily predict postdivorce parent-child relationships by extrapolating from the predivorce situation.

One thing, though, is clear. Conventional custody creates casualties. Growing awareness of the limitations inherent in the traditional approach to custody has led some families and courts to explore other avenues that allow for more father participation. These families are in the vanguard of the custody revolution.

# MAXIMIZING CHILDREN'S CHANCES: FIVE COPING FACTORS

Despite the psychological risks that attend growing up in a mother-custody home, some children cope more successfully than others. Which children do best depends, in large measure, on their parents. Throughout this chapter, I have mentioned various ways parents affect their children's adjustment. These are important enough to merit emphasis. Also, because these factors help predict outcomes for children, mental-health professionals and courts should weigh them in their custody deliberations.

**1.** *Sufficient access to each parent to enable children to maintain high-quality relationships with both.*

This ensures that children do not lose a parent as a result of the divorce. Through word and deed, a parent can support access to the noncustodial parent. Siblings should be given the opportunity to have some time alone with each parent. A mother should convey to her children the belief that contact with their father is to be valued highly. The easier she makes it for the father to maintain contact with the children, the more likely he is to do so. She should have the children ready on time. And she should avoid unpleasant confrontations with her ex-spouse when the children are picked up or dropped off. Such confrontations make children anxious and detract from the value of their contact with their father.

One of the most difficult issues for mothers is the loss of control they feel when the children are under the father's supervision. Often the mother and father have different ideas about appropriate diet, behavior, etc. The father may have his new romantic interest accompany him when he sees the children. Unless the children are being abused, the mother should recognize the advantages of their contact with their father, no matter how she feels about his way of doing things.

For his part, a father should do what he can to make it more likely for the mother to support his contact with the children. He should be consistent and reliable, arriving on time to pick up the children and bringing them back as scheduled. He, too, should avoid using the transfer of the children as an excuse to argue with his ex-wife.

Both parents should be flexible (within reason) and willing to accommodate each other when occasional schedule changes are requested. (But parents should stick as closely as possible to the schedule and not request last-minute changes casually or frequently.) If the mother is going to be away from the children at a time when they are not scheduled to be with their father, she should offer him the chance to take them. And the father should welcome this opportunity to be with his children, rather than complain about being used as a babysitter. Neither parent should make a big deal out of a few minutes' lateness in picking up or dropping off the children.

If parents can't agree on custody, courts should try to determine which parent is more likely to foster the children's contact with the other parent. This factor should receive considerable weight in the custody decision.

**2.** *A cooperative, low-conflict relationship between the parents.*

This may be the most difficult thing for divorced parents to accomplish, but it is also the greatest gift they can give their children. If parents cannot let go of their anger, the children will wonder if any purpose was served by the divorce. Children whose parents maintain high levels of conflict are more likely to feel torn between the parents and suffer painful loyalty conflicts. They also feel more anxious and have less self-control.

Parents and attorneys often ask, "How can two people who could not get along with each other in marriage, cooperate with each other after their divorce?" My response is that most of us have learned to be courteous and get along with people we don't like—co-workers, sales personnel, casual acquaintances. If parents can treat strangers with common decency, surely—for the good of their children—they can make the same effort with their former spouses.

**3.** *Skilled and sensitive child-rearing practices.*

All children, regardless of their parents' marital status, function best with what psychologists call "authoritative parenting." This has three basic components: warmth, firmness, and consistency. Authoritative parents relate to their children with empathic understanding of their emotional needs, nurturant, attentive involvement, and extensive verbal give-and-take, while at the same time setting and enforcing clear limits. This parenting strategy is linked with children's higher self-esteem, maturity, and social responsibility. Authoritative parents avoid the two extremes of being overly permissive or excessively harsh and punitive.

**4.** *Minimal changes for the children.*

Divorce changes many things for children. If parents can remain in the same geographical area, their children will at least maintain the same friends, neighborhood, and school. Most important, the children will still have access to both parents. If the parents do not maintain a commitment to live within easy commuting distance from each other, the result will be the children's loss of regular contact with one parent.

**5.** *Good social-support systems for children and parents.*

Divorce undermines children's confidence in the permanence of love. This can be offset, in part, through the continued love and involvement of relatives. Parents also can use support to cope with the emotional strains and demands that accompany divorce. The best assistance a single mother and her children can have is the active and supportive involvement of the noncustodial father. Grandparents can offer children reassuring stability and love and a safe haven from parental hostilities. Most parents fail to discuss the divorce with their children's teachers. This is usually a mistake. A compassionate teacher can give a child needed support during family crises. Parents should request that their child be placed with a nurturing teacher who runs an orderly, structured, and predictable classroom. Children who see little of their fathers can benefit from a warm relationship with a male teacher.

Good substitute child care can be a major support for children while giving their single mother needed relief. It enables children to receive a greater amount and a higher quality of adult attention, both from the additional care-givers and from their mother (because her emotional resources will be less depleted).

Finally, groups such as Parents Without Partners can provide parents with emotional support. By exposing them to others who have coped successfully with the challenges of divorce, such groups help divorced parents maintain hope during a time of crisis.

# PART 2

## FATHER-CUSTODY FAMILIES

# 4

## PIONEER
## FATHERS

*Most fathers don't want custody and could not take it
on even if they thought they wanted to.*
**—Anonymous reviewer, American Journal of Psychiatry, 1981**

*It would be very difficult for a man to raise two boys
like a woman can, therefore, I'm going to name [the
mother] as managing conservator [custodian] of the children.*
**—Family-court judge, Waco, Texas, 1982**

**R**aising children is women's work. Or so we are programmed to believe. When a woman seeks custody of her children, it seems natural and we don't think twice about it. But when a man seeks custody, we are filled with doubts and questions. Why does he want custody? How does he handle the job? How are his children affected?

Let us begin our portrait of custodial fathers by looking at their various motives for seeking custody.

## WHY FATHERS SEEK CUSTODY

Occasionally I am called into a custody dispute to conduct a psychological evaluation. In the course of my examination, among other goals, I must try to uncover the father's reasons for pursuing custody. Because in our culture it is unconventional for a single father to want to be actively involved in raising his children, many people assume that such a father has bad motives for seeking custody. This stereotype is belied by the many fathers I have met over the years who were motivated primarily by love of their children and concern for their welfare. Unfortunately, I have met some fathers who fit the stereotype—fathers who were using the custody issue as a means to other ends. Although in my experience they are in the minority, I would like to describe some of the more reprehensible characters I have encountered in this line of work before discussing the benevolent motives of the majority.

## Bad Reasons for Seeking Custody

Eight types of fathers seek custody for what I consider the wrong reasons.

**The Negotiator and the Cheapskate.** The "negotiator" acts as though he wants custody of his children. But his objective is something quite different. What he really wants is to gain the upper hand in the divorce negotiations. His strategy is to threaten his wife with the prospect of a costly and public custody battle. If he succeeds in intimidating her, then he agrees to withdraw his request for custody in exchange for a more favorable financial settlement.

Incidentally, fathers are not the only parents guilty of this tactic. I recall interviewing one vindictive mother embroiled in a custody dispute for six years. (Tragically, in some families custody litigation continues until the child is an adult.) This mother surprised me by declaring that her ex-husband could see his son as much as he wanted if he would only give her a one-time payment of $1,800. It was not her extortion attempt that surprised me, but the open admission of her ulterior motive. This strategy is usually played with more finesse.

A character as unscrupulous as the negotiator is the "cheapskate." He seeks custody mainly for the purpose of avoiding child-support payments. Either he underestimates the difficulty of raising children alone, or he plans to remarry soon after the divorce and expects his new wife to assume the child-care responsibilities.

**The Bluffer and the Clinger.** A variant of the negotiator is the "bluffer." This father, too, seeks custody when he does not really want it. But he is not looking for a better divorce settlement. In fact, he does not even want a divorce. Like the bluffer in poker who makes the hand too expensive for the other players to continue, this father raises the stakes of the divorce by threatening his wife with the loss of her children. He hopes that, instead of taking this risk, she will fold her cards and return to the marriage.

When a man has no hope of convincing his wife to return to him, yet he still cannot let go, he may adopt the strategy of the "clinger." This father wants custody so that he can have more frequent contact with his ex-wife. Not only will he see her every time she comes to visit the children, but he will telephone her frequently under the guise of discussing the children's needs. The hope for reconciliation lingers in his mind.

**The Avenger and the Narcissist.** The "avenger" responds differently to a rejecting wife. Instead of clinging to her, he wants to punish her. And what better way to do so than to win custody? The typical avenger is bitter because his wife has left him for another man. Some men take their revenge by filing for divorce on the grounds of marital infidelity and then having the satisfaction of proving this publicly in a court of law. If, however, a wife is granted a no-fault divorce, her "wrongdoing" will be considered irrelevant in the courtroom and the man will be deprived of this form of revenge. For this reason, some legal scholars believe that no-fault divorce is partially responsible for the recent increase in custody litigation. The custody battle replaces the divorce trial as an outlet for the husband's anger.

Even when there is little hope of winning custody, a custody trial offers a man the opportunity of denigrating his wife by laundering in public all the dirty linen of the marriage. One vindictive father who lost his bid for custody told me confidentially that he would not have kept custody if he had won. He believed that the children should live with their mother, but he gloated about seeing "her mask of virtue slipping" during the bitter custody hearing.

The "narcissist" regards custody as a vehicle to prove his worth to the world, to his ex-wife, and to himself. Although he may pay lip service to the children's needs, he is more concerned with his own image. The narcissist's ego, already fragile, is dealt an additional blow by the failed marriage. To compensate, he self-righteously aggrandizes his own contribution to the children while belittling his wife's role.

**The Atoner and the Loner.** Two types of fathers who seek custody for the wrong reasons deserve more sympathy than those discussed above. The "atoner" wants a divorce, but feels guilty about breaking up the family. He seeks custody in order to assuage his guilt. In essence, the atoner chooses to live with his children in order to live with his conscience.

The "loner" wants custody in order to receive emotional support from his children. Ralph was a typical loner. A chemical engineer for a large corporation, Ralph was far more competent with test tubes than with people. When it came to social skills, he and his wife, Susan, were opposites. Susan made friends easily; Ralph often said that, were it not for her, he would have no friends. Although he enjoyed spending time with people, he relied on Susan to generate their social contacts. When Ralph and Susan separated, his social life deteriorated and he grew more lonely and depressed. To relieve his loneliness, Ralph sought custody of his children. He knew that the children's presence on a daily basis would keep him from feeling isolated. Although his wish for custody was genuine, Ralph was less concerned about what he could *give* the children than what he could *get* from them.

I have described the eight groups of fathers as pure types, but in reality most parents have mixed motives for seeking custody. Some motives they express openly, and some they hide, at times even from themselves. In fact, the most powerful motivating forces may exert their influence unconsciously. For example, a man may convince himself that his bid for custody is solely for the benefit of his children, when simultaneously he is unconsciously driven by a wish to punish his wife. Furthermore, his motive for keeping custody may change over time. Initially he may seek custody solely to punish his wife, but then discovers the gratifications of greater involvement with the children. As we shall see, fathers frequently "grow into" the role of custodial parent.

If it is difficult for a father to know his true reasons for pursuing custody, the difficulty is multiplied for judges. Because it is not always possible to

---

## BAD REASONS FOR SEEKING CUSTODY

1. To extract a better financial settlement.
2. To avoid child-support payments.
3. To force your spouse to stay in the marriage.
4. To have more contact with your spouse after the divorce.
5. To punish your spouse.
6. To prove your worth to the world.
7. To alleviate your guilt about the divorce.
8. To relieve your loneliness.

---

determine when a father is hiding less-than-noble motives, a judge may assume that a father litigating for custody probably wants to avoid child-support payments or hurt his wife. In most cases, this assumption would be incorrect.

## Benevolent Motives for Seeking Custody

Every study that has investigated this issue has revealed that most fathers who seek custody feel strong bonds with their children and cherish these bonds. Custody, for them, is a way to maintain the strength of these ties. These men take their child-rearing responsibilities seriously and believe they can provide a good home for their children. One man volunteered this advice to other fathers: "What is your real basic motive in wanting custody? . . . Taking a shot at the wife is the wrong reason. If you feel you can do a better job of parenting, then that's a good reason. It's not a piece of cake so be sure you want to do it."

Similar sentiments are expressed by most custodial fathers. Wreaking vengeance on an ex-spouse or avoiding child-support payments is little compensation for the tremendous expenditure of time, energy, and money required of custodial parents. A plumber, whose wife allegedly drank heavily and neglected the children, spent $10,000 on legal fees for his custody battle. He told an interviewer, "I had to take out a loan, and my parents had to take out a loan. But it was worth it. I would have done anything to get my children back. It was hell for me those eight months while they were with her. I was worried to death about them." This man's commitment is typical of the attitude many fathers have toward custody.

Brock Henry is a professor of government at a university in California. His prior experience with traditional custody taught him a bitter lesson and left him determined never to relinquish custody again. I will let him tell you his story in his own words.

"I had been married before—I'd gotten married and had a child in my early twenties. I was much too young to have had any business getting married, much less have a child, or know how to raise one. When that marriage broke up after a few years, it was a disaster—my wife just moved out one day, taking the child with her. I would have visits with him, but at one point his mother simply disappeared with him. I found out after a year that she was living in another state. We finally finalized a divorce, and I simply accepted what I thought was the standard deal available, as worked out by the lawyers—she would have custody, and I would pay child support and have visitation rights.

"The problem was, she continued to move from place to place, but always several states away, so visitations were special occasions, fraught with tension and significance—I had no real, normal contact with my son. At one point, my ex-wife essentially dumped him on me for six months, while I was living alone in a small apartment. It was difficult to suddenly integrate a six-year-old into the independent life style I had evolved, and I didn't do a very good job of refocusing my energies toward child-rearing.

"Then my ex-wife suddenly appeared again and whisked my son away, and I'm afraid I didn't put up much of an argument. So he was raised by his mother in another state, eventually with a stepfather and stepsibling, and we would talk on the phone once a week and have visits once a month or so, but the relationship always seemed both somehow artificial, because of the distance, and pressured, because of my need to make it mean something when we did have contact.

"My son grew up with socialization problems, and with a lot of un-resolved anger. I had remarried, but it remained difficult to integrate him into my life—my city apartment was small even for a married couple, and there were tensions between my son and my new wife. We tried a board-ing school, but he got himself expelled after two years, and wound up living by himself in Los Angeles, in various social undergrounds. He's since got his high-school equivalency, and has been taking courses at a local college. But he still walks around with a lot of unresolved anger that he won't admit to himself, and he is prone to unpredictable and some-times self-destructive impulses. I ascribe much of this to the chaotic experience that he had as a child, moving from place to place, and to my absence from his life and upbringing in any meaningful day-to-day man-ner.

"So, after this disastrous and heartbreaking experience with conven-tional custody, I was determined that, if I ever had another child, it would not be this way again."

Brock did have a child by his second wife. Unfortunately, this marriage, too, ended in divorce, and this time Brock did not relinquish custody. "It seemed to be absolutely essential that my daughter not lose her connec-tion with me as her father, and that we would continue to have a normal family relationship, the kind that's defined by all those apparently trivial activities like getting breakfast, picking out clothes for the day, talking about what happened in school, bedtime stories, etc. This was what I had missed with my son, and the lack of this normal family experience seemed to have prevented normal family intimacy with him, and to have deprived him in some way of a point of moral reference in his life."

It should come as no surprise that fathers can be dedicated parents. The preceding chapter demonstrated that fathers can and do develop strong attachments to their children. We saw the heartbreaking anguish of noncustodial fathers suffering from the involuntary child-absence syndrome. The evidence is clear: We have no reason automatically to assume malevolent motives on the part of a father who seeks custody of his children.

As we have seen, some fathers do pursue custody with less-than-honorable intentions. But are we justified in doubting the sincerity of *all* men seeking custody? Clearly not. Continuing this prejudice is equivalent to presuming a man is guilty until proven innocent. Only the motherhood mystique allows such a blatant form of sex discrimination to be practiced in our courts.

## HOW CUSTODIAL FATHERS COPE

Fathers planning to keep custody wonder what their lives will be like after divorce. In most families, the initial breakup of a marriage sends a shock wave with reverberations that are felt by everyone in the family for many months, sometimes many years. This is no less true for men with custody of their children. In the wake of the divorce, and in common with other divorced parents, custodial fathers struggle with anger, guilt, anxiety, loneliness, and depression. Fathers who think that keeping custody will shield them from the stress of divorce are sadly mistaken. As most divorced mothers know, with custody come additional challenges. And because it is unconventional in our culture, father custody brings with it certain *unique* problems.

## FATHER CUSTODY AND THE WORKPLACE

At work, custodial fathers frequently encounter unsupportive attitudes from supervisors and co-workers. Employers expect men to regard their jobs as their top priority; little tolerance is shown for a father who must juggle work and child-care responsibilities.

In a job interview, one recently divorced father emphasized his inability to work past five o'clock because he had to pick up his children from day care. During his first week on the job, his employer asked him to stay later; when he explained why he could not stay, he lost his job. It seemed that his employer was so unaccustomed to the idea of a father with primary child-care responsibility that he had not taken the father seriously during the job interview.

Even if they do not lose their jobs, men who refuse to work overtime because of their child-care responsibilities are perceived as less valuable employees and suffer reduced opportunities for advancement.

Co-workers are sometimes highly critical of a father whose child-care duties are evident in the workplace. This occurs, for example, when a father leaves work to retrieve a sick child from school. Although the criticisms are usually couched in terms of the inconvenience to others on the job, hidden motives often fuel such negative attitudes.

The custodial father's strong commitment to his children threatens the self-esteem of fathers who are not so committed. Many men, particularly divorced fathers with traditional visiting schedules, feel guilty about devoting little time to their children. They deal with this guilt through various rationalizations. They may tell themselves that their careers do not permit greater involvement with their children, or that raising children is women's work. The mere existence of custodial fathers exposes these rationalizations as flimsy. To ward off their own discomfort, some fathers will disparage men with custody, as if to say, "It is your life style that is wrong, not mine."

Male co-workers are not the only ones in the workplace to express hostility toward custodial fathers. Women with traditional attitudes about sex roles, or divorcees whose ex-husbands have threatened or actually initiated challenges to the custody of their children, often resent fathers with custody and have a psychological stake in proving that the father-custody life style is not viable.

Custodial fathers can better withstand the criticisms of co-workers if they understand the hidden motives behind the criticisms. The same motives drive some attorneys and psychotherapists to discourage divorced fathers from seeking more access to their children. If you are working with a lawyer or therapist who holds such attitudes, you should bring it up with him or her. If you continue to doubt your lawyer or therapist's ability to empathize with your concerns, you might want to get a second opinion, from a professional who is more sympathetic to your goals.

It should come as no surprise that fathers can be dedicated parents. The preceding chapter demonstrated that fathers can and do develop strong attachments to their children. We saw the heartbreaking anguish of noncustodial fathers suffering from the involuntary child-absence syndrome. The evidence is clear: We have no reason automatically to assume malevolent motives on the part of a father who seeks custody of his children.

As we have seen, some fathers do pursue custody with less-than-honorable intentions. But are we justified in doubting the sincerity of *all* men seeking custody? Clearly not. Continuing this prejudice is equivalent to presuming a man is guilty until proven innocent. Only the motherhood mystique allows such a blatant form of sex discrimination to be practiced in our courts.

## HOW CUSTODIAL FATHERS COPE

Fathers planning to keep custody wonder what their lives will be like after divorce. In most families, the initial breakup of a marriage sends a shock wave with reverberations that are felt by everyone in the family for many months, sometimes many years. This is no less true for men with custody of their children. In the wake of the divorce, and in common with other divorced parents, custodial fathers struggle with anger, guilt, anxiety, loneliness, and depression. Fathers who think that keeping custody will shield them from the stress of divorce are sadly mistaken. As most divorced mothers know, with custody come additional challenges. And because it is unconventional in our culture, father custody brings with it certain *unique* problems.

## FATHER CUSTODY AND THE WORKPLACE

At work, custodial fathers frequently encounter unsupportive attitudes from supervisors and co-workers. Employers expect men to regard their jobs as their top priority; little tolerance is shown for a father who must juggle work and child-care responsibilities.

In a job interview, one recently divorced father emphasized his inability to work past five o'clock because he had to pick up his children from day care. During his first week on the job, his employer asked him to stay later; when he explained why he could not stay, he lost his job. It seemed that his employer was so unaccustomed to the idea of a father with primary child-care responsibility that he had not taken the father seriously during the job interview.

Even if they do not lose their jobs, men who refuse to work overtime because of their child-care responsibilities are perceived as less valuable employees and suffer reduced opportunities for advancement.

Co-workers are sometimes highly critical of a father whose child-care duties are evident in the workplace. This occurs, for example, when a father leaves work to retrieve a sick child from school. Although the criticisms are usually couched in terms of the inconvenience to others on the job, hidden motives often fuel such negative attitudes.

The custodial father's strong commitment to his children threatens the self-esteem of fathers who are not so committed. Many men, particularly divorced fathers with traditional visiting schedules, feel guilty about devoting little time to their children. They deal with this guilt through various rationalizations. They may tell themselves that their careers do not permit greater involvement with their children, or that raising children is women's work. The mere existence of custodial fathers exposes these rationalizations as flimsy. To ward off their own discomfort, some fathers will disparage men with custody, as if to say, "It is your life style that is wrong, not mine."

Male co-workers are not the only ones in the workplace to express hostility toward custodial fathers. Women with traditional attitudes about sex roles, or divorcees whose ex-husbands have threatened or actually initiated challenges to the custody of their children, often resent fathers with custody and have a psychological stake in proving that the father-custody life style is not viable.

Custodial fathers can better withstand the criticisms of co-workers if they understand the hidden motives behind the criticisms. The same motives drive some attorneys and psychotherapists to discourage divorced fathers from seeking more access to their children. If you are working with a lawyer or therapist who holds such attitudes, you should bring it up with him or her. If you continue to doubt your lawyer or therapist's ability to empathize with your concerns, you might want to get a second opinion, from a professional who is more sympathetic to your goals.

## TASK OVERLOAD

Custodial fathers have a number of problems in common with custodial mothers. They must single-handedly assume the household and child-care responsibilities usually shared by two parents, while continuing to meet the demands of an occupation. It is no wonder that custodial fathers complain of being overloaded with too many things to do and not enough time and energy to take care of everything. Psychologists call this "task overload." Its effects are debilitating. In the words of one father, who could have been speaking for any custodial parent, father or mother, "There's lots of times when it feels like a big burden, it really does. . . . It's just a lot of work. Everything I do by myself. It seems as if the enormity of the task of arranging things becomes magnified greatly."

The combination of emotional stress, job demands, household tasks, child-care responsibilities, and dating means less time and attention for the children. Children react to diminished parenting with frustration and insecurity. They express these feelings by becoming more demanding, angry, and difficult to manage. And this, of course, creates more stress for the parents, thus perpetuating a vicious cycle. At this point, many divorced parents begin to wonder if the divorce was a mistake. Many also consult psychotherapists in an attempt to interrupt the steady deterioration of family relationships.

## SOLE RESPONSIBILITY FOR CHILDREN

It is not just the amount of work that is oppressive, or the logistics of juggling a job, housekeeping, and child care. An additional psychological burden stems from the awareness that you are solely and totally responsible for the children. You have no other parent to lean on, with whom to discuss problems and decisions concerning the children; no adult to serve as an emotional buffer between you and the children when your relationship becomes too strained, as it inevitably does in all families from time to time.

In one study, custodial fathers ranked "feeling totally responsible" for their children as more stressful than the problem of combining work and child care. If you are a married parent, you can better understand this by thinking for a moment about the many decisions you make concerning your children and about the comfort you derive from discussing these decisions with your spouse.

## LONELINESS

Not having anyone with whom to share child-rearing responsibilities leaves custodial fathers feeling quite lonely. In fact, custodial fathers rank loneliness as the chief stress factor following divorce. As one man told the interviewer: "You asked me what it was like suddenly having three kids alone. I didn't think of it like that. The only thing on my mind was—what am I doing here alone? I felt abandoned."

The responsibility for taking care of his job, household, and children leaves the custodial father with little time to pursue an active social life. Dating is infrequent, compared with the average noncustodial father, and the children often accompany their fathers on dates, thereby further restricting the opportunity for emotional intimacy. As one researcher put it: "It is difficult to have a romantic dinner in one room while the children are making popcorn and watching *Dallas* in the other."

Men who had been very dependent on their wives for emotional and social support are hit the hardest. Although living with their children helps to relieve some of the loneliness of divorced fathers, the children cannot be expected to meet their parents' needs for emotionally sustaining involvements with other adults. In fact, custodial parents who lean too heavily on their children for nurturance place the children in a psychological bind that stunts their emotional growth and leads to special problems in family relationships. I will have more to say about this in chapter 8.

## FINANCES

In one respect, the average custodial father has a distinct advantage over most custodial mothers—money.

Although custodial fathers rarely receive child-support payments, men do not suffer the substantial drop in income after divorce that is typical for women. Divorced men tend to stay in the same jobs with stable incomes. Men with custody generally hold high-status positions and have incomes to match. This means that they are not constantly preoccupied with money worries, and their children do not suffer the economic deprivations imposed on the average child living in a mother-custody home. Naturally, we are speaking here of average families. Some custodial fathers *are* financially strained and must contend with economic stress in addition to the other stresses.

## SELF-CONCEPT

One of the advantages of keeping custody is enhanced self-esteem. Indeed, one of the more devastating consequences of divorce for a noncustodial father is the damage to his self-concept triggered by the change in his relationship with his children. An important part of any father's identity is derived from his role as a parent. When he loses custody of his children, this role is reduced in the eyes of the law, and his identity as a parent is undermined. Consequently, his self-esteem suffers. When society relegates you to the status of second-class citizen vis-à-vis your children, it is easy to doubt your worth as a father. The doubts are reinforced when you see your relationship with your children deteriorate or become more superficial—as often occurs under the constraints of the typical visiting schedule.

The father who retains custody has a clear advantage in this regard. As a rule, he is not plagued with these types of self-doubts. Because of the greater commitment he has made to his children, his identity as a parent is strengthened, not weakened, and his self-esteem is enhanced.

According to Dr. Nathaniel Branden, a leading theoretician on the psychology of self-esteem, self-esteem can be thought of as the integration of two components: self-confidence and self-respect. Divorced fathers benefit in both aspects when they retain custody. Self-confidence increases as a result of mastering the many tasks associated with full-time parenting, tasks that the father may not have been called on to perform during the marriage. Self-respect, the sense of personal worth, is enhanced as a result of facing a difficult challenge and honoring a sense of responsibility to one's children despite society's proscriptions against such involvement.

We have been discussing how fathers grow in self-esteem after retaining custody, but we should add that a strong sense of self-worth and confidence in parenting abilities is often a precondition for seeking custody. Regardless of whether or not fathers possess high levels of self-

---

# SHOULD YOU SEEK CUSTODY?

**Advantages and Rewards**

**1.** Having daily contact with your children.
**2.** Maintaining an in-depth, meaningful relationship with your children rather than the superficial relationship that often results from the traditional "visiting" arrangement.
**3.** Enjoying the gratification of sharing in your children's triumphs and achievements.
**4.** Developing the inner satisfaction that comes from helping your children cope with life's inevitable trials and disappointments.
**5.** Retaining greater input into decisions that affect your children.
**6.** Avoiding the sense of loss that comes from living apart from your children.
**7.** Enhancing your self-esteem and strengthening your identity as a parent.

**Problems, Complaints, and Dissatisfactions**

**1.** Conflict between work and child-care responsibilities.
**2.** Unsympathetic attitudes from co-workers, bosses, and society in general.
**3.** Too many things to do and not enough time to do them.
**4.** Less time and attention for the children.
**5.** Having to make all the child-rearing decisions on your own.
**6.** Restricted social life.
**7.** Stress, stress, stress.

---

esteem to begin with, the observation stands: Custodial fathers seem to escape the inner turmoil suffered by noncustodial fathers around the issue of their identity as parents.

In regard to their personal adjustment to divorce, then, it appears that, on the average, custodial fathers are somewhat better off than noncustodial fathers and no worse off than custodial mothers. Fathers and mothers with custody face similar challenges, although fathers have the disadvantage of society's negative attitudes and the advantage of better financial status. A father's personal adjustment, though, is just one aspect of his life as a custodial parent. Many observers worry that the real risks of father custody will become apparent when the focus turns to the father's performance in housekeeping and child care.

## CAN FATHERS MANAGE HOUSEWORK?

Comical images of bungling fathers helpless when facing housework are part of our national consciousness. These images are reflected in, and fueled by, television situation comedies such as those from the 1950s and '60s. Ward Cleaver in *Leave It to Beaver* and Jim Anderson in *Father Knows Best* are never shown doing housework. Similarly, the single fathers on *My Three Sons*, *Bachelor Father*, *The Andy Griffith Show*, *Family Affair*, and *The Courtship of Eddie's Father* all had live-in housekeepers. And despite the efforts of the women's movement and media accounts of the "new father," recent surveys indicate that the typical husband of the nineties shares very little of the housework, even when his wife is employed outside the home.

Since most men have little experience in doing housework during their marriage, we naturally expect that, when they are divorced and have custody of their children, they will be inept in performing household tasks, and will rely on hired help or the children to do the bulk of the work. Even professionals are not immune from such stereotypes. As divorce researcher Dr. Deborah Leupnitz candidly admitted: "I predicted at the outset that divorced mothers would be taking for granted their domestic tasks and that *fathers* would be going mad trying to cook and keep house."

Once again the facts do not support the popular assumptions. Men may not be doing much housework in two-parent households, but apparently many have the requisite know-how. Half of the fathers in Leupnitz's study said they did not have to learn any new domestic skills after the divorce. Even more significant was the relaxed attitude expressed by all the men about household tasks. One father of two teenagers captured the essence of this attitude:

> *I don't worry. No matter how poor you are at those things, you're going to get by. You're not going to die if you don't know how to fix*

*up the house. I'm sure I could have done more fixing up, and it would be neater and nicer here—but it wouldn't make any real difference. We survive on pizza and sandwiches. Everyone is happy, and it's been five years. If I don't like to cook, I can't expect them to like it. I've never heard them complain.*

Dr. Leupnitz's data on custodial fathers refuted her predictions. Referring to the fathers in her study, Leupnitz concluded, "It was not the case that single parenthood found them frantically burning pancakes or shrinking clothes in the dryer. Nor had these fathers hired housekeepers as substitute wives."

Do fathers with custody delegate extra household chores to their children? Opinion is divided about whether or not such extra responsibility is good for children, but apparently this is more typical in mother-custody homes than in father-custody homes.

Contrary to expectations, custodial mothers were having more problems with domestic chores than custodial fathers. Leupnitz attributed this to the fact that most of the new tasks men had to perform were made simpler through technology, such as microwave ovens and permanent-press clothing. Again quoting Leupnitz, "Technological innovations have made it easy for men to learn 'women's work'—but not vice versa. There are no quick automated solutions for changing storm windows or repairing roofs. The tasks the mothers had to learn involved more complex skills, more danger, and greater expense."

I think that poor housekeeping abilities should not disqualify a parent from having custody; by the same token, being a consummate homemaker does not entitle him or her to a Custodial Parent of the Year award. Unless we are considering the extremes of housekeeping—so dirty or messy as to be unhealthy or dangerous, or so compulsively neat and clean as to be unsuitable for children—how parents deal with their physical surroundings should not be regarded as a very significant criterion of fitness for custody. Far more important are parents' skills and sensitivities in relating to their children. It is in this domain, more than any other, that society holds negative expectations for custodial fathers.

## SOCIAL BIASES

Custodial fathers are well aware of these attitudes. Often it feels to them as if they are living on a stage, with a cadre of self-appointed critics in the audience eager to give their performance as parents a scathing review. Are the children dressed properly? Do they eat balanced meals? Are they late for school? What happens when they are sad? Does anybody soothe their hurts or are they left to fend for themselves? The image of physically and emotionally neglected children looms large in the minds of many adults who come in contact with father-custody children.

For example, one psychologist tells this story about a custodial father he interviewed. The father repeatedly took his son, Abdo, to the pediatrician because the boy's teacher thought he was ill. After each visit, the father reported to the teacher the doctor's conclusion that the child was in good health, yet the teacher remained unconvinced. Finally, the doctor reported directly to the school that Abdo was healthy and growing properly. Only then did the teacher stop complaining to the father about his son's health.

Ten-year-old Martha lives alone with her divorced father. Her best friend, Amy, never accepts Martha's invitations to sleep over. The reason? Amy's parents do not want their daughter spending the night in a home where no mother is present. Somehow a divorced man is regarded as less trustworthy than a married man in taking care of children. Without the support of a mother in the home, the father loses his status as a loving, competent parent. Of course, this very attitude leads our society to discount the value of a divorced father's involvement with his children.

We may scoff at Abdo's teacher and Amy's parents, recognizing that they are acting out of ignorance and fear. But their concerns are genuine and their attitudes toward father custody are not unusual. In fact, in most parts of the country their opinions would be considered mainstream. Is there any basis for such concerns?

## CHILD-REARING

The stereotypical man is an emotional clod when it comes to nurturing children. This stereotype finds expression in the behavior of athletic coaches who are so preoccupied with winning that they lose sight of the emotional impact of their behavior on the children.

The image of such men leads many judges and mothers to the assumption that in a father-custody home, without a woman's touch, the children's emotional needs will go unmet. Although this belief is an offshoot of the motherhood mystique, there is some basis in reality for concern. In fact, custodial fathers themselves have similar worries.

Cultural stereotypes of masculinity and femininity can function as self-fulfilling prophecies. When we believe that raising children is "women's work," we teach our sons to ignore their parental feelings and deprive them of valuable experience as care-givers. Girls, on the other hand, gain experience playing with dolls and babysitting younger children, which provides an enjoyable outlet for rehearsing nurturing behaviors.

Also, in order to meet society's expectations of what "real" men should be like, boys learn to disown their more tender feelings. This may render them, as adults, less in tune emotionally with their children. For instance, in our culture boys are taught to feel uncomfortable about crying, so that many men are incapable of fully experiencing their sad feelings. A man who cannot easily recognize his own sadness will have a difficult time empathizing with sadness in others, including his children. This may be particularly true with regard to young children, who are less able to communicate feelings verbally to their parents.

As a result of their upbringing, therefore, men who gain custody may initially be handicapped in their ability to respond to the emotional needs of their children. Does this weaken the case for father custody? I don't think so.

The important question is not whether men already *have* the skills to nurture children, but whether they can acquire such skills. Dr. Michael Lamb's research suggests that these skills can be learned. He studied parents shortly after the birth of their first child and observed no initial differences in competence between mothers and fathers. Over time, however, the mothers became more competent. Dr. Lamb attributed this, not to a maternal instinct, but to the fact that parenting skills are learned "on the job" and mothers were "on the job" more than were fathers.

Does being "on the job" help fathers with custody improve their parenting skills? Apparently so, according to interviews with fathers and their children. Custodial fathers generally feel they are doing a good job of raising their children and have less difficulty meeting the emotional needs of their children than "average" fathers. The children concur and rate their single fathers as more nurturing than children in two-parent families rate either parent.

Although such impressions may be biased, some credibility may be indicated by the fact that these fathers were not reluctant to discuss problems in other areas. For example, some reported concerns about their own depressive reactions after the divorce. Also, the studies that portray custodial fathers as competent parents number more than a dozen. We should not easily dismiss such consistency.

The strongest evidence for custodial fathers' care-giving competence comes from the Texas studies conducted by Dr. John Santrock and me (see appendix). These studies corroborated the results of prior studies by supplementing parent and child interviews with psychological tests and direct observations of parent-child interaction. On four separate measures, custodial fathers were rated just as nurturant as custodial mothers.

Have these fathers learned parenting skills "on the job" after acquiring custody, or were they more nurturing in the first place? Since no study has observed custodial fathers immediately after they were awarded custody, a definitive answer must await future research. For the present, we must rely on fathers' recollections of this period. The picture they paint generally resembles the situation in the film *Kramer vs. Kramer*. Initially inept men gradually learn to be effective full-time parents and, in the process, develop deep emotional bonds with their children. Beginning with a peripheral involvement, they increasingly make their children's welfare their top priority.

Skill in nurturing is only one component of good parenting. It is also important to consider how effectively custodial fathers manage their children's behavior. In this area it is well established that custodial fathers outperform custodial mothers. In fact, in many divorced families children, particularly boys, are sent to live with their fathers when their mothers can no longer control their problem behavior.

Custodial parents, fathers and mothers alike, become more lenient after the divorce. Under the sway of guilt over the divorce, sympathy for their children's pain, and sheer exhaustion, parents relax their enforcement of the limits they set. In mother-custody homes this contributes to an increase in discipline problems as children learn they can get away with misbehavior. Not so in father-custody homes. Despite their increased leniency, custodial fathers are less permissive and less likely to allow their children to control them than are custodial mothers. Also, children are in general more likely to comply with their father's requests. Most of us remember the extra measure of fear aroused by mother's threat: "Wait until your father comes home!" Because children invest their fathers with so much authority to begin with, they keep their behavior within acceptable bounds even when the limits are not strictly enforced.

Another facet of being a good parent is giving proper attention to children's physical needs. Are these needs neglected in father-custody homes? To answer this question, the Texas project asked teachers to complete extensive questionnaires on each of the children studied. We reasoned that teachers, despite their own biases, are in a relatively good position to evaluate the care given to children's physical appearance. Children may be dressed in their Sunday best when meeting with our project staff, but their appearance in school is a more reliable indicator of the day-to-day attention given to these matters. If a parent is lax in this regard, the child's teacher is apt to be the first to notice.

Here again, our findings support the case for father custody. Teachers rated children from father-custody homes just as healthy, clean, and neat in their appearance as children from mother-custody homes.

## SATISFACTION WITH CUSTODY

Despite the daily hassles of single parenting, most parents with custody say they are happy to be custodial parents and are not interested in a change. Judging from the results of several studies, it appears that custodial fathers are even more satisfied with custody than are mothers.

There are three reasons for this. First, custodial fathers often do not have the financial problems that plague custodial mothers. Single mothers rank money worries as the number-one stress factor in their lives. Second, children are better behaved with their father. The strain of custody is vastly reduced when you are not constantly engaged in struggles with your children. Third, fathers who keep custody benefit from an increase in their self-esteem. This plays a key role in their enjoyment of custody. Dr. Branden is clear on this point: "A high level of self-confidence and self-respect is intimately related to the ability to enjoy life and to find sources of satisfaction in our existence."

Fathers with custody are pioneers. They assume an unconventional role for men in our culture and thereby challenge the traditions of the past seventy years. What can parents expect when the father keeps custody? The evidence is clear that, allowing for variations in men, the average father will be able to acquire the necessary skills and attitudes to cope with housework and raise his children competently. He will probably shift his priorities and allocate more time to his children, and in the process his confidence as a parent will grow.

Compared with the average custodial mother, he will be more in control of his children's behavior, but otherwise will be doing neither better nor worse in caring for his children's physical and emotional needs.

These findings by themselves are not sufficient to make the case for father custody. Fathers may be as competent as mothers; but if children need their mothers more than their fathers—if the motherhood mystique is reality—then, no matter how skilled a father is, his children will suffer more problems living apart from their mother than if they lived apart from him.

For this reason, we must complement the preceding analysis of custodial fathers with an in-depth look at their children's psychological development. This is the bottom line in any assessment of father custody. How well are children coping in father-custody homes, and how do they compare with children in mother-custody homes? Before tackling these questions, though, we need to focus our spotlight on the other parent in a father-custody family—the mother without custody.

# 5

# MAVERICK
# MOTHERS

No description of father custody would be complete without a portrait of the noncustodial mother. Or, rather, portraits—because mothers without custody are no more homogeneous a group than are fathers with custody. They arrive at their situation by different paths, for different reasons, and with different outcomes.

One thing many share, though, is what one author calls "the tragic equation": the noncustodial mother's own guilt reinforced by society's rejection. And rejection there is. Plenty of it. Women who live apart from their children are social outcasts: They face a constant barrage of irrational accusations and scorn from family, friends, and even strangers.

One Milwaukee woman was so upset by people's reactions that she expressed her outrage in a letter to Ann Landers:

> Dear Ann Landers:
>
> *Recently I made the decision to give custody of my three children to my ex-husband. The responses I've gotten from family and friends ranged from insensitive to cruel. Society seems to assume that a woman who doesn't have custody of her children doesn't love them, or that she is a child abuser.*
>
> *I've been asked, "What did you do that was so terrible that you weren't allowed to keep your children?" I am appalled that so many people rush to make a judgment with no information. . . .*

*Let me say this to those who have the nerve to ask such a question.
You are not entitled to an answer. It's none of your business. Please,
don't be so quick to pass judgment until you have walked in my
shoes.*

What compels people to pass this judgment? The motherhood mystique. Women who live apart from their children openly affront our most
cherished notions about motherhood. *If mothers are uniquely suited to care
for their children, then noncustodial mothers aren't doing their job.* If children
need their mothers more than their fathers, then these mothers are subjecting their children to terrible deprivation.

We know now that such views are greatly mistaken. The scientific
evidence is clear: Fathers make good custodial parents, and their children
are no more deprived than those raised in mother-custody homes. But
even if our response to the question "How could a mother give up her
children?" is not the conventional one ("She must be a horrible mother"),
the question is still valid and deserves a response based on reason rather
than hysteria.

A related question also merits our attention: What happens to a mother
when she relinquishes custody? How does it affect her life? A woman
contemplating this option will want and need to know what she can
anticipate. Will she become accustomed to living apart from her children,
or will it always weigh heavily on her heart? How will this decision affect
her relationship with her children? Will the children feel abandoned? Will
they hate her? How will she get along with her ex-husband? And, most
important, will she regret her decision?

Learning the answers to these questions is not easy. Many women who
relinquish custody remain "in the closet." To avoid stigma and to deflect
condemnation, they quickly learn to conceal their custodial status; some
don't even tell their own parents! For a reliable account of the causes and
consequences of the decision to relinquish custody, we must look at the
results of systematic studies. The best of these, and the one I draw from
the most in the subsequent discussion, is the doctoral dissertation of Dr.
Maria Constantatos. Her study, conducted in Dallas, and other studies
conducted throughout the country, offer us a glimpse behind the closed
door into the world of noncustodial mothers.

## WHO GIVES UP CUSTODY, AND WHY?

Some women lose custody in court; but the vast majority of women who live apart from their children voluntarily choose this option.

Like all unconventional behavior, it is not well understood by most people. In place of understanding, fear and prejudice dominate society's opinions of nonconformists. Chapter 4 showed how fathers who seek custody are often accused of malevolent motives. Mothers who give up custody must be prepared for a double dose of criticism. Typical assumptions: They are immature women who just want to escape the responsibility of being a parent. Or they have abandoned their offspring in order to pursue a life of sexual promiscuity. Or they are hardhearted women who lack maternal feelings and place their careers and their own freedom before their children.

As usual, the stereotypes miss the mark. Psychological tests comparing women with and without custody reveal no differences in emotional maturity, warmth, or nurturing, "motherly" feelings. And no study has found even one woman who left her children for a lover. If such women do exist, they have somehow eluded the researchers, and they most certainly are not representative of noncustodial mothers.

If the stereotypes don't fit, then what could prompt a mother to give up custody of her children? In reality, the decision is complicated and usually reflects the interplay of a number of considerations rather than just one motive. The Milwaukee mother who wrote to Ann Landers gave several reasons for her decision: "My former husband earns twice what I make. I could never have kept my family going on my earnings, even with child support. He is just as good a parent as I am, in some ways better. We both love the kids. They are as comfortable living with him as they would be with me."

According to Dr. Constantatos, this mother's explanation is very typical of the women she studied. Most point to their ex-husbands' financial resources and parenting abilities as major factors in their decision. Also, the majority believe that keeping custody would interfere with their pursuit of a career or educational goals.

But this cannot be the whole story. After all, most divorced women have career or educational aspirations, and most have less money than their ex-husbands; these circumstances do not prevent them from retaining custody. In fact, most women never think twice about custody; they just assume they will keep the children and adapt as best as they can to the demands of the role. When asked to explain the reasons behind their custody choice, custodial mothers react with mild surprise: "It was never an issue. It was a given that I would keep the children." Another mother says, "There was never any doubt. I wouldn't have it any other way."

The critical difference between mothers who retain and those who relinquish custody has more to do with attitudes toward motherhood than with practical concerns such as finances. Mothers who continue to live with their children regard their mothering role as an essential aspect of their identity. It is inconceivable for them to abandon this part of themselves. "It would be like cutting me in half if Julius and René lived somewhere else," said one custodial mother, putting her own twist on the tale of Solomon.

Noncustodial mothers, on the other hand, are more ambivalent about motherhood. Their opinion of motherhood is best expressed by: "It is not all that it is cracked up to be." For these women, motherhood has not been the source of pride and accomplishment that it has been for others. They derive less personal satisfaction from child-rearing and are far less likely to feel fulfilled in the role of mother.

We must not confuse these women's feelings about motherhood with their feelings toward their own children. There is no doubt that they love and care deeply for their children. What they don't love as much is the role of full-time mother. One woman explains, "I found motherhood an enormously oppressive task—not physically, just the responsibility of it."

Maternal ambivalence may have roots in the mother's relationship with her own mother. More noncustodial mothers say they have conflictual ties with their own mothers and feel their mothers were themselves less satisfied with motherhood. "My mother always regretted giving up her career . . . and we all knew that," said one woman who was living apart from her children.

Many mothers who relinquish custody want to explore a new life style freed from the restrictions of primary child care. Some also seek a new, multifaceted identity. But, contrary to stereotype, this quest does not indicate emotional immaturity or severe disturbance. It merely represents a conscious effort to step outside the bounds of full-time motherhood. Almost always this decision is accompanied by much agonizing soul-searching and made with the conviction that it is best for the entire family. Let us not forget that it takes courage to choose a life style that fails to conform to cultural norms.

Electing to give up custody also requires confidence in the father's ability to manage the job. In the Dallas study, 85 percent of the noncustodial mothers cited their ex-husbands' parenting skill as one consideration in their decision to leave the children with him. Although there were no differences between noncustodial and custodial mothers in how adequate they felt as parents during the marriage (both gave themselves high marks), a majority of the noncustodial group did feel they would be unable to handle the strains of single parenthood and this was a factor in their decision. By contrast, none of the custodial mothers admitted to these self-doubts, and a majority believed that their ex-husbands were not capable of managing the responsibilities of custody.

To summarize, in most cases there is no one factor that motivates a mother to relinquish custody. A mother who does so may want to explore her potentials by adopting a new life style. She may feel ambivalent about motherhood. She is probably comfortable leaving her children with their father because she believes her ex-husband can handle custody at least as well as she can. Most definitely she is not insensitive to her children's needs. Objecting to the stereotypes, one woman wrote, "Noncustodial mothers are maligned. We are not tramps, unfit mothers, or dirt. We love our children, and it is this love which has given us strength to realize that we made the decisions based on what was best for the children (and at a great expense, sacrificing what may have been best for us)!" Dr. Constantatos unequivocally supports this view: "The noncustodial mothers in this study were not found to be characterologically or clinically unsound. They are not unfeeling or unfit mothers. They are simply not conventional mothers."

## WHAT HAVE I DONE WRONG?

Some noncustodial mothers, about one in five, do not so much *choose* to relinquish custody as they *acquiesce* to their child's request to live with Daddy. The only path to giving up custody that is more difficult for a mother to accept is to be declared an unfit mother by a judge. Indeed, many a mother in this situation feels that her child's request brands her as an unfit parent.

The typical response is to feel hurt and humiliated. Many mothers in this position feel an acute sense of loss. Self-blame is common. Just as the bereaved are plagued by thoughts of what they could have done to prevent a loved one's death, so the mother will blame herself for her child's preference. In some cases, the mother's guilt results from an incomplete understanding of the reasons for her child's desire to live with the father. She can only assume that she has failed as a mother. (After all, the motherhood mystique keeps us from recognizing that a child may yearn for more contact with his father.) In other cases, the guilt is an attempt to cope with helpless feelings. Feeling guilty allows the mother to believe that she did something to cause her child to develop a preference for the father's home; if she caused it, perhaps she can reverse it.

Yet, in most cases, the mother has little, if any, control over her child's preference. If the father remains in the home and the mother moves to another community, her child may wish to live with the father in order to avoid all the changes that accompany a move—new home, new neighborhood, new school, and new friends. When the preference requires a shift in living arrangements, it most likely reflects the child's need at his or her age to cement a closer relationship with the father. In some families, it may *appear* that a child's desire to move is prompted by excessive conflict with the mother. We must appreciate, however, that the conflict itself may be the result of the child's need to maintain some psychological distance from the mother. As discussed in chapter 8, a boy may actively push his mother away in order to preserve a strong masculine identification, especially if he is the only male in a female-headed household. When the fighting does not accomplish this goal, the boy may feel he has no alternative but to move out of the home. Other children may be attempting to escape what seems to them an unbearable stepfamily situation.

Often the child himself is unaware of the major reason he wants to move to his father's house. For example, one fifteen-year-old boy insisted on moving in with his father six months after his mother remarried. The boy seemed to get along fine with his stepfather and mother and could not really articulate why he felt he had to move. A year after he moved, he figured out, with the help of a therapist, that he had been having strong unconscious sexual feelings toward his fourteen-year-old stepsister. To avoid temptation, he felt he needed to get out of the house. When his mother understood this, she felt less hurt by his move, although she still wished there were some other way to resolve the situation.

In general, when the mother understands her child's true reasons for wanting to move, it is easier for her to accept the decision. Still, the sense of loss is great. Her child's readiness to leave the nest catches the mother off guard. As one mother of a ten-year-old remarked, "I always knew my

# WHAT TO DO IF YOUR CHILD ASKS TO LIVE WITH DADDY

**1.** First, don't panic. And don't assume this means you are a bad mother or your child doesn't love you. It is probably best to give yourself some time before you respond to the startling announcement. Let your child know that you are collecting your thoughts and that you will talk about it when ready.

**2.** Often this request is blurted out in the midst of a heated argument. When this is the case, resist the temptation to say, "Fine! You want to live with your father? Good riddance!" Instead, acknowledge the request but postpone discussion of it and return to the issue at hand. "Let's finish what we were talking about. If you still want to discuss moving to your father's, we can do that some other time." This helps to sort out spurious requests, which are actually weapons in the current battle, from more stable desires to live with the father.

**3.** Keep the lines of communication open. Your child must know that you have not ignored the request and consider it important enough to discuss. Reacting too emotionally can frighten your child into silence, but the feelings do not disappear with the silence.

**4.** Try to help your child articulate the reasons for his or her preference. Does the decision reflect primarily a desire to be with the father, or a wish to leave your home?

**5.** Don't automatically give in to your child's request. Generally, the older the child, the more weight we would give to his or her preference. The younger the child, the more we suspect that the decision is temporary and fails to take into account a wide range of factors. For example, upon returning from a visit in which she was showered with gifts, a five-year-old girl asks to live with her father. Her request is most likely influenced not by any balanced assessment of the merits of living with her father, but by the unrealistic prospect of daily visits to the toy store.

**6.** If you are thinking seriously of honoring your child's request, withhold this from your child until you know your ex-husband's position. ("Why don't we see what your father thinks about this?") It would be disheartening for your child to hear that you think he should move in with his father, and then learn that his father does not want him.

**7.** If the transfer of custody takes place, don't indicate that it must be an irreversible decision. People are allowed to make mistakes, especially young people. Your child should know that if the move does not work out he is welcome to return to your home. Avoid punishing him for his decision by withholding your love or your home. On the other hand, it is reasonable to discuss a fair trial period that will give everyone a chance to test out the new arrangements. You don't want your child shifting custody every time he gets mad at a parent.

**8.** Reassure your child of your continuing love. Try not to take the request as evidence of your failure as a mother. Remember, children do not reach a decision like this easily. Shifting custody is probably the only way they know to accomplish some emotional goal.

child would grow up and leave home someday. I just wasn't prepared for it to come so soon. What have I done wrong?" Another woman poignantly told me that when her son asked to live with his father she felt as though someone had died: "I am really grieving. With Rebecca going off to college, I was looking forward to spending some time alone with Adam. Over the past few months, I have had time to prepare myself psychologically for Rebecca's departure, but for this I am not at all prepared. Adam leaving now would be a tremendous loss."

## LIFE WITHOUT CUSTODY

Is this loss something from which a mother can expect to recover? What happens to a woman after she relinquishes custody? What price does she pay for defying the motherhood mystique? What benefits does she reap?

## Did I Do the Right Thing?

As you might expect, the consequences of giving up custody are neither all positive nor all negative. Every mother who is contemplating this choice should carefully consider this major drawback: *There is a fifty-fifty chance that she will be dissatisfied with, and doubt the wisdom of, her decision.* At an average, three and a half years following the breakup about half of the Dallas group of noncustodial mothers were not at peace with their decision; by comparison, only 5 percent of the custodial group felt this way.

Why did the noncustodial mothers regret their choice? Mainly they missed their children and longed for a larger place in their children's lives. Being away from their children was more difficult than they had anticipated. "There is a great yearning and emptiness. A void. And, oh, the *pain* on his birthday," said one noncustodial mother. It was apparent that this woman was suffering from the same "child-absence syndrome" that afflicts many noncustodial fathers. It seems that most loving parents, men and women, experience pangs of sorrow when forced to live apart from their offspring. This is the highest price parents have to pay for the failure of their marriage.

But not all noncustodial mothers pay the same price. Half of the Dallas group were relatively comfortable with their decision, a finding that agrees with those of other studies. According to a nationwide survey, the most satisfied noncustodial mothers are those who believe that they have a good relationship with their children and that their children are better off living with their fathers.

Also important are the reactions the mother receives from those around her. It helps when relatives and friends accept her decision and offer emotional support. By the same token, being the target of censure for "abandoning" her children creates an additional strain. Repeated criticism undermines the mother's sense of having made the correct move. Naturally the criticism will have less impact on a mother who is more sure of her choice.

It is interesting to note which factors did *not* affect a mother's satisfaction with her decision. The age, sex, and number of children in the family had no bearing on the issue. Mothers who had relinquished custody of young children or daughters, for example, were no more likely to regret their decision than those who lived apart from older sons. The degree of choice the mother felt regarding the divorce or the custody arrangements also did not affect her satisfaction. And the passage of time neither alleviated nor worsened the mother's discomfort with her decision.

## Promises Fulfilled and Unfulfilled

Noncustodial mothers may be more dissatisfied with their custody decision, but they are also less stressed as a result of their choice. They get along better with their ex-spouses and their children than custodial mothers do, and, although advancing no further in their careers, they reach career goals more easily.

One reason noncustodial mothers are less stressed is that they don't worry as much about making ends meet financially. Of course, as a group they are by no means free of financial worries. But it is far less stressful to worry only about yourself than it is to worry about whether you will be able to feed and clothe your children as well.

After the divorce, noncustodial mothers give their ex-husbands high marks as parents; custodial mothers, on the other hand, continue to rate their ex-husbands as less adequate. As might be expected, along with the greater respect comes more cooperation, more sharing, and less conflict. These are significant benefits not just for the noncustodial mother but also for her children. We have already seen that divorced parents who get along relatively well give their children a distinct advantage.

Noncustodial mothers are also relieved of the daily hassles that inevitably arise between parents and children who live under the same roof. Fears that their children will hate them for leaving are not realized. Instead, as with noncustodial fathers and their children, the reduced time together makes for more harmonious and less conflictual—albeit limited—interaction. As a result, noncustodial mothers enjoy their time with their children more than custodial mothers. Whereas custodial mothers want and need more time *away* from their children, noncustodial mothers long for more time *with* them. Though this longing is itself a source of stress, the flip side is the relief that comes from having less responsibility.

Freedom from full-time child care also makes it easier for these women to pursue their career goals and their social life. This does not mean that they are more satisfied with their accomplishments in these spheres. In fact, though career aspirations are often cited as one reason for living apart from the children, noncustodial mothers advance no further in their careers than custodial mothers. After the failure of their marriages, both groups increase their investment in their chosen occupations and regard their work as a major source of self-esteem and life satisfaction.

With social activity, too, we find more similarities than differences between the two groups of women. The stereotype of the noncustodial mother who has no time for her children because of her busy social life is not borne out by the results of research. Although custodial mothers express more frustration with the restrictions that their parental duties place on their social life, they are actually as socially active as mothers without custody. As for the notion that women who live apart from their children are sexually promiscuous, research indicates no difference between mothers with and without custody in the frequency of sexual relations.

In other respects, relinquishing custody appears to make no difference to a woman's adjustment after divorce. When custodial mothers are compared with noncustodial mothers, no differences are found in their overall satisfaction with life, their psychological health, or their self-esteem.

## WHAT'S A MOTHER TO DO?

Choosing to live without your children is a frightening decision. It should be made carefully and with full consideration of the likely outcomes. If you are looking to ease your financial stress, you will find this accomplished. If you think your ex-husband can take good care of your children, you are probably correct. If you have career goals in mind when leaving your family, you won't necessarily be more successful than if you keep custody, but you will find an easier path toward your goals.

If your decision reflects ambivalence about your role as a mother, you should know that you may continue to feel torn about being separated from your children and less involved with their daily routines and activities. When you are with them, however, you can expect to enjoy a pleasurable relationship.

Based on her investigation Dr. Constantatos concludes, "For some women the relinquishment of custody, though not problem-free, can still be a viable custody option. It may fulfill their personal needs without necessarily being detrimental to their families."

I am still troubled, though, by the high proportion of noncustodial mothers—50 percent—who come to regret their decision. Even those who do not lament the decision find it painful to live apart from their children for long periods of time.

If this were clearly the best arrangement for the children, then we could regard their mothers' suffering as a price worth paying. It would then be easier to endorse father custody when the mother is ambivalent about keeping custody.

As things stand, though, I regard the total relinquishment of custody as an unsuitable option for most women and do not generally recommend it. This is not because fathers can't do a good job raising their children, or because children invariably suffer more in father-custody homes. The preceding chapter retired the first of those myths; the next chapter will address the second. Instead, my reluctance stems from the conviction that, in the vast majority of cases, two parents are better than one. Just as a single father needs to spend more time than four days per month with his children in order to meet his needs and those of his children, a single mother needs more time with her children than she would typically spend as a noncustodial parent. When this is not feasible, the mother may then be faced with the most difficult decision she will ever make. Such was the dilemma that brought Joyce back to my office.

Joyce first consulted me just after deciding to divorce Nathan, her husband of thirteen years. Together they had three boys, ages eleven, seven, and five. Joyce and Nathan had grown apart in recent years, and Joyce wanted out of the marriage. Two years earlier, she had completed her graduate education as a medical researcher in a highly specialized field. Joyce's work had already shown much promise. Her career kept her busy, and she enjoyed her work. But she felt guilty about not having more time for her children.

Joyce had heard about joint-custody arrangements in which parents shared child-care responsibilities. She asked me if this was suitable for her family. Nathan had always been a very involved father. He was present in the delivery room during all three births. When the children were young, he participated in feeding, changing diapers, and bathing. Now that they were older, Nathan helped with homework, took a strong interest in the children's sports activities, and attended most school functions. In fact, he was the class "mother" for their youngest son's kindergarten.

Although Nathan was surely capable of caring for the children, he was unsure about the impact of joint custody on them, and he was particularly hesitant about having them live apart from their mother for any significant amount of time. I told Joyce that I thought their family was well suited to a joint-custody arrangement (chapter 9 details the arguments, pro and con, for this option, as well as the circumstances in which joint custody works best). When Joyce and Nathan came in together the next week, I reiterated my recommendation and helped them work out a reasonable parenting plan. Nathan was relieved that he would be able to continue his involvement with the boys and that this arrangement would benefit them as well. We also discussed how they could prepare their children for the upcoming changes.

After an initial adjustment period, things went exceedingly well for the entire family. Joyce became involved in a collaborative research project with a top laboratory on the East Coast. This necessitated frequent trips out of town, some of which occurred at times when the children were scheduled to be with her. Fortunately, Nathan moved into a sales position that allowed him to arrange his own schedule. When Joyce traveled, the boys stayed with their father and he was able to come home early most afternoons.

For the first year and a half, the custody arrangement was a model of cooperation and flexibility and the children thrived. Although they regretted the loss of their intact family, they did not feel that they had lost a parent.

Then Joyce called me.

She was being considered for a prestigious position in the East Coast lab. The job was based in the lab but required extensive travel to other labs and professional conferences. Because her field was so specialized, Joyce could not look forward to many more such opportunities. This position would ensure her future professional success. Taking the job meant, of course, the end of the shared-custody arrangement. But what should take its place? Take the boys with her, or leave them with Nathan?

Nathan, by this time, was convinced that the boys would be better off staying with him. But he was not about to subject himself and his family to any legal battles. Even if he was willing to go to court, he figured that his chances of being awarded custody were slim, since Joyce was by no means an unfit mother. Therefore, the decision was in Joyce's hands.

Two months later, in January, Joyce was offered the coveted position. She accepted the offer but decided to postpone a decision about custody. Since it was in the middle of the school year, she agreed to allow the children to finish the semester in their current schools before subjecting them to a move. Besides, beginning a new job, setting up a new residence, and establishing roots was going to be stressful and time-consuming. She would probably not be in the best frame of mind to help her children adjust.

In June, the decision had to be made. If the children were going to move to the East Coast, they would be spending the summer with their father. If, on the other hand, they were going to continue living with their father, arrangements needed to be made for them to spend the summer with their mother.

By this time, we had additional information to help with the decision: The past five months had allowed the family to experience a "trial" father-custody arrangement. On the negative side, Joyce found it difficult to be away from the children for so long. It was especially painful saying goodbye at the end of the ten-day visit during spring break. On the positive side, Joyce enjoyed the challenges of her new job and admitted that it was easier to devote the time she wanted to the lab when she knew her sons were not at home waiting for their mother. Nathan had no major difficulty adjusting to the situation, since he was already used to caring for the children on a regular basis. As for the children, they all seemed to be doing very well. They continued to make good grades in school and showed no overt signs of emotional or behavioral problems.

The two older boys told both parents that they wanted to continue living with their father. The youngest boy, if he had a conscious preference, was not volunteering it to anybody. I interviewed the children and determined that the preference of the two boys to remain where they were was not based solely on a fear of the unknown. I asked them whom they would want to live with if their mother moved back home and their father were transferred to another state. They replied that they would choose to move with their father. Apparently they felt very attached to, and comfortable with, their father. There was no sign that the boys had been coached or "brainwashed" by their father to say these things. (Sad to say, this is such a frequent occurrence in custody disputes that psychologists must always entertain the possibility when consulting on custody issues.)

Despite the good adjustment of the children, I thought it was unfortunate that Joyce's career move necessitated an alteration of the joint-custody arrangement that had worked so well. But only Joyce could assess the benefits of her new position relative to the drawbacks to her family. Only she could assess the new job's impact on her life satisfaction. If she had turned down what looked like the opportunity of a lifetime, her children would have gained the physical presence of a parent, but the gain might have come at the expense of living with an unhappy, unfulfilled mother. And how would Joyce cope with the awareness that the needs of her children were keeping her from achieving the professional success for which she had longed and worked so hard? This might have put an excessive strain on what had so far been a good relationship between Joyce and her children.

Custody decisions are rarely clear-cut. Trade-offs are inevitable. It may take years for parents to know if they made the correct decision. And they may never be certain. Although I couldn't make the decision for them, after weighing all the factors I told Joyce and Nathan that it seemed reasonable for the children to remain with Nathan. I had several reasons for this opinion.

Research has demonstrated certain advantages to keeping boys with their fathers (see chapter 7). Research has also demonstrated that geographical stability helps children cope better after their parents' divorce (see pages 71 and 198). Living with Nathan would entail the least amount of change and loss for the children. They could continue to profit from the emotional roots they had established in their home, neighborhood, and school. They would not have to give up their friends. Nathan had already demonstrated to everyone's satisfaction that he could well manage the responsibilities of custody. And Joyce's work would continue to require out-of-town trips, at which time the children would be without either parent if they were in her custody. The strongest argument for leaving the children with Nathan was how well the children were doing after living with him these past five months.

In the end, this is what tipped the scales for Joyce. In what was surely a gut-wrenching decision, she opted to let the children stay with Nathan. It was not an easy call. Joyce was a good and loving mother. Although the children might have adjusted well to a move, they would always have longed for their father.

I believe the motherhood mystique made Joyce's custody decision even more difficult. Had the shoe been on the other foot, with the father moving out of town, few would doubt the propriety of keeping the children with their mother. Why uproot the children when they were already doing so well?

But such logic does not hold its own in a society that frowns on a mother's living apart from her children. Like all women, Joyce had been raised with the expectation that her husband would not play as central a role in parenting as she. Thus it seemed unnatural for the children to live with Nathan. Years of conditioning made it difficult for Joyce to shake the sense that what she was doing was terribly wrong.

Joyce's decision took inner strength and the willingness to think for herself, a talent that contributed to her success as a scientist. It also took

## SHOULD YOU RELINQUISH CUSTODY?

**Benefits**

1. Less stress.
2. Fewer financial worries.
3. More freedom to pursue career options.
4. More enjoyable, less conflictual relationship with your children.
5. Better relationship with your ex-husband.
6. Fewer restrictions on your social activities.

**Drawbacks**

1. Pain of missing your children and longing for more contact.
2. Less participation in your children's daily activities and routines.
3. Less input into decisions that affect your children.
4. More superficial relationship with your children.
5. High likelihood of regretting your custody decision.
6. Guilt over "abandoning" your children.
7. Social stigma.

courage to violate cultural norms. In the context of the twentieth-century United States, Joyce's decision is unconventional, unpopular, and sure to be met with disapproval.

## A New Double Standard

It shouldn't have to be this way. Women in Joyce's position should not have to suffer any more than men who choose to live apart from their children. Noncustodial mothers who regret their decision blame society's negative attitudes for much of their discomfort.

We should acknowledge that society's attitudes have changed substantially in this regard during the past quarter-century. Before then, most women could not even conceive of the possibility of voluntarily relinquishing custody. Society's mores held relatively few options for the average woman. With the rebirth of the women's movement came a new vision of women's potential. It became respectable for mothers to pursue fulfillment outside of the home and family. And this set the stage for some women to go a step further by giving priority to the search for personal and career fulfillment.

In the 1950s, Joyce would have been resigned to her fate as a housewife. She most certainly would not have become a dedicated medical researcher, and even if she had, she would never have thought of moving away from her children. In the 1990s, Joyce pursues her career without hesitation. She conceives of the option of relinquishing custody, but expects no moral support for this life style.

Wouldn't feminists approve of her choice? After all, the women's movement laid the groundwork for making this option available. Ironically, if Joyce turns to the women's movement for support, she may not find a sympathetic ear. After years of advocating the elimination of the traditional sex-stereotyped division of roles—of teaching that a woman's place is not just in the home, and that there is nothing in a man's nature than prohibits him from cleaning, cooking, or nurturing children—some feminists (but not all) are calling for a new type of double standard: one rule for married parents, a different rule for divorced parents.

Married women should encourage and allow their ex-husbands to assume more responsibility for raising the children. But divorced women should discourage and oppose their ex-husbands' efforts in this direction. Married men should defy tradition and get more involved with their children. But divorced men should respect tradition, curtail contact with their children, and leave to their ex-wives the daily chores and responsibilities of raising the children.

Of course the position is not usually phrased in this manner. If it were, the implicit chauvinism would be apparent. Those who hold the position do not really want to deprive women of the opportunity to rearrange their priorities or to live an unorthodox life style. For them, the real issue is power. They want to preserve and expand women's sphere of influence. To them, relinquishing or even sharing custody means giving up one of the few prerogatives that women retain in our society. Hence, the women's movement has not been particularly vocal in support of father custody and joint custody as alternatives to sole mother custody.

One can hardly blame noncustodial mothers for feeling ostracized in our society. Fortunately, they do not have to stand alone. Over ten thousand women have sought solace through Mothers Without Custody, a nationwide network of self-help groups organized to provide emotional support to these maverick mothers. Groups such as this can help, but they cannot eradicate the anguish of a mother separated from her offspring, They cannot fill the void left by her children. They cannot satisfy her wish for more involvement with her children in spite of her choice to give up full-time parenting.

As I indicated earlier, relinquishing custody is a tough choice with both benefits and drawbacks. I have discussed the disappointments that accompany this decision in order to help parents make fully informed decisions. But nothing I have written should dissuade a woman from electing this option when it is clearly the best course for her family. Although 50 percent of noncustodial mothers regret their decision, 50 percent are satisfied with their status.

The lesson to be taken from this chapter is that in many cases giving up custody is a reasonable alternative with an undeserved bad reputation. Most women who choose this path deserve our respect. But, as with all difficult choices, it should be made with full awareness of the likely consequences.

## COPING STRATEGIES FOR MOTHERS WITHOUT CUSTODY

**1.** If at all possible, stay in the same geographical area as your children. The potential for meaningful contact with them is multiplied severalfold when you live in fairly close proximity.

**2.** Attend your children's school functions and extracurricular activities such as athletic events and music recitals.

**3.** Be punctual and conscientious when it comes to spending time with the children. More than words, your actions will tell them how important they are to you and how secure they can feel in your love. For children in father-custody families, the mother's reliability carries special significance. Reliability about visits will also foster a better relationship with your ex-husband.

**4.** Bridge the gap between visits with telephone calls and letters.

**5.** If your life situation changes, explore the possibility of increasing your time with the children.

**6.** Look into support groups sponsored by Mothers Without Custody and Parents Without Partners.

**7.** Recognize that there is no perfect custody disposition; every arrangement has its advantages and drawbacks. If your children are having problems when living apart from you, don't assume that the custody situation is responsible. In general, research indicates that children are just as likely to develop problems in mother-custody homes as in father-custody homes.

**8.** If you must live in a different geographical area from your children, ask their teachers to send you copies of school announcements and report cards. Teachers are more likely to comply with this request if you give them self-addressed, stamped envelopes. Let the children know, by telephoning and writing letters, that you are thinking of them. Many mothers find that disappointments are minimized if phone calls are made on a prearranged schedule.

**9.** Do whatever soul-searching is necessary to come to terms with your custody status. Although a sense of loss and grief is to be expected, it helps neither you nor your children for you to remain chronically unhappy about your life style. If you have trouble making peace with your decision, get professional assistance.

# PART 3

## WHAT ABOUT THE CHILDREN?

# 6

# FATHER CUSTODY VERSUS MOTHER CUSTODY

Judge O'Donald had just about made up her mind. She had already heard the testimony of each parent and their respective witnesses. Earlier she had met with their son, Kirk, in her chambers. He was a cute seven-year-old redhead, complete with freckles. Although nervous and shy, Kirk answered all her questions about his school, his home, his parents, and their divorce. Now the judge listened to the psychologist testifying about the strengths and weaknesses of each parent. Results of the psychological interviews and testing confirmed the judge's impressions.

The weight of the evidence favored the father. Judge O'Donald was confident that he was in a better position to meet Kirk's needs and had a better relationship with his son. Nevertheless, after six years on the bench, Judge O'Donald was aware of a familiar, nagging doubt. Convinced that Kirk would be better off living with his father *at this point in time*, she turned her thoughts to the boy's future. "What are the long-term consequences of living apart from his mother?" she wondered. "What kinds of problems can we expect to develop in boys raised by their fathers?"

Judge O'Donald had no answers to these questions, yet she had to base her decision, in part, on what she expected the future to hold. Of course, skill at fortunetelling is not a prerequisite for becoming a family-court judge. How, then, do judges make these predictions? Most are guided by implicit assumptions or biases, often ideas that are never consciously articulated.

One such assumption is that the parent who best meets the child's needs in the *present* is the parent with whom the child would do best in the *future*. This implies a static view of people and relationships in divorced families—i.e., that each parent and child will remain the same after the divorce. We know from our discussion of mother-custody families, though, that this assumption is false. In particular, parent-child relationships undergo massive upheavals after parents separate. Judges who do not take into account these predictable changes may unwittingly reach decisions that benefit children in the short run but cause damage to their long-term development.

Judges are aware of this problem. So are divorcing parents who try to agree on the best custody arrangement without fighting it out in court. They need a rational basis for predicting the likely outcome of different custody dispositions. I am often consulted by parents in this situation. During our talks, when a certain living arrangement is proposed, one of the questions I am asked most frequently by parents is "How will this arrangement affect my child's future development?"

Lacking a crystal ball, I of course can never answer with certainty. What I rely on in making such predictions is the next-best thing to a crystal ball—the experiences of several thousand children who have lived with different types of custody. Many of these children have been studied by research psychologists; others have been followed by clinicians. These children have taught us a great deal about life in father-custody, mother-custody, and joint-custody homes. Such knowledge helps professionals predict the best custody arrangement for each child—and it will help you do the same.

## THE CRISIS OF SEPARATION: WHEN CHILDREN STAY WITH FATHER

Every loving parent contemplating a marital separation has wondered, "How will the children react?" Research has led us to expect a period of great distress and turmoil when children stay with their mothers. But what happens when children stay with their fathers? Is the separation any less traumatic for them?

The parents we interviewed in Texas answered with a resounding "No!" And their answers agreed with those of parents interviewed in California, Massachusetts, Pennsylvania, and Virginia.

Father custody does *not* spare children the pain of divorce. They react with the same range of feelings and behavior as do children in mother-custody homes. Although every child reacts somewhat differently, and much depends on the child's age, certain symptoms are most common. These include anger, confusion, worry, and grief. Tears come easily to these children, so parents should expect more frequent crying. Young children in father-custody homes are likely to exhibit regressed behavior, such as bed-wetting, thumb-sucking, and increased demands for attention from their parents and teachers.

Take Nina, for instance. She was six years old and in first grade when her parents announced their decision to separate. Her parents agreed that it would be better for Nina to remain in the family home with her father. Nina's mother moved out on Saturday, and after a few tears Nina seemed to have accepted the situation. She showed little reaction during the remainder of the weekend. On Monday, when the school bus arrived, Nina went to give her father a goodbye kiss as she always did. But instead of the usual quick-kiss-and-out-the-door, little Nina clung steadfastly to her father, sobbing as though her life were ending. Her father was flabbergasted. This was like the time when Nina was two years old and refused to stay with the new babysitter.

Dramatic reactions such as Nina's can be quite alarming to parents who are not prepared for them. It is perhaps only somewhat reassuring for parents to know that, for most children, these reactions are temporary. Also, not all the changes are negative. About one-third of the parents in the Texas study said that, at the time of the separation, their children showed more self-control and mature behavior, in addition to some adverse reactions. In Iowa and Missouri, custodial fathers who left very stressful marriages reported that their children were relieved and happy after the breakup.

Despite reports of some positive outcomes, it is clear that divorce is a major stressful life event for most children and that parents should expect a wide range of reactions. What is also clear is that these reactions are no worse in father-custody homes than in mother-custody homes.

*Contrary to popular assumption, mothers do no better than fathers in easing the immediate stress of divorce for their children.* Naturally, when making custody decisions, we are more concerned with *long-term* consequences than with immediate reactions. Do father-custody children have a harder time coming to terms with the divorce? In the long run, how do father-custody children fare psychologically?

## FATHER-CUSTODY CHILDREN SPEAK OUT ON DIVORCE

If you want to learn about how father-custody children cope with divorce, a good place to begin is to ask the children. That is exactly what we did in the Texas project. We interviewed elementary-school children from father-custody and mother-custody homes and compared their outlook on their parents' divorce and its effect on their lives.

Some answers were predictable; others challenged conventional wisdom regarding how children are "supposed" to feel about divorce. No doubt their parents would be astonished by some of the answers. Even psychologists are having to rethink long-held views about children and divorce in the light of current research.

For instance, there is a popular notion that children are so resilient that they can easily bounce back from any crisis, including divorce. Not true. If children were writing the books about divorce, we would see fewer upbeat titles like *Creative Divorce* and *Happiness Through Divorce*. One thing is clear: *Parents may view the divorce as a solution to their marital problems, but the majority of children view the divorce as the problem.*

Nancy was seven years old when her father told her that her mom was moving out. Her immediate reaction was surprise: She thought he was joking. But when she saw the tears in his eyes, she knew it was true. Nancy often overheard her parents arguing, and she figured this was how all parents acted. Lately her mother had been talking a lot more about needing her "space": Nancy wasn't exactly sure what this meant, but she guessed it had something to do with Mom's moving out.

At first Nancy cried a lot. She even cried at school. She was feeling very sad and very little. When her teacher heard about the divorce, the teacher appointed her the class monitor two days in a row and let Nancy sit in her lap. This helped a little.

When she came home from school, things were very different. Her mother used to sit down at the kitchen table while Nancy ate her snack and they would talk about the school day. Now her mother wasn't there. Dad had set up a studio in the spare bedroom so he could be home for Nancy. He was a landscape designer. He made good snacks for her, but they weren't always ready when she came home. She complained a few times, and he started getting better about it. But he didn't always have time to talk with her. Sometimes the phone rang and he had to go back to the studio. The rest of the afternoon, he worked and she was on her own. Dad said this was better than going to day care. Nancy wasn't sure exactly what day care was like, but her friends didn't like it so she figured she wouldn't either.

The week after Mom moved out, Nancy developed new fears. She was afraid to enter her bedroom alone, even during the day. She would run in quickly, get the things she needed, and run back to the family room. She couldn't walk into the bathroom unless the light was already on. And at night she was afraid to be left alone in her room. Dad usually kept her company until she fell asleep, but sometimes he got mad at her and told her to stop acting like a baby. If she got up in the middle of the night, she went to Daddy's bedroom and slept in Mommy's old place. When Dad woke up, he took her back to her own bed. But sometimes he was too tired and let her remain. Dad said they might move into a smaller house one day, where the bedrooms were closer together. Maybe this would help. She hoped the new house would have a backyard large enough for her swing set. Lately she spent more and more time on the swings.

The biggest change was that she only got to see her mom every other weekend and Wednesday nights for dinner. Mom was always happy to see her. But it always seemed that, just when Nancy was getting used to being with Mom, it was time to go back home. One of the hardest things for Nancy to accept was the idea that Mom had a boyfriend. It wasn't the man that bothered her so much; it was the fact that he had a daughter just about Nancy's age, and sometimes when Nancy was with her mom, Tracy was there, too. Nancy didn't think it was fair that she had to share her mom with these people. And she hated the idea that Tracy sometimes got to be around Mom when Nancy didn't. "Maybe Mom doesn't love me so much anymore," she thought. When she asked her dad about this, he said she shouldn't worry, that her mom loved her more than anything. But she still worried. If Mom loved her so much, why did she have to move out? Maybe, just maybe, Mom would change her mind and move back.

Recall that over one-half the children interviewed in the California study of mother-custody families preferred things the way they had been before the divorce. The Texas children echoed these sentiments. Cavette, nine years old, lived with her dad. She spoke for many of the children in our study when she remarked, "Things were bad before the divorce, but now they're terrible." Cavette's major complaints were that she missed her mom and that she had to stay in day care after school. She also told us that her father was not as much fun to be around since the divorce. In our studies, two out of three children thought life had been better before the divorce. Even more children, five out of six, longed for their parents to reunite, and most expressed strong desires to see more of the noncustodial parent. The children's attitudes about the divorce were not affected by the custody arrangements: *Mother-custody children were just as likely as father-custody children to view the divorce as an unwelcome intrusion in their lives.*

It is tempting to dismiss these negative attitudes as merely temporary reactions, fresh psychic wounds destined to heal over time. This might be justified if the attitudes were expressed by children whose parents had recently divorced. Unfortunately, such was not the case. These children were interviewed an average of *three and a third years* after their parents' separation. Guided by conventional wisdom, their parents would have predicted that the children had long since come to terms with the divorce. They would have been wrong. I have talked with adults ten, twenty, thirty years after their own parents' divorce who confess that they still wish their parents would get back together!

One of the more disturbing findings of our research was the extent to which many parents were unaware of their children's feelings about the divorce. More than half the parents thought their children had given up their reconciliation wishes. If the parents don't know how their children feel, how can they help them cope with their feelings?

Not every child we interviewed expressed intense suffering over the divorce. But the majority revealed a lingering and touching sadness, a sadness that respected no adult convention about the presumed importance of mothers versus fathers. Fathers were missed as much as mothers, and the intact family, once taken for granted, was now a cherished memory.

## FATHER CUSTODY VERSUS MOTHER CUSTODY

Knowing how our children feel about divorce puts us in a better position to help them cope successfully with the trauma. Nevertheless, we cannot rely on children's feelings to answer our central question, "How does father custody affect children's future psychological development?" Feelings are no substitute for objective measures. Proponents of the motherhood mystique can argue that, although being in the custody of their mothers does not help children *feel* better about the divorce, the children *do* better in the care of their mothers.

To respond to this argument, we must examine the results of careful laboratory observations and psychological tests. Nine scientific studies, all but one conducted within the past decade, have compared children raised in father-custody homes with those raised in mother-custody homes. These studies measured a broad range of psychological traits in children aged two through twenty and used standard techniques well respected by the scientific community. This body of research provides the best test of the assumption that children do better in the custody of their mothers after divorce. If the assumption is correct, then, on the average, the mother-custody children will look better adjusted than the father-custody children. If, on the contrary, the children in father-custody homes equal or surpass those in mother-custody homes, the popular preference for mother custody is not warranted.

Of the many possible psychological traits to study, the one that has received the most attention from divorce researchers is self-esteem. Why? Look beneath the surface of any child's emotional and behavioral problems and you will find low self-esteem. This was evident in the California study of mother-custody families. When divorce resulted in psychological problems for those children, the principal symptom was low self-esteem. Thus it was clear that psychologists interested in father-custody children would have to study their self-esteem.

The results were unanimous. In every study, the self-esteem of father-custody children was comparable to that of mother-custody children. The same was true for every feature of psychological development assessed! Not one difference was found between father-custody and mother-custody children—not in their level of maturity, independence, anxiety, frequency of behavior problems, number of psychosomatic complaints, behavior with interviewers, and not in their relationships with custodial parents, teachers, and peers.

Regardless of what trait was measured, and how or by whom it was measured (there were male and female investigators), in all nine studies the psychological status of children living with their fathers was comparable to children of the same ages living with their mothers.

Father-custody children, on the average, do not look any better than mother-custody children and they do not look any worse. Averages, though, do not tell the whole story. Common sense tells us that some children cope more successfully than others with their parents' divorce.

# FATHER CUSTODY VERSUS MOTHER CUSTODY: CHILDREN'S PSYCHOLOGICAL DEVELOPMENT

Following is a list of reactions, attitudes, traits, and behavior that psychologists have studied in children from divorced homes. On none of these factors were there overall differences that favored father-custody or mother-custody homes.

1. Sadness.
2. Distress.
3. Longing for the intact family.
4. Strong wishes for parental reconciliation.
5. Self-esteem.
6. Maturity.
7. Independence.
8. Anxiety.
9. Behavior problems.
10. Psychosomatic complaints.
11. Custodial parent-child relationships.
12. Teacher-child relationships.
13. Peer relationships.

Here, too, the similarity between father-custody and mother-custody families is striking. The five coping factors that maximize children's chances in mother-custody homes (pages 81–83) also help children in father-custody homes cope better. Parents, mental-health professionals, and judges should take note of these factors, which cushion the divorce experience for children:

1. Sufficient access to each parent to enable children to maintain high-quality relationships with both.
2. A cooperative, low-conflict relationship between the parents.
3. Skilled and sensitive, "authoritative" child-rearing practices.
4. Minimal changes for the children.
5. Good social-support systems for children and parents.

When we consider the research discussed in this chapter, along with the work discussed in previous chapters, one conclusion is inescapable: *We have no grounds for discriminating against fathers in custody matters.* We have seen that a custodial bias in favor of mothers cannot be defended by appeals to history, theory, or research.

Mother custody, far from being a historical imperative, was virtually unknown to our ancestors. The belief in a mother's singular importance to her children arose in response to economic pressures and was buttressed by sentiment, unproven theories, and faulty interpretation of earlier research. Recent research has underscored the father's immense contribution to his children's development and documented the psychologically harmful effects of his absence. Research with father-custody families has proved that fathers are able to manage competently the responsibilities of single parenting and that their children are no worse off than their peers in mother-custody families.

In the light of this evidence, reason beseeches us to revise the cultural and judicial standards that have guided custody decisions during the past seventy years. It is time we release judges, attorneys, and divorced families from the grip of the motherhood mystique.

# 7

# THE GENDER
# CONNECTION

◆

$\mathbf{E}$d Stein and his daughter, Alice, were fifteen minutes late for their first appointment at the university. While waiting, we reviewed the information Ed had given us during our initial phone conversation. He was a thirty-seven-year-old insurance agent whose lawyer had referred him to our custody project. Alice had just turned eight and was in the second grade. Three years earlier, Alice's mother had chosen to return to college and leave (Ed called it "abandon") her husband, home, and child.

A parent's sudden departure creates an emotional storm that takes many months to subside. We were curious about how the Steins had weathered that crisis. But we were more interested in how they were doing now. Three years was long enough, we thought, for the dust to settle. Long enough for father and daughter to come to terms with their loss. Long enough for us to learn about everyday life in a father-custody household. By letting us observe, interview, and test them, the Steins, and volunteers like them, would help us learn how a father managed the task of raising a daughter on his own and how his daughter coped without her mother at home.

Ed walked in first, out of breath and apologizing for their lateness. He was a large man, large enough for a slim second-grader to hide behind, which is exactly what Alice was doing. With his dark suit, white shirt, tie, and well-trimmed beard, Ed looked like a man who was not accustomed to being late for appointments.

Alice wore a white ruffled sundress, appropriate for our hot Texas sun, white shoes, and pale-green socks. Her light-brown hair was cropped short. Pink-framed glasses shielded her large brown eyes.

While her dad was reading and signing the forms giving consent to participate in the study, we tried to coax Alice out of hiding. We were unsuccessful. We knew how to help shy children feel more comfortable, but Alice wasn't just shy; she was petrified. Watching Alice cling to her father's pants, we wondered how she would behave when left alone with him to work on the routine tasks we assigned to parents and children. Would she relax and work effectively with her father, or would she continue her anxious and immature behavior? Unfortunately, it was the latter.

Through the two-way mirror, we watched as Alice sat in the seat closest to her father. She held on to the sides of her seat and began swinging her legs as though preparing for takeoff.

"What are you so nervous about?" asked her father.

She swung faster.

"I hate my nose," Alice said, looking at her reflection in the mirror. When she wiped her nose with the back of her hand, Ed chastised her for not bringing her little purse with Kleenex in it.

As if to bridge an imagined gap created by the rebuke, Alice suddenly got up, plopped herself on her father's lap, and gave him the type of bear hug that melts a parent's heart. But then the hum that accompanied the strong hug grew in pitch and intensity until it was a loud siren. Ed's discomfort mirrored our own. Demonstrating remarkable patience, he waited for about sixty seconds before asking her to get off his lap.

Alice refused.

Her father tried to make the best of a difficult situation. "You look like a puppet, you know, the guy with the thing sitting on his knee. He pulls the strings back here and the mouth moves." Ed held Alice's jaw in his large hand and moved it up and down, simulating a ventriloquist's dummy. Perhaps Ed was expressing his wish for a more compliant daughter.

When Ed removed his hand, the puppet's jaw stopped moving, and the siren continued. He couldn't hide his annoyance any longer. It came out indirectly.

"Why are you wearing green socks with a white dress?"

In response, Alice climbed down from her father's lap. She began skipping around the room, periodically stopping to press her face up against the mirror, trying to see the video camera on the other side. Next she crawled under the chairs, all the while giggling. Ed tried, unsuccessfully, to engage Alice in working on the tasks we had assigned. Someone who did not know she was eight would have guessed she was much younger.

Toward the end of the session, Alice hopped back up on her father's lap. He looked at her with an anxious expression that read, "Now what?" As though to answer, Alice began making farting sounds with her mouth and giggling over her performance.

"Now, that's not nice."

"Me has to go to the bathroom," Alice said in a voice much younger than her eight years. She belched out loud, and the session closed on that note.

During the subsequent interview with Ed, we learned that the immature behavior we had observed was not unusual for Alice. "She's been like this ever since her mother left. She just doesn't act her age. And she's never as relaxed as the other girls in the neighborhood. Her teacher said that Alice needs to work more independently. Alice is always asking for help, even when she doesn't really need it."

Like many of the custodial fathers in our study, Ed had never met any other divorced man who had custody of his children. He asked if his problems with Alice were typical of father-custody families. Since our project was the first to observe father-custody children directly, and we had not yet begun our data analysis, we did not have the answer. Now we do.

I have already discussed (in chapter 6) our comparisons of children in father-custody and mother-custody families. We found that the psychological health of the *average* child in a father-custody home was comparable to the *average* child in a mother-custody home. As a group, father-custody children have neither more nor fewer problems than mother-custody children. This discovery is revolutionary. If children are as well off in father-custody homes as in mother-custody homes, there are no grounds for discriminating against fathers in custody matters. With this knowledge, judges, attorneys, and divorced families are released from the grip of the motherhood mystique.

Nevertheless, Alice's experience reminds us that averages do not tell the whole story. We need to go beyond discussions of "average" children if we want to understand father-custody families better. Otherwise we will be oversimplifying what is fundamentally a complicated psychological picture.

The five coping factors discussed in chapters 3 and 6 tell us what divorced parents can do to help their children cope better. But what about the children? Do some children do better in one type of custody than in the other? If so, can we predict which custody arrangement will work best for which type of child? Answering these questions would allow us to provide more specific guidelines to divorcing parents and courts—one of the most important goals of our research. To meet this goal, we had to search beyond global comparisons of father-custody and mother-custody children.

We were not prepared, though, for the results of the search. More precisely, we were not prepared for the intensity of public interest and controversy generated by our results. As discussed in the preceding chapter (page 134), we discovered several attributes common to families with high-functioning children. But one finding in particular struck a chord and stirred up much interest among parents, lawyers, and journalists: *Children in the custody of the same-sex parent, father-custody boys and mother-custody girls, were better adjusted than children in the custody of the opposite-sex parent.*

Of course it was no surprise that girls had fewer problems than boys in mother-custody homes; that difference is consistent with the mother-custody research discussed in chapter 3. But psychologists had always assumed this meant that boys just have a harder time than girls coping with their parents' divorce. A false assumption, according to the evidence provided by our study. It is not *divorce* in general that gives boys a harder time than girls. It is *mother custody.* *Boys* living with their fathers after divorce do not have the problems so characteristic of boys living with their mothers. On the other hand, *girls* living with their fathers after divorce face more problems than do girls living with their mothers. So Alice's immaturity, while definitely not representative of father-custody children in general, is fairly typical of girls in father-custody homes.

As you can imagine, these results are welcome news to fathers seeking custody of their sons and mothers seeking custody of their daughters. A well-known television commentator closed her interview with this warning to me: "You know that you are going to be deluged with requests from attorneys for your testimony." She was correct. Nearly every week, I receive inquiries from parents and attorneys involved in custody battles, all hoping to use our research to strengthen their case.

Such attention presents me with a dilemma. On the one hand, I am gratified that my work is having an impact on the world outside the laboratory. On the other hand, I have serious misgivings about the marriage of the laboratory and the courtroom. Throughout history, custody decisions have been based on the sex of the parent. Will our research perpetuate this tradition by helping fathers win custody of their sons and mothers win custody of their daughters merely on the basis of sex?

Certainly this wouldn't represent progress in custody policy. We would be merely substituting a new mystique of "sex matching" for the seventy-year-old motherhood mystique. The appeal of such mystiques is not difficult to understand; they offer the promise of ready-made solutions to difficult problems. But they overlook the needs and circumstances of individual families. My patients have taught me much about the suffering caused by the indiscriminate application of a single formula to all divorcing families. I do not want my work to support a new formula that would continue to oversimplify the complexities of custody decisions.

To guard against such oversimplification, we have been careful to note, in our scientific reports, that our findings may not apply in all situations. Although the evidence justifies giving considerable weight to the sex of the child in custody decisions, it is only one factor, among many, that affects the success or failure of a custody arrangement. Not all boys are better off in the custody of their fathers, and not all girls are better off in the custody of their mothers. Unfortunately, such qualifications have not prevented the misuse of our research findings.

Testifying in the sensational Pulitzer custody battle, a psychologist referred to "the Warshak study" in defending his recommendation of the father as primary custodian. Roxanne Pulitzer, aided by court transcripts, described this testimony in her account of the case: "He said the studies showed that boys with fathers as primary custodian did better in their academic work, were better adjusted and were better accepted by their friends than boys raised with mothers as their primary custodian." In his final judgment, awarding custody to the father, the judge characterized this psychologist's testimony as "very impressive."

I do not agree. I am not impressed with this testimony, because I know it is not entirely accurate. I have never reported that father-custody boys enjoyed better academic performance and peer acceptance than mother-custody boys. Nor am I aware of any other study that has reported better academic adjustment for father-custody boys.

Mrs. Pulitzer may have erred in her recollection of the doctor's testimony. Nevertheless, before giving testimony that would forever influence the happiness and well-being of two children and two parents, I wish this psychologist had called to discuss the research with me, or to ask why I myself would not testify in the Pulitzer case, or to clarify his understanding of my findings.

Despite the potential misuse of custody research, the evidence does favor a radical change in custody policy away from the prevailing preference for mothers. In previous chapters I have shown that the typical custodial father is doing *as good* a job as the typical custodial mother. Now I am going beyond that observation. With a consensus of studies to back me up, I am proposing that many boys (but not all) may actually be *better off* living with their fathers after divorce. Girls, on the other hand, may be worse off.

This was the pattern in the Texas studies. Compared with children in the custody of the opposite-sex parent, children in the custody of the same-sex parent were rated more mature, sociable, cooperative, and independent. They were less anxious and less demanding, and had more self-esteem. And they were more satisfied with their living arrangements. In other words, these children were more at peace with themselves and with the world. This pattern of sex-linked adjustment has now been corroborated by four independent investigations of father-custody children and numerous investigations of mother-custody children around the country.

Alan walked confidently into the laboratory for his first interview. His smile matched his relaxed body posture. Apple-polished cheeks, complete with freckles, brought to mind a Norman Rockwell painting. Alan sat close to the interviewer and warmed up easily. In a clear, self-assured voice, he responded to the initial questions: He is ten years old and attends fifth grade in his neighborhood public school; he likes his teacher, but thinks she is sometimes too strict; he has one older brother and several close friends, and enjoys playing football and soccer and watching television; his favorite show is *Bewitched.*

Alan showed perseverance in the face of frustration as he continued working on a difficult puzzle we asked him to assemble. When we asked him to create original stories, Alan had no trouble exercising his imagination. Dr. Marla Isaacs has found a drop in creativity for some children following their parents' separation. Fortunately, Alan suffered no such loss.

Toward the end of the interview, we asked children to tell us how they felt about their parents and about the divorce. Alan's mixed feelings mirrored those of most of the children in our study.

"The best thing about the divorce is that we don't have to hear Mom and Dad argue so much."

"And the worse thing about the divorce?"

"I don't get to see Mom enough."

"How do you feel about living with your father?" we asked.

"I like it. We get along pretty good. We both like sports, and he doesn't fuss a lot. Probably most girls would want to stay with their mom if their parents got a divorce. But it's different for boys. Moms don't like to watch football or anything." Alan paused. "What I really wish is that Mom and Dad would get back together. Then I could live with both of them."

"Do you think that will ever happen?"

"No," he said, "but I wish it would. I wish it a lot."

That Alan should feel this way some two and a half years after his parents' separation was not in itself remarkable. Consistent with studies around the country, 84 percent of the children we interviewed expressed the wish, usually strong, for their parents to reunite. Of the 16 percent who did not, all but one created an imaginary story in which a child of divorced parents hoped they would reunite. We took this to mean that, at some level, these children really did long for their parents' reconciliation.

What distinguished Alan from other children of divorce (and adults, for that matter) was his remarkable ability to stay in touch with his thoughts and feelings without seeking refuge behind self-created walls of denial and rationalization. And more: With minimal prodding from his interviewer, he could openly talk about the changes in his life brought on by his parents' divorce. Yet one would not say Alan was preoccupied with the breakup. True, given three wishes, his first was to have his parents reunited. But the second and third wishes were for "a sports car and lots of money"—quite typical for a fifth-grade boy.

Alan is, no doubt, an exceptionally well-put-together youngster. But his behavior during the interview was representative of the father-custody boys and mother-custody girls we came to know through our research. As a group, these children were easier to interview than mother-custody boys and father-custody girls. They were more cooperative. Our interviewers felt an easier rapport with them, and found them more appealing. Our confidence in the accuracy of the interviewers' impressions was increased when independent judges observed videotapes of the interviews. These judges rated father-custody girls as having the least self-esteem and the most anxiety of all the children in our study.

When we observed children and their parents together, children in the custody of the same-sex parent acted more mature, independent, and sociable and less demanding than children in the custody of the opposite-sex parent. There was an unmistakable spirit of camaraderie between custodial fathers and their sons, and between custodial mothers and their daughters. Their easy give-and-take would be the envy of most single parents living with children of the opposite sex.

Ike and his father were a good example. When asked to discuss the main problems in their family, Ike pinched his nostrils, turned to his father, and said, "Your smelly socks. Phew!" This gave them both a good laugh and served to reduce their tension.

We expected this task to generate a certain amount of anxiety. After all, what family wouldn't be nervous discussing their problems in front of a video camera? One of the things we wanted to learn was how parents and children dealt with their anxiety. Ike and his dad used humor to cope, and it worked. After laughing, they were able to identify and discuss their major concerns in a serious manner.

Other parent-child pairs were less capable of managing their anxiety. For some the tension was so high that it kept their attention from the task at hand.

Barry and his mother spent the time discussing movies instead of family problems, as we had asked them to do. Only once did his mother try to steer the conversation around to the assigned task; Barry ignored her and they went right on talking about movies. We learned later that Barry and his mother considered each other "best friends" and that Barry did not respect his mother's authority.

In some cases, joking dominated the session and problems were never addressed. In other cases, the tension resulted in participants' being overly critical of one another. In still other cases, one or both participants would clam up and say little during the interaction. Father-custody girls and mother-custody boys were particularly likely to handle their anxiety by acting silly and immature, as did Alice.

It was not only their behavior that distinguished children living with the same-sex parent from those living with the opposite-sex parent. We have reason to believe that the children living with the same-sex parent also *felt* more satisfied with their living arrangements.

Measuring a child's preference for living with his or her mother or father is a delicate matter. Many children would have no problem stating a preference; a few would feel great anxiety if they even thought about having a preference. To protect children from feelings of disloyalty, I instructed our interviewers to refrain from asking any child to state a preference. Instead, we borrowed a time-honored technique from child psychology—an indirect approach called a "projective" task.

Working on the same principle as the well-known Rorschach Ink Blot Test, a projective task is so named because children project their personalities through the task, as movies are projected on a screen. In this case, the task was to create stories to accompany a series of pictures. We were interested not only in children's ability to exercise their imagination freely, but also in the product of their imagination. Children usually become absorbed in their stories and say things about the characters that actually reveal their own innermost feelings.

To elicit children's deeper attitudes about divorce, we showed them a picture of a man, woman, and child and told them that this was a picture of a mother and father getting a divorce. After their story was completed, we asked several questions, including, "Who does the child want to live with after the divorce?" Here is how they answered.

*Every* father-custody boy said the boy in his story wanted to live with his father. *Every* mother-custody girl said the girl in her story wanted to live with her mother. *Not one child* in the custody of the same-sex parent created a story in which the child preferred to live with the opposite-sex parent.

What about children who were living with the opposite-sex parent— father-custody girls and mother-custody boys? Did they project a preference, in their stories, to live with the opposite-sex parent? Some did, but more did not. More than half (57 percent) said the child in their story wanted to live with the same-sex parent, the parent from whom, in reality, they were separated.

If these stories express the children's own feelings, then they indicate that children place a high value on contact with the same-sex parent.

Additional support for this conclusion came from the interview, when children discussed their attitudes about visits with the noncustodial parent. Although many wanted more frequent visits, this desire was more prevalent among father-custody girls and mother-custody boys. In other words, children valued contact with the same-sex parent more highly than contact with the opposite-sex parent. The next chapter explains why.

To recap, as a group, children in the custody of the parent of the same sex were more satisfied with their living arrangements and were in better psychological shape than children in the custody of the parent of the opposite sex.

. . .

Can we be confident that these findings accurately reflect the reality of father-custody and mother-custody families? I believe we can, for several reasons. First, we employed precise, state-of-the-art, scientific safeguards to ensure the validity of our conclusions. (These are described in the appendix.) Second, the findings were robust: The better adjustment of children living with the same-sex parent was evident in different contexts using a variety of measures. None of the Texas studies indicated more favorable outcomes for father-custody girls or mother-custody boys. And third, the identical pattern of sex-linked adjustment has been confirmed by four independent investigations comparing father-custody and mother-custody children and by numerous investigations demonstrating that the ill effects of mother custody are more pervasive and enduring for boys than for girls.

*No study has ever concluded that boys adjust better in mother-custody homes or that girls adjust better in father-custody homes.*

"Boys from mother-custody homes and girls from father-custody homes . . . displayed the highest levels of aggression and behavioral problems," according to Drs. Kathleen Camara and Gary Resnick, Tufts University psychologists working under the auspices of the National Institute of Mental Health. These children, like those we studied in Texas, had the least self-esteem and were the least sociable. They tended to be rejected by other children, particularly by their same-sex peers. During school recess, for example, compared with the other children studied, mother-custody boys and father-custody girls were more likely to play with children of the opposite sex. These children are probably caught in a vicious circle. Aggressive behavior leads to peer rejection, which produces frustration, which leads to more aggressive behavior.

Dr. Judith Wallerstein and Sandra Blakeslee wrote about one boy who took part in a California study of children from divorced homes. "Kevin was twelve when his parents brought their stormy marriage to an end. For as long as the boy could remember, his mother and father yelled, screamed, and hit one another amid mutual accusations, probably justified, of infidelity." When his father moved out, Kevin, who adored him, changed from a model student to a behavior problem. He refused to complete assignments. He spent his time fighting with other children and became the school bully.

Kevin's father rarely visited his son and instead made promises about the things he would do with and for Kevin. He never kept these promises, and Kevin eventually felt betrayed by his father. According to Wallerstein and Blakeslee, by seventeen "Kevin regularly drank and smoked pot, had been caught breaking and entering, and had even forged one of his grandmother's checks." By twenty-two, Kevin had been in jail three times—"for drunk driving, dealing dope, and beating up his girlfriend."

The behavior problems of mother-custody boys do not always disappear in adolescence. Along with Kevin, *one out of three boys* in the California study got into some trouble with the law. Delinquency in boys has long been attributed to "broken homes," but we now have evidence that the type of custody has a lot to do with the likelihood of such problems. Boys raised by their single fathers are less likely to become delinquent than boys raised by their mothers, but girls raised by their fathers are more likely to become delinquent. This was the conclusion of a survey of eleven thousand Minnesota high-school students reported in 1965. The survey also found that children raised by the opposite-sex parent are more likely to drop out of high school.

The problems of girls raised in single-father homes were documented, once again, in a nationwide study of children in the 1980s. Father-custody girls, but not boys, engaged in more antisocial behavior and were more vulnerable to depression. The only study comparing father-custody and mother-custody children after high school found higher levels of anxiety in female college students raised by single fathers.

Study after study reports the same pattern. Whether we look at independence, maturity, self-esteem, sociability, anxiety, aggression, delinquency, or depression, one conclusion is inescapable. On the average, boys do better in the custody of their fathers and girls do better in the custody of their mothers; therefore, *the child's sex is one factor that should carry significant weight in custody decisions.*

I am aware that many judges, lawyers, and parents will find this conclusion controversial. It is too easy to mistake it for a sexist view. Some feminists object to the idea of any woman's losing custody of her child, because this is seen as a loss of power. And some fathers'-rights advocates may object, because the results of my research do not lead to unqualified endorsement of father custody.

So be it. Facts are facts. We cannot alter the results of scientific research to accommodate the philosophical and political preferences of those who have a stake in the outcome of the research.

Even some psychologists, until recently, had strong reservations about applying these results to custody decisions. In the face of mounting evidence, though, the experts are publicly giving up their reservations and proclaiming the obvious.

Child-development specialist Dr. Ross Thompson captures the prevailing attitude among our colleagues:

> *Historically, there has been much judicial abuse of [sex guidelines] concerning custody disputes, partly because they can be so indiscriminately applied. For this reason one is hesitant to recommend the child's gender as an important factor in custody decision making. . . . Even so, the weight of the evidence, drawn from studies of fathers in traditional as well as nontraditional families, must certainly be taken seriously in judicial considerations.*

Before our work, the establishment view was that divorce was generally harder on boys than on girls. Following our reports, the prestigious National Academy of Sciences and the National Institute of Child Health and Human Development commissioned a study to evaluate all the evidence that bore on the question of sex differences in divorce adjustment. This study's outcome can be taken as a scientific "seal of approval" for my proposal to assign more weight to the child's sex in custody decisions.

"Boys do indeed respond more negatively to parental divorce," the 1989 report reads, "both immediately and over a period of years, *if* they are living with an unremarried mother; whereas in . . . father custody, girls fare worse. The major conclusion of this review is that both research and practice with children of divorce must consider gender differences in divorce reactions in relation to postdivorce family forms."

## IMPLICATIONS OF CUSTODY RESEARCH

Practically speaking, what does all this mean?

First, we can predict that in the typical family a boy will have an easier time adjusting to divorce in the custody of his father than in the custody of his mother.

Second, guided by the above prediction, serious consideration should be given to increasing the divorced father's involvement with his sons when this would not result in the separation of brothers and sisters (i.e., in families with no daughters). Whether this involvement should take the form of sole custody or joint custody is a matter to be taken up in a later chapter.

Third, living arrangements that reduce a boy's contact with his father or a girl's contact with her mother should only be attempted with full awareness of the psychological risks involved.

After hearing these recommendations people invariably ask certain questions.

*"Does this mean that all boys living with a single mother and all girls living with a single father are doomed to suffer serious psychological problems?"*

No. Research findings, such as those discussed in this volume, deal with averages, not individual cases. Certainly some boys do well in mother-custody homes and some girls do well in father-custody homes. The next chapter explains why most children have a harder time living with the opposite-sex parent and what parents can do to help minimize problems in these situations.

*"Should all fathers have custody of their sons and all mothers have custody of their daughters?"*

No. The child's sex is only one among many factors to consider when choosing an optimal custody arrangement. Circumstances such as the quality of the child's relationship with each parent may override the weight given to the child's sex. For example, no one would want an abusive father to receive custody of his son. Each case must be decided on its own merits. In chapter 6, page 134, I describe other factors that parents and judges should consider when making a custody decision.

*"Should custody of siblings routinely be split along sex-related lines (brother with father and sister with mother)?"*

Since few families have tried this approach, we don't have enough information about its effects on the children to make any general recommendations. Adrift in the turmoil associated with divorce, children may welcome the company of siblings, who are "in the same boat." On the other hand, in selected cases, splitting custody of siblings makes enormous sense. Before separating siblings, I recommend that parents consult a professional who will conduct a complete family evaluation and advise the parents about the benefits and hazards of such an arrangement. Some of the issues that bear on this decision are discussed at greater length in chapter 9 on joint custody (pages 199–200).

· · ·

*"Should fathers who currently lack custody of their sons and mothers who lack custody of their daughters instantly petition the court to change the custody arrangements?"*

Probably not. Such changes, and the legal battles that often accompany them, may be more detrimental to children than living with the opposite-sex parent. In many families, though, modification of the court-ordered living arrangements occurs informally, by mutual agreement of both parents, and often at the request of their child. In fact, I believe this is so prevalent that it deserves its own label; I call it "flexible custody." In some cases, this helps children. In other cases, it multiplies their problems. Chapter 10 provides suggestions to parents on how best to handle custody changes.

*"Should fathers have custody of babies?"*

Results of father-custody research should not be indiscriminately applied to children and families who differ significantly from those who participated in the research. In the Texas and Tufts University studies the children were an average of five years old at the time of their parents' separation. We have very little information about younger children in father-custody families. Although, as we have seen, fathers in intact families are quite capable of caring for infants and toddlers, this is a far cry from recommending that they have sole custody of their baby boys in the event of a divorce. Custody of infants is a complicated issue, which I will address later in the book.

*"Does race affect the pattern of children's adjustment to divorce?"*

Most of the divorced families that participated in the research are white. Some psychologists have argued that the results of this research may not be applicable to nonwhite families. Although I agree that cultural traditions may influence the manner in which a child experiences divorce, I see no reason why the dynamics that create problems for children living with opposite-sex parents would be different for children of other races. These dynamics are discussed, in the next chapter.

*"Does the difference in adjustment between boys and girls change when a parent remarries?"*

In families where the custodial parent has remarried, the differences in adjustment between boys and girls may not fit the same pattern. Many other factors come into play in determining whether the remarriage helps,

## MAKING THE GENDER
## CONNECTION WORK FOR YOU

**1.** When determining living arrangements after the divorce, try to maximize your child's contact with the parent of the same sex.

**2.** If it is not feasible or desirable for your child to live with the parent of the same sex, do what you can to facilitate the child's sense of attachment to that parent. Frequent visits or long visits during school vacations, frequent telephone calls, letters, and tape-recorded messages can all contribute to a sense of connection. It is also important to include the other parent in school conferences and to keep that parent informed of important events in your child's life, such as sports activities and music recitals.

**3.** Avoid automatically choosing father custody for boys and mother custody for girls. Although important, the sex of your child is just one factor to consider when choosing the best custody arrangement.

**4.** Caution should be exercised when splitting up brothers and sisters. The support afforded by a sibling can outweigh the advantages of being paired with the parent of the same sex.

**5.** The importance of your child's relationship with the same-sex parent should not be used to discount the importance of the other parent in your child's life. Children need mothers *and* fathers; those who lose a parent as a result of divorce deserve our sympathy . . . and so do their parents.

hinders, or makes no difference to a child's psychological well-being. These factors include the child's age, the quality of the child's relationship with each parent and stepparent, the stepparent's personality and style of parenting, the health and stability of the new marriage, whether or not the stepparent has children from a previous marriage who live in the household and, if so, how the stepsiblings get along with each other, the grandparents' attitude about the remarriage, whether or not the remarried couple have a child together and, if so, how they treat that child in relation to the child from the previous marriage, and the relationship between the remarried couple and the noncustodial parent.

To illustrate: Generally, the younger the child, the more he or she is apt to accept emotionally the entry of the stepparent into the family. Particularly if a boy has little contact with his father, he is likely to welcome the presence of an adult male in the home. On the other hand, the child who enjoys regular contact with the nonresidential parent is apt to resent the remarriage if it results in less contact with the other parent or if the stepparent denigrates the other parent. A stepparent who supports the child's relationship with the nonresidential parent, and who does not try to move into a disciplinary role too quickly, has a better chance of forging a solid and rewarding bond with his or her stepchild.

We still have a long way to go in understanding the impact of remarriage on a child's development. However, because so many additional variables affect a child's outcome in a stepfamily, the child's sex should be given much less weight in deciding the living arrangements for children in remarried families.

By formulating guidelines that will result in more divorced fathers' maintaining more involvement with their offspring, I realize that I am challenging the tradition of the past seventy years and thereby asking a lot of parents and judges. But, then, parents who divorce are asking a lot of their children. Surely, for the sake of the children, our society can summon the courage to rise beyond the outmoded stereotypes that currently dictate custody decisions. We owe our children no less.

# 8

## PSYCHOLOGICAL MINEFIELDS: COPING WITH THE GENDER CONNECTION

◆

**W**hen Jimmy, age five, was introduced to his mother's boss, the first man he had seen her with since his father abandoned him, Jimmy punched the unsuspecting gentleman in the nose. At the time, his mother and her boss thought this was cute and got a good laugh out of it.

What Bill did, at age eleven, was not so cute, and his mother, Evelyn, was not laughing when she told me the story. Evelyn had arranged to spend an evening with her date at home, watching videotapes. Despite their efforts to involve Bill, he refused to talk to her date or even eat his pizza in the same room as him. Bill then provoked an argument with Evelyn over something minor, and became so worked up during the argument that he began yelling, much to his mother's embarrassment, "All you care about is men, men, men!" One would have thought that she had paraded a succession of dates in the home.

As if this were not enough, when Evelyn returned from a brief walk with her date, she found a note nailed to the outside of her apartment door: "To My Mother—You don't care about your children. You never pay us any attention. You go out all the time. All you are interested in is men, men, men." The note was signed, "Your *ex*-son, Bill." Now all the neighbors would think that Evelyn was living life in the fast lane while neglecting the welfare of her children.

In reality, Evelyn was anything but a neglectful mother. Like most single mothers, she was struggling to carve out a decent life style for herself and her three children. This meant working long hours on her job to make ends meet. The child-support checks from her ex-husband came sporadically and were less than adequate. Ever since he had moved to another state, the children's visits with him had been less frequent. Thus, Evelyn rarely had the time out from parenting that some other custodial mothers enjoy. Preoccupied with licking the emotional wounds of the divorce, earning a living, and raising her children, Evelyn had chosen to keep her social life on hold for the two years since the divorce. Only recently, and reluctantly, had she begun to date.

Evelyn was worried about the impact of her dating on her son. Nevertheless, she was appalled that Bill would begrudge her the chance to relax and enjoy herself. "How can he be so selfish?" she asked. Doesn't he realize how much I care about him? I do so much for him. The children have always come first. But I'll never find another husband if I don't date. Why doesn't Bill realize that having a man around the house would make life easier for all of us? Then he'll have someone to do things with, you know, the things that guys are interested in. It's not my fault that his father skipped town."

Bill, however, was enraged that his mother would choose to spend time with a date when her work already kept them apart so much of the time. "I hardly ever get to see her. She makes me go to stupid day care every day after school. When she picks me up, she says she's too tired to do anything with me. If she's so tired all the time, how come she has the energy to go out with other men?"

Evelyn was not a bad mother and Bill was not a bad kid. But both were caught up in a delicate situation that neither understood very well. They were stepping through one of the psychological minefields that dot the landscape for divorced families.

Psychological minefields are hazards that can trigger emotional and behavioral troubles. We know from the preceding chapter that children in the custody of the opposite-sex parent experience more of these troubles. Now we learn why. The minefields discussed below pose the greatest risks to children living with the opposite-sex parent. It is my hope that this discussion will act as a minesweeper, helping parents anticipate the dangers and thereby avoid or defuse them.

## GROWING UP TOO FAST

One common minefield results from the breakdown of the usual boundaries between parent and child. Feeling lonely, emotionally deprived, and stressed, some custodial parents turn to their children for companionship, advice, and solace. In effect, the children are expected to act as quasi-spouses.

When his wife moved out after twelve years of marriage, Morris told his nine-year-old daughter, Stella, that now *she* was "the lady of the house." In addition to expecting her help with household chores, Morris treated Stella as a friend and confidante. During dinner, he spoke to Stella about his problems on the job, his back pain, and his worries about Stella's younger brother. When company was present, Morris relied on Stella to act as hostess.

Comparing the family to a corporation, Harvard sociologist Dr. Robert Weiss has observed that, after divorce, children frequently shift from the role of subordinate member of the household to that of junior partner. In effect, they are promoted to a position in the family with more authority and more responsibility. In carrying out this new role, some children begin to display more mature behavior. But many develop serious problems.

Relatives warned Morris that Stella was growing up too fast, that she was missing out on her childhood. But Morris didn't see the problem. He felt that Stella's new responsibilities made her more independent and better prepared her for life. Besides, Stella was not complaining. In fact, Stella seemed to enjoy her camaraderie with her father and began acting more mature around him.

Stella's teacher, though, saw a different side of the girl. In class, Stella became whiny and belligerent. Her newfound maturity turned out to be a thin veneer, behind which lay a very insecure little girl. Stella was paying a heavy price for her new role in the family structure. Her relatives were correct: Stella was indeed growing up too fast.

To a certain extent, the circumstances of the custodial parent set the stage for a shift in roles. If the parent is working full-time, it may be necessary to share traditional parental responsibilities with the children. Many single parents, for example, cannot afford optimal child-care arrangements and may see no alternative to leaving the oldest child in charge of a younger sibling, even though both may need adult supervision. Or the parent may have no one else with whom to share worries. This was the case with a parent interviewed by Dr. Weiss:

> *You're hit with these bills and who can you talk to about it but the kids? You have to have someone to share it with and so you share it with the people that you're doing it for. And, every so often, if they're bugging me for something that costs too much money, that's out of proportion to what I can afford, I take the bills out and show them the bills, show them what we get in monthly and say, "Now you make sense of it."*

Children, too, contribute to the problem. Often they take pride in their new status as their parents' peers. Chuck came for his therapy session one day after having spent the weekend with his mother house-hunting. He described the house he liked best, but regretfully added that the terms of purchase required $40,000, more "equity" than his mother could afford. Another house they were considering needed only $7,000 down and payments of $750 per month for twenty-seven years. All this was said in a matter-of-fact tone. For a moment, I had to remind myself that Chuck was only ten years old. How many other children his age need to concern themselves with such matters of family finance? Despite *my* reservations about Chuck's involvement in the mortgage deliberations, *he* was eager to participate, although he was subjecting himself to a new set of worries.

Even where it appears that the pressure for a role shift emanates from the child, I believe that the parent plays a larger part than he or she may wish to admit, particularly if the situation lasts a while. Looking beneath the surface, I invariably find in these cases that the parent who does not overtly encourage the role shift either covertly fosters it or at the very least tacitly accepts it.

Morris was correct when he claimed that Stella was eager to assume the responsibilities of "middle management." In fact, her willingness to play the quasi-wife role made it more difficult for Morris to recognize the problems it was creating for her. But, for his part, Morris welcomed Stella as his confidante, and he was not prepared to give this up until he found another woman to take the place of his ex-wife.

Not all custodial parents encourage their children to assume authority for managing the household. Dr. Weiss tells of one mother whose oldest son said, upon the separation of his parents, that he was not about to become the man of the family for her. To which she replied, "I just got rid of one. Why should I want another?"

# AVOIDING THE MINEFIELD: ROLE SHIFTS

**1.** Set reasonable limits for your child, and enforce them. Don't give in to the temptation to abandon your standards of acceptable behavior because you feel sorry for your child. Even if your child presses for more independence, she needs to have clear boundaries or she will become anxious. Make it clear to your child that the limit-setting does not work both ways; children should not ordinarily be setting limits on their parent's behavior. For example, don't allow your child to admonish you to be home by a certain time.

**2.** Assigning additional responsibilities to your child may be a necessary and reasonable response to the burden of single parenting, but your expectations should not exceed what is appropriate for your child's age. When in doubt, here is a good rule-of-thumb to follow: *Do not ask your child to assume responsibilities that, in the marriage, would have been assumed by your spouse.*

**3.** When assigning additional household chores, do so without delegating "managerial" authority to your child. You should continue to maintain authority for supervising the successful completion of chores.

**4.** Don't delegate to your child the task of providing basic meals. Children can assist with shopping or prepare an occasional meal. But they should not have primary responsibility for preparing most of their meals. Symbolically, the provision of food is experienced by children as one of the most basic acts of parental nurturing. It is too much to ask a child to give up such nurturing, even as an adolescent.

**5.** *Don't* use your child as a sounding board for your day's frustrations and worries. Find another adult to serve this purpose. *Do* be available to listen to your child's worries.

**6.** Don't ask your child for advice about decisions related to your work or your social life. Your child cannot become your confidant without sacrificing too much of his or her own childhood. When children become their parents' confidants, they are unfairly deprived of their childhood.

**7.** Encourage your child's friendships with other children. Healthy peer relationships help your child maintain her identity as a child and not a "junior parent." Also, if your child is very involved with friends, she is less likely to become overinvolved in your personal life.

**8.** Treat your child *as a child*. Your daughter is not "the lady of the house," your son is not "the man of the house," and they should not be told that they are.

**9.** If you are too distressed or depressed to follow the above guidelines, seek professional help. Your situation will only get worse if you expect your child to take care of you.

When the role shift does occur, it can be a heavy burden, particularly for younger children. Missing out on a (relatively) carefree childhood is just one of the unfortunate consequences. Parents' reliance on children for emotional comfort and companionship inevitably leads to mutual frustration. The reason is simple. Most children are not capable of meeting their parents' emotional needs on a regular basis. The parents, then, are disappointed, and the children feel inadequate and guilty. This leads to more strain and conflict between parent and child. And the children's self-esteem is diminished, because they experience themselves as incompetent to meet their parents' expectations. If these children generalize from their family-life experiences to the world in general, as adults they may have to contend with a deep-seated conviction that they are unable to meet the needs of the opposite sex. This attitude will create barriers to achieving and maintaining emotionally intimate and gratifying heterosexual relationships.

It might be objected that some mothers with custody rely on their daughters for emotional nurturance and some fathers with custody rely on their sons. This is true. Nevertheless, because the child is a psychological stand-in for a spouse, it is most often children of the opposite sex whom parents place in this position. Also, for reasons that will become clear as we discuss the next minefield, opposite-sex children are more troubled by the shift in roles.

Children in the custody of the opposite-sex parent have more behavior problems, more anxiety, and lower self-esteem than children in the custody of the same-sex parent. We can now begin to understand why this is so: It is simply asking too much of children to fill the shoes of an ex-spouse.

Even when these children do manage to meet some of their parents' emotional needs, it is often at the cost of stunting their own emotional growth. Dr. Weiss describes this process: "Many of these children have had to learn to suppress their need for a parent, to prevent their yearning for a parent's nurturance from reaching expression because they know the parent cannot respond." And when the child does communicate a wish for nurturance, it is in a disguised manner. "Neither the child nor the parent may then be able to identify quite what it is that the child really wants. Interchanges between child and parent become frustrating, and degenerate into quarrels whose origins are baffling to both child and parent." In other words, they are caught in a psychological minefield.

A parent who needs a child's closeness too much, and for too long, may have difficulty letting go and fostering an appropriate degree of independence in the child. The child may come to feel that it would be disloyal to become too attached to persons outside the family. If this conflict is not resolved, the child grows into an emotionally handicapped adult who is unable to love another without feeling anxious and guilty.

## SEX AND THE SINGLE PARENT . . . AND CHILD

In some families, the boundaries between child and parent become so blurred that another, even more explosive, minefield is entered—an upsurge of sexual tension.

Many families live with an undercurrent of sexual attraction and possessiveness between a child and the parent of the opposite sex. Normally these feelings are kept under control and out of conscious awareness, in part because of our culture's incest taboo, and in part because of the inhibiting presence of the other parent. For example, a father generally makes it clear to his son that there are limits to the boy's relationship with his mother; he may not sleep with his mother or relate to her as a husband. These limits help the boy grow up to be a man who is free to form a loving relationship with a woman.

When his father is absent from the home, a boy may have more difficulty giving up his wish to possess his mother exclusively. He may actively strive for a closer relationship with her. If his mother accommodates him, for example, by allowing him to share her bed, the result is a higher level of tension between them, fueled by sexual feelings. This is why relaxing child-parent boundaries creates more of a problem for children in the custody of the opposite-sex parent. Extreme closeness between a mother and her children, while never desirable, causes less anxiety for her daughter than it does for her son.

Another source of tension between a divorced mother and her son is the mother's social life. In addition to threatening the boy's fantasy of exclusively possessing his mother, her dating activity heightens his awareness of her as a sexual being. Although children in television sitcoms are depicted as being fully comfortable with their single parents' dating (certainly more comfortable than their parents), in reality this causes children more anxiety and grief than many parents realize. The behavior of Jimmy and Bill, described earlier, attests to this. And psychotherapists who treat divorced families will confirm that these children are by no means atypical.

The intensification of sexual feelings is not limited to custodial mothers and their sons. Similar problems exist between custodial fathers and their daughters, and for the same reasons. We saw evidence of this in our research.

A nine-year-old girl who lives alone with her father put her hands under her dress and pushed it out in front of her to simulate a protrusion from her belly. She then paraded seductively in front of her father and announced that she was pregnant. This behavior seemed to arise spontaneously from the girl, and not in response to any provocation from her father. If anything, as you might imagine, her father was quite uncomfortable with his daughter's behavior.

Some parents, though, do sexually stimulate their own children, sometimes without being aware of it, often without admitting it. A psychiatrist reported about one boy he treated whose mother exposed him to numerous sexual stimuli. The boy had developed nervous twitches which the doctor thought were related to the mother's sexual provocations. This mother believed in open nudity around the house and did not miss an opportunity to titillate her son with references to sex. For example, when she and her son were looking at a magazine advertisement that had a picture of an island, the mother wondered aloud whether there were nude beaches on the island. Her son's twitching became worse. When the psychiatrist tried to help the mother become aware of the connection between her comment and the twitching, she accused the doctor of being obsessed with sex and took her son out of treatment.

This brings us back to the unpleasant topic of incest—the most extreme and devastating loss of boundaries between parent and child. The entire question of incest between divorced parents and their children must be approached with caution. The past ten years have seen a tremendous increase in the number of allegations of sexual abuse made by parents involved in custody litigation. This is in keeping with a general trend in the mental-health field toward more recognition and acknowledgment of the prevalence and trauma of sexual abuse. But false allegations of sexual abuse have also been discovered to be an effective weapon in child-custody battles. The accusation alone is often sufficient to separate a parent from a child, pending the results of a lengthy investigation. Even if the accused is found innocent, the damage to the alleged perpetrator and the child can be irreparable.

When incest does begin in the aftermath of divorce, it is a product of pre-existing, but dormant, psychological tendencies that become triggered by the collapse of child-parent role boundaries. Although incest certainly exists in nondivorced families, there is no doubt that some parents who are able to control these impulses in the context of a marriage lose such control when the spouse is no longer in the home. These parents need to be especially conscientious about not allowing psychological role shifts to occur.

Unfortunately, to minimize the possibility of being accused of sexual abuse, some custodial fathers inhibit their expressions of affection to their daughters. They may become stiff and physically remote, which can be experienced by their children as a withdrawal of love. This may be another factor contributing to the emotional difficulties of some father-custody girls. Most fathers need not worry about being affectionate with their daughters; the majority of men are able to show their love to their children in an appropriate and healthy manner. When a father sexually abuses his daughter, it is an expression not of affection but of a deep-rooted personality problem.

## BECOMING A MAN

Common sense dictates that it is harder for a boy to develop a strong and comfortable sense of masculinity without a father around to teach him. Common sense, in this case, is confirmed by years of psychological research.

Conflict with gender identification is one of the most troubling mine-

# AVOIDING THE MINEFIELD: SEXUAL TENSION

**1.** Avoid excessive nudity. If you have previously taken a laissez-faire attitude toward being nude in front of your opposite-sex child, now would be a good time to re-evaluate the policy.

**2.** Do not allow your child to share your bed on a regular basis. This does not mean that young children should not come into their parent's bed on weekend mornings for some cuddling. But if your child sleeps with you regularly, he or she may become sexually stimulated.

**3.** Sharing their mother with other men, or their father with other women, is troubling to children. To avoid fueling jealousy, you would be wise to restrict your child's access to your casual dates. This will also protect your child from becoming too attached to someone who may not be around for very long.

**4.** Exercise discretion if a date spends the night. Particularly with adolescents, who struggle with their own sexual impulses, parents need to be sensitive to the messages that their actions convey about appropriate sexual behavior.

**5.** Do not treat your opposite-sex child as a substitute spouse. A little boy is not, and cannot be, "the man of the house." The same goes for little girls.

**6.** If your child shows signs of excessive sexual preoccupation, examine your own behavior to determine if you have unknowingly been seductive or overstimulating.

fields for boys living in the custody of their mothers. Often it is difficult to detect or to avoid.

Any discussion of gender identity is troublesome, because of our rapidly changing standards of what is properly masculine or feminine. Please bear in mind that the following discussion does not pertain to specific traits stereotypically associated with being male. Rather, the focus is on a sense of comfort and acceptance of one's sex, feeling worthwhile within one's role as a male, and the difficulties experienced by boys in achieving this when they live apart from their fathers.

In order to understand these difficulties better, let us look briefly at how gender identification normally develops. Most infants and toddlers are cared for primarily by their mothers. Spending all this time with her, they begin to identify with her and take on certain of her characteristics. Young girls *and* young boys enjoy imitating their mothers and even wearing their mothers' clothes.

Boys, though, at an early age come to understand that they are supposed to become more like their fathers than their mothers. To accomplish this, boys begin patterning themselves after their fathers. Girls continue to regard their mothers as the models for appropriate female behavior.

If his father is physically present, and they have a good relationship, a son will have the desire and the opportunity to observe and emulate him. By so doing, the boy will come to value himself as a male and feel confident in that role. His mother plays an important role in this process by encouraging, and expressing pride in, her son's masculine behavior. Although she contributes to her son's gender identity, it is primarily by identifying with his father that a boy achieves an inner feeling of being appropriately masculine. This inner feeling does not come easily when the identification with the father is strained, as it is with boys who are raised by their single mothers.

It is an unfortunate fact of divorced life that mother-custody children see progressively less of their fathers with the passage of time. This means that there is less opportunity for a boy to learn from and feel close to his father. Even when the father observes a court-awarded "liberal visitation" schedule, as we have seen, his contact with his son often feels unnatural and superficial and lacks the emotional richness that characterizes strong relationships. Michigan psychologist Dr. Neil Kalter describes the risk from the point of view of the son:

> A boy growing up in a [mother-custody] household faces the likelihood of a weakened or unrealistic tie to his father. Day-to-day modeling of masculinity, even when father and son are not necessarily the primary characters in some interaction, is diminished. Father becomes a peripheral player in the ebb and flow of daily experience, and thus may be experienced as an idealized, distant, and unrealistic figure. . . . Though many continue to love their father, are often concerned about him and his welfare, and long to be close to him, there is nonetheless a sense of distance and loss that permeates the child's experience of his father.

In his attempt to compensate for the loss and bridge the gap between himself and his father, a boy may unwittingly generate more conflict between himself and his mother. This is what happened with Bill, the boy who accused his mother of being preoccupied with men. Possessiveness and jealousy were not the only reasons he reacted so negatively to his mother's dating. Puzzled by Bill's behavior, Evelyn asked me if her son realized that her dating was a path to remarriage, an event "that would make life easier for all of us." What Evelyn did not know was that Bill realized this all too well—and it was the last thing he wanted.

To make up for having so little contact with his father, Bill held to a secret belief that his parents would someday reunite. This was his attempt to maintain some link with his father, even if only in fantasy. If his mother remarried, Bill would be forced to relinquish his fantasy, and face the painful reality that he would never again live with his father. This was something that Bill was not yet prepared to do.

Bill had another reason for shunning his mother's boyfriend. He felt that it would be an act of disloyalty to his father if he allowed himself to get close to another man. Bill's overriding need to identify with his father was evident in the note to his mother that he nailed to the front door. Recall that Bill signed the note, "Your *ex*-son," thereby unconsciously identifying with his absent father—the other "ex" in his mother's life.

We have seen the damage to a child's identification with the noncustodial parent when that parent is not available on a regular basis. And the converse is true: Research with mother-custody preschool boys has found that frequent contact with father is linked to stronger identification with the masculine role.

But what about the mother who does not want her son to identify with his father? Evelyn, for one, could not understand why Bill insisted on idealizing his father. From her point of view, Bill's father was far from ideal. He was a poor husband and a poor father, delinquent in his child support and uninvolved with his children—definitely not the sort of man she wanted her son to emulate. Another mother put it more bluntly: "He's a bum! Why would I want my son to turn out like him?"

This mother's negative opinion of her former spouse, if conveyed to her son, can do more harm to his gender identification and his self-esteem than can the lack of contact with his father. A father's absence deprives his son of *opportunities* to identify with him; a mother's critical attitude toward the father may undermine the boy's *desire* to identify with his father. For it is not just that his mother devalues his father. If she is like many mothers in this position, she may subtly—or not so subtly—encourage her son to adopt these negative attitudes himself. And this puts the child in a major psychological bind.

On the one hand, he wants to please his mother and learns that he can do so by joining her in devaluing his father. On the other hand, he needs to feel good about himself, and he cannot do so if he devalues his father. Why? Because a central part of a boy's psychological makeup, his sense of who he is, derives from his identification with his father. In the very act of renouncing his father, therefore, he is renouncing this central part of himself. *Rarely does a boy hold a predominantly negative opinion of his father without holding the same opinion of himself.* This helps to explain why so many boys raised by single mothers suffer from feelings of self-depreciation. When Evelyn understood this, she was able to have more sympathy for Bill's struggle to hold on to his father, which went a long way toward easing the strain of their relationship.

In fact, most mothers would never deliberately undermine their sons' self-esteem. They just don't seem to realize that *to encourage a son to turn against his father is to encourage him to turn against himself.*

This became clear to me years ago, when I was consulting with a family-court judge about one of the cases that was before him. Mrs. Pellegrino wanted the judge to stop all visits between her seven-year-old son, Tony, and his father. She claimed that Tony hid under his bed and refused to come out when his father arrived at the house for his scheduled weekend visit. She told the judge that she thought her ex-husband might be abusing Tony. Mr. Pellegrino admitted that Tony hid from him when it was time for the visits, but he could not understand why, since Tony always seemed to enjoy himself when they were together. He adamantly denied abusing his son and resented the accusation.

While I was meeting with Mrs. Pellegrino, she went to great lengths to convince me that she really regretted stopping the visits, because she knew it was important for Tony to have a close relationship with his father. Tony, who was playing in a corner of my office, looked up briefly. But then, in a poisonous tone, Mrs. Pellegrino proceeded to denigrate the boy's father, ending with the statement "I know Tony should love his father, but *I* have no use for that man." Hearing this, Tony tucked his head between his shoulders, turtlelike, as though he wished he could disappear.

Next week, I saw Tony alone in my office. He acted reserved and gave brief responses to my initial questions. When I asked him to tell me about his dad, though, he immediately launched into a recitation of his father's sins. His speech sounded canned, not at all the words of a seven-year-old, and it lacked the ring of truth. I asked Tony how he knew all this about his father, and he said that "lots of times" he heard his mother talking to her friends about his father. Just as she had done in my office the week before, without addressing her comments to Tony, Mrs. Pellegrino indirectly let him know how despicable his father was. Tony was being exposed to a subtle but insidious process of "brainwashing."

Psychological testing confirmed my impression that Tony really did love his daddy and thought of himself as similar to him. (In fact, there was a strong physical resemblance between the two.) But at the same time, the similarity threatened Tony. When he heard his mother say, "I have no use for that man," Tony took this to mean, "I cannot love you if you take after your father." Without realizing it, this mother was rejecting her son.

Feeling insecure about his mother's love, Tony thought he had no choice but to agree with her that his daddy was a bad man. Otherwise Mommy might get rid of him like she did Daddy. To preserve his mother's love, Tony rejected his father. And in so doing, Tony undermined his own budding sense of masculinity and his self-esteem.

In Tony's case, his mother made her feelings about his father clear and left Tony to draw the conclusion that he would not be loved if he too closely resembled his father. Many times, though, the mother's rejection of her son's connection to his father is more explicit. A mother may tell her son, in a contemptuous tone, "You're acting just like your father." Although this mother is venting upon her son the anger she feels toward her former husband, the child perceives it as a personal rejection.

The wound from such a rejection cuts deep. I have seen it in my consulting room. Just two days after writing the above, I listened as a man in his forties recalled the shame and confusion he had felt thirty-five years earlier when his mother had told him that he was, just like his father, worthless. He was still struggling to break free of this assessment.

Even worse for a boy is his mother's rejection not just of his father but of "men" in general. This attitude may lead her to discourage any signs of masculine striving in her son, such as the rough-and-tumble play that is generally more typical of boys than of girls. The anguish of the son whose mother disparages all men was captured in a poignant scene from the 1989 motion picture *Parenthood*.

Julie runs away with a boy, has a fight with him, and returns home, to cry to her mother. Helen, played by Diane Wiest, commiserates with her daughter. Helen herself has not had a successful relationship with a man. She hugs her daughter and agrees, "Men are scum." Just at that moment, she glances up and sees her teenage son, Gary. The look on Gary's face tells Helen that he has heard, and she realizes what her blanket criticism must mean to him. He feels like an outsider in his own home. Shortly thereafter, Gary telephones his father and asks for permission to move in with him.

Let me hasten to add a girl does not emerge unscathed by the absence of her father and her mother's disparagement of him. But the harm is of a different sort, and it shows up at a different age. With girls, the ill effects are usually not apparent until adolescence, when relationships with boys begin to take on special importance. At this age, and later, a girl who has not had a good relationship with her father may doubt her attractiveness to males and feel insecure about being able to keep a male interested in her (for a fuller discussion of this, see pages 44–45).

But before adolescence the average girl is better able than the average boy to cope with a disruption in her relationship with her father. A girl can disown her identification with her father and still retain her core identity as a female. A boy gives up more; when he disowns his identification with his father, he undermines his core identity as a male.

Without having his father present on a daily basis, a boy runs the risk of becoming too dependent on his mother, which further threatens his sense of masculinity. Many of the behavior problems we see with mother-custody boys are a reaction to the intensity of the mother-son relationship and to the boys' masculine self-doubts. By acting defiant and disobedient, a boy accomplishes two goals. First, he gains psychological distance from his mother. Second, by standing up to his mother, he "proves" that he is powerful and not submissive. Some boys resort to even more extreme measures to reassure themselves of their manliness. Research has shown that an exceptionally large proportion of juvenile-delinquent boys come from father-absent homes. Often their violent and delinquent acts are desperate attempts to prove they are "real men." We need to realize that what looks like a *problem* to us is frequently a child's attempt at a *solution*—in this case, a misguided effort to bolster self-esteem and masculine self-confidence.

Misbehavior may serve another hidden purpose, as I learned from one of the first patients I saw in my private practice, a seven-year-old boy named Harris. Harris lived with his mother and two older sisters following the recent departure of his father, and his sense of masculinity was reeling under all the feminine influence. He was brought for treatment because he had begun stealing money and urinating in the corner of his room. When his mother caught him in the act, he dared her to call his daddy: "He'll come over and spank me." For Harris, the pain and humiliation of a spanking seemed a small price to pay for his father's return.

Although defiant boys are a challenge for their parents, I worry more about another group of boys in mother-custody homes—those who resolve their masculine self-doubt by taking an opposite path. Instead of pulling away from their mothers, they draw closer. Instead of struggling to achieve masculine self-confidence, they identify too much with their mothers' femininity. Instead of posing as super-macho, they inhibit their assertiveness and passively let themselves be dominated by others. Often the mother and her son enjoy their closeness and see no need for change. These families are thus harder to help than families in which the boy actively resists his mother's influence.

People call these boys "mama's boys." Some become so frightened to leave the safe "womb" of their mother's home that they refuse to attend school. They usually have difficulty getting along with other boys and prefer to play with girls and younger children (see the case of Bruce on pages 43–44).

In extreme cases, a boy becomes so identified with his mother that he suffers from what psychologists call a "gender-identity disorder." This child does not just have difficulty feeling competent as a male; he does not even want to be a male. Oregon psychiatrist Dr. William Sack reported on a six-year-old boy from a divorced home who expressed the wish to be a girl. The boy was taken for treatment after he was seen wearing a dress. His father was upset by the boy's feminine gestures and his preoccupation with a Wonder Woman doll.

Some children with this disorder grow up to be transsexuals—people who want to be rid of their genitals and live as members of the other sex. I must emphasize, though, that gender-identity disorder and transsexualism are rare. Most boys are able to find other ways to deal with their gender-role conflicts.

Up to this point, we have been discussing how children identify with their parents. But the process of identification works both ways. Parents also identify with their children, and most parents identify more strongly with a child of the same sex. Generally, fathers feel more confident in their ability to contribute to their sons' development. Because they can draw on their own experiences in growing up, the territory seems more familiar. Most fathers, though, feel that they have less to offer their daughters. Most mothers feel the same about sons.

THE CUSTODY REVOLUTION

Recognizing this limitation, one mother encouraged her son to form close relationships with his male relatives. When he became interested in contact sports, she expressed concern about his safety but supported his involvement. Throughout the years, without implying any weakness on her part, she emphasized the differences between her son's "masculine" interests and her own. As a result, this boy was able to retain a solid sense of comfort with his male identity, while enjoying a close and caring relationship with his mother.

## BECOMING A WOMAN

Although single fathers with daughters and single mothers with sons are equally vulnerable to the minefields of role shift and sexual tension, when it comes to gender-identity problems the situation for girls raised by single fathers is not exactly parallel to that of boys raised by single mothers. As we have seen, most boys form an identification first with their mothers and then with their fathers and, because of this, are vulnerable to conflict if the tie to their fathers is weakened.

Girls, on the other hand, are less vulnerable to such conflict. Unless a girl has been raised by her father since infancy, her initial identification is with her mother, and she is able to retain this primary identification even when living apart from her mother. Although many girls take after their fathers in many respects, very few are so identified with their fathers that they worry about their "womanliness" in the same way that boys may worry about their "manliness."

Another reason why father-custody girls run less risk than mother-custody boys of a weak gender identity is that girls in our culture generally have more extensive contact with same-sex adults than do boys. Most elementary-school teachers are female, as are most babysitters and day-care attendants. Girls, then, can more readily find substitute role models.

If a father-custody girl faces hazards on her path to womanhood, these probably have more to do with her father's anxieties than her own. As mentioned earlier, most parents identify more strongly with a child of the same sex. Some custodial fathers doubt their ability to nurture their daughters adequately or to teach them the things most girls learn from their mothers.

A father's anxiety about not having as much to offer a daughter as he does a son is beautifully illustrated in the musical *Carousel*. The carnival

# AVOIDING THE MINEFIELD: GENDER-IDENTITY CONFLICT

**1.** Do what you can to maintain meaningful contact between your children and their other parent. With rare exceptions, such as in the case of a severely disturbed parent, it is desirable for boys and girls to have access to both of their parents.

**2.** When talking to your children, balance your criticisms of your former spouse with statements about his or her good points.

**3.** If your child does not have frequent access to the parent of the same sex, find others who can serve as models for identification. This can be a relative, scout leader, athletic coach, high-school student, or someone from the Big Brothers and Big Sisters organizations.

**4.** Make it clear to your children that the divorce is between their mother and father and that you do not expect them to choose *between* their parents but to continue loving both.

**5.** If your child reminds you of your former spouse, take extra care not to demean the child for this. Avoid references to the other parent when reprimanding your child. Statements such as "You're just like your father" or "You remind me of your mother" do too much damage. Remember, your child is not responsible for the misdeeds of your former partner.

**6.** If the divorce has left you bitter and distrustful of all members of the opposite sex, this attitude will probably spill over into your relationship with your opposite-sex child. Psychotherapy may be indicated to help heal your emotional wounds.

**7.** If your child shows signs of emotional or behavioral troubles, seek consultation with a mental-health professional. Low self-esteem, overly defiant behavior, excessive anxiety, immaturity, physical symptoms (such as frequent headaches or stomach-aches) for which no physical cause can be found, and school problems all can signal the presence of psychological problems. Pay special attention to your child's peer relationships, since these are highly sensitive to emotional disturbances. If your child has no friends of the same sex, this can be an early warning sign of gender-identity conflict. When in doubt, it is best to have your child examined by a competent professional.

barker Billy Bigelow is exhilarated at the prospect of becoming a father. In a stirring soliloquy about "my boy Bill," he sings of the many things he will teach his son. But then, with a start, he realizes that he might have a daughter instead. His hope turns to worry about whether he can fulfill her needs.

Those who eschew sexual stereotypes may balk at this type of thinking, but I believe it reflects a profound psychological reality for many men. We should take it seriously, because fathers' anxieties about raising daughters alone may have a lot to do with the higher levels of anxiety exhibited by girls raised in father-custody homes. Nowhere is the custodial father's anxiety more evident than in his attempt to discuss sexual matters with his daughter.

A man who raised two daughters wrote, "I had to swallow hard when it came to facing situations that mothers more naturally deal with. To help me discuss menstruation, I ordered a kit that consisted of hygiene samples and a pamphlet. When I mustered the courage to ask if there were any questions, I was relieved when my daughter embarrassedly said 'no.' "

Most parents feel awkward and embarrassed talking with their children about sex, some more than others. In a two-parent home, the parent who has the harder time with this can pass the responsibility to the other parent. But in a divorced family, this may not be possible. Single fathers who feel uneasy about discussing such sensitive matters with their daughters can benefit from the following advice, applicable to all parents.

Psychologists Seymour and Rhoda Lee Fisher suggest that parents establish a clear and comfortable limit on how open they wish to be in communications about sex. For example, one father told his daughter that his own sexual behavior was private and that he would answer her questions about sex with information but not with personal history. The Fishers believe such limits help parents handle these situations with less embarrassment, less anxiety, and more composure. If a father cannot bring himself to discuss sex with his daughter, he should arrange for someone else to do the job. This can be a female friend of the father, a teacher, a school counselor, or a relative.

. . .

The point of this chapter is not to suggest that boys need their fathers more than they need their mothers, or that girls need their mothers more than they need their fathers. It takes two parents to create a child and, in the best of circumstances, the two parents together will raise their child. But divorces do occur, and when they do parents and their children travel down a rough road. We have seen that the journey is even rougher for children in the custody of the opposite-sex parent. Still, it is not always possible, or desirable, for the same-sex parent to keep custody. Other factors may outweigh the consideration given to the child's sex. Many single mothers are raising their sons, and more and more single fathers are raising their daughters. In detailing the psychological minefields facing such families, my purpose is not to alarm or depress parents. Rather, my intent is to alert parents to the potential trouble spots so that they may anticipate the hazards and thereby avoid or minimize them.

Children *can* cope successfully with their parents' divorce. But to ensure that successful coping is the rule and not the exception, we need a major overhaul, a revolution, in the way custody is handled.

# PART 4

## THE CUSTODY REVOLUTION

**G**iven the problems with conventional custody, parents and courts should entertain viable alternatives rather than pigeonhole every family into the identical custody arrangement. For some families, father custody is the best solution. Avoiding this option in deference to tradition makes little sense. When it comes to managing custody, we have seen that fathers are as capable as mothers and that, on the average, children in father-custody homes suffer no more than those in mother-custody homes.

But many do suffer, especially when they lose a parent as a result of divorce. Four days per month (or less), whether with Daddy or Mommy, are not enough to meet most children's need for a parent. We know it is not enough for the noncustodial parent. And it also places an unfair burden on the custodial parent, a burden that was not part of the original agreement, when the couple first decided to have children.

There has got to be a better way to handle custody.

There is. But it requires more than minor changes in the current system. It requires an entirely new approach to custody, a revolution in both the substance of custody decisions and the process of making these decisions—in *what* we decide, and in *how*, *when*, and *why* we decide it. We turn now to the blueprint for this revolution.

# 9

## JOINT CUSTODY: PANACEA OR PANDEMONIUM?

Throughout history, people have assumed that after divorce only one parent should have custody of the children. The rise in the divorce rate has forced an entire generation to take notice of the problems with "sole custody"—overburdened custodial parents, angry noncustodial parents alienated from their offspring, and children sadly longing for a deeper, more authentic relationship with the absent parent. The solution most often proposed, and gaining increasing national attention, is *joint custody*. To date, thirty-four states recognize joint custody as a valid option, and sixteen of these give some degree of preference to joint custody over sole custody. It would seem that joint custody is sweeping the nation, yet the proportion of children living with their mothers after divorce has not changed: It is still nine out of ten. How is this possible? The answer is to be found by unpacking the phrase "joint custody."

### WHAT IS JOINT CUSTODY?

Ask ten people to define joint custody and you'll likely get ten different answers. Of all the terms used to describe custody, joint custody (sometimes called "shared custody") is the most confusing. One source of confusion lies in the distinction between joint *legal* custody and joint *physical* custody. Although fathers have a better chance of winning joint legal custody, mothers are still the preferred recipients of physical custody. This is why the proportion of children living with their mothers remains nine out of ten, despite the popularity of joint custody.

Joint legal custody means that parents share authority over major decisions affecting their children, in areas such as medical treatment, education, and religious training. Millie and Jack had joint legal custody. When their son Myron was having trouble in school, his pediatrician recommended a consultation with a psychologist. Before the appointment could be made, Millie and Jack had to agree on whether or not to follow the doctor's advice, and then on which psychologist to consult. When the psychologist recommended that Myron be enrolled in a special school for gifted children with learning disabilities, Millie and Jack had to agree on that decision as well.

In some cases, parents divide authority so that each retains the right to make decisions in some sphere. One mother was willing to share decisions regarding medical care and education, but she insisted on retaining the sole right to select her children's place of worship. Joint legal custody also means that both parents are legally responsible for the actions of their minor children. This arrangement may or may not include joint physical custody.

Joint physical custody (also called "joint residential custody") implies that the children's time in each parent's household is more evenly balanced than occurs in sole custody, and approximates a fifty-fifty split. Usually parents who share physical custody also share legal custody. However, joint-physical-custody plans can work in many different ways. The phrase "joint physical custody" is not reserved for any particular distribution of time or frequency of shifts between households. Thus joint physical custody can mean a fifty-fifty split, a sixty-forty split, a seventy-thirty split, or any variation in between. The children can shift residences as often as twice each week or as seldom as once a year. For example, I sometimes recommend that a child stay with one parent every Monday and Tuesday, the other parent every Wednesday and Thursday, and alternate weekends. This arrangement has the child shifting homes twice weekly, but gives him or her five consecutive days with each parent two times each month. At the other extreme, I know of a family where the children alternate primary residences every six months. When they are based at one home, they still spend a significant amount of time with the nonresidential parent.

In rare cases, it is not the children who move back and forth between households, but the *parents* who rotate in and out of a main home where the children remain. To make matters more confusing, a divorce decree can designate an arrangement as joint physical custody when, in reality, the specified living arrangements differ in no substantial way from sole custody.

Because of the many ways in which the term "joint custody" is used, it is crucial that parents determine exactly what their lawyers and ex-spouses mean when using the label. *Joint custody does not necessarily mean that both parents will be equally involved in their child's upbringing.* If you assume that it does, without reading the fine print, you may be in for a rude awakening.

To avoid confusion, the subsequent discussion relies on the term "joint custody" to designate a situation in which parents share decision-making authority *and* the child's time with each parent is divided more evenly than in the typical sole-custody arrangement, with no greater disparity than a two-thirds–one-third split. The phrase "joint legal custody" indicates a situation in which parents share decision-making authority but the child has a primary residence with one parent.

We shall see, though, that the best joint-custody arrangements reflect more a state of mind than the parents' legal rights or the distribution of time between them. These arrangements are distinguished by a high degree of cooperation and flexibility in which the parents acknowledge the reality of their *mutual* importance to their children. Divorce does not change this fact. At a time when they most need it, their children are reassured of the continuing love of both parents, neither of whom is primary or has authority over the other.

## HOW PARENTS FEEL ABOUT JOINT CUSTODY

Let us begin by describing parents' perspectives on joint custody. It is generally agreed that joint custody has both advantages and disadvantages for mothers and fathers. Parents need to weigh the pros and cons carefully before making their decision. Because joint custody is most frequently posited as an alternative to mother custody rather than to father custody, for the sake of simplicity the following discussion focuses on the benefits and drawbacks of joint custody as compared with sole mother custody. We can assume that identical considerations would apply to a comparison of joint custody with sole father custody.

## Joint Custody: The Man's View

"I have always been very close to my son. The divorce wasn't my idea, but if it had to happen I wanted to make sure that we wouldn't lose our closeness," one man says. He was describing why he chose joint physical custody. "I didn't want to become like so many divorced fathers you see—the ones who schedule two days of entertainment to make up for seeing their kids only twice a month. I was not going to be a 'Disneyland daddy.' I'm proud to say that I'm not."

Joint custody allows men to avoid the superficial relationship that typifies "visits" between children and noncustodial fathers. It is just not possible to pack two weeks' worth of living into two days. Poignant conversations which draw father and child closer together occur spontaneously. These moments cannot be scheduled like items on a conference agenda.

Men who have experienced both noncustodial and joint-custodial status agree that sharing physical custody is a very different experience from seeing their children every other weekend. The extra time makes possible a qualitative change in the parent-child relationship. Men with joint custody, like those with sole custody, enjoy a genuine intimacy with their children that can only come from living together. Their connection is based not on movies and pizza but on the rhythm of daily routines, habits, negotiations, and accommodations that give one a sense of really "knowing" the other. A father with custody can tell you the difference between his son's mood on a school morning and a Saturday morning. He can tell you when his son is worried, ashamed, scared, sad, proud, excited. He learns when to give more direction and when to back off. And his son observes his father happy, playful, and supportive, but also tired, frustrated, impatient, and angry. The negative interactions are certainly not pleasant for either father or child, but they are a necessary part of any real relationship.

Brock Henry, the professor of Government quoted in chapter 4, is one father who tried conventional custody, thought it was disastrous, and now has joint custody. He clearly prefers his current arrangement: "For me, the experience constantly confirms my sense that 'quality time' can't exist separately from the flux of daily life, housekeeping, chores, etc. The little pleasures of friendship and affection with a child pop up at any time— they don't follow a schedule. Sarah talks about her delights, her worries, her dreams when they cross her mind—when she's in the middle of playing, or doing chores, or having breakfast—and if a father isn't there, involved in this, he doesn't really know what's going on." Brock also likes having a stronger voice in shaping his daughter's sense of right and wrong: "I believe that all kinds of attitudes about fairness, values, moral behavior get passed on in the flux of life, or in talking about what the kids did at school today, or answering theoretical questions. This kind of exchange and communication just can't be duplicated on weekend visits."

Joint-custody fathers avoid the sense of loss and devaluation that afflicts many noncustodial fathers. They prize their right to have an important say in their children's education, medical care, and religious training. They enjoy shepherding their children through life's inevitable disappointments. They enjoy witnessing their children's attainments. As a group, fathers with joint physical custody are proud of their involvement with their children. You will not easily find a man with joint custody who does not agree that it is well worth the extra effort.

But make no mistake about it: Sharing physical custody does require a lot more effort than being a noncustodial parent. One shares not only the rights and rewards but the responsibilities and chores. A man with joint custody must devote significantly more time and energy to his children. He must take off from work or arrange for child care when his children are ill on school days. He must forgo opportunities for career advancement that require moving to a new locale: This may result in lower financial status. He must arrange his social schedule to accommodate his time with the children. And he must communicate much more frequently with his ex-wife.

Not all divorced fathers want to take on these obligations, and not all fathers are capable of doing so. As is true of fathers with sole custody, many joint-custody fathers "grow into" the role. They learn as they go along how to recognize and how best to respond to their children's emotional and physical needs. Men with custody learn, as all parents do, that the rewards of child-rearing are often overshadowed by the daily hassles and conflicts. For example, men who have frequent access to their children should be prepared to be the target of more of their children's anger than if they were seeing them only twice each month.

Nevertheless, as I indicated earlier, most fathers who elect joint custody do not regret the decision. For most, the advantages far outweigh the drawbacks. From the beginning, Brock understood the trade-offs that go with joint custody: "I knew that this arrangement was going to be harder than some other options. It would mean limiting myself to staying in the Los Angeles area as long as Sarah was growing up. I'd have to give up career opportunities elsewhere. I knew that being a single-parent caretaker, even for part of the week, was a demanding job that would put stress on professional pursuits and social life. But I felt the rewards of continued close contact with my daughter would more than make up for these difficulties."

And how does Brock feel now about his decision? "Although it's been harder in some ways," he says, "and I have had to give up some social and work life, it's been very rewarding to have the sole responsibility for taking care of Sarah when she's with me. I think a lot of fathers let things slide, let their wives pick up the slack in the day-to-day job of child-rearing. I have had these tendencies myself, and I'm grateful in some ways that this living arrangement has rescued me from that. I know that Sarah gets a lot of full-time attention from me." At the same time, Brock appreciates the advantages of shared custody over sole custody. "I'm glad that Sarah still has her mom to relate to, to take care of her half the time, so that I do have some freedom. I'm glad that Allie is there for me to bounce ideas off of, to talk about problems, that there's someone else who loves Sarah as much as I do, who will enjoy hearing about her triumphs and delights."

Most fathers with joint custody would agree with one father who, after thoughtfully weighing the pros and cons said, "Sure, it's a lot of work. Even more than I expected it to be. I've had to adjust my priorities, give up some things. But it's worth it. Ricky and I get along better now than we did before the divorce. When we first separated, I didn't spend as much time with Ricky. His mother used to complain about how many things she had to do. At the time, I though she was just trying to make me feel guilty about the divorce. But now I know what it's like for her. It's hard on all of us, but I think it would be much worse if my ex-wife did it alone. I know that wouldn't be fair to her either. But don't get me wrong. I'm not doing this for her sake. It's as simple as this: I like being a father."

## Joint Custody: The Woman's View

By tradition, child-rearing has been considered a woman's province. An important goal of the women's movement was to introduce more flexibility in such matters, so that women were free to assume additional roles beyond wife, mother, and homemaker. The reciprocal prescription was for men to expand their roles by becoming more involved in nurturing their children and helping with housework. Most fathers, however, have not yet gotten the message. Surveys show that, even when a father intellectually endorses the idea of an enlarged role in child care, his liberated words are not often matched by deeds. Nonetheless, married women welcome their husbands' support, when it is forthcoming. Raising children is rewarding but demanding, time-consuming, and emotionally draining; most mothers appreciate having help with the job. This is no less true after divorce. In fact, when a mother is on her own, the father's assistance is even more crucial.

## Sole Mother Custody Revisited

Let us briefly review the job description of a typical single mother. (For a more complete portrait, see pages 72–73.) She is solely responsible for the physical and emotional care of her children when they are at home, and she is responsible for selecting adequate substitute care when they are not with her. She coordinates their schedules and makes sure they get where they need to be when they need to be there. She is ultimately responsible for the running of the household, including laundry, cleaning, grocery shopping, and bill-paying. All of this is in addition to her breadwinning outside the home, and possible pursuit of a social life.

The mother with sole custody bears a heavy work load as well as the burden of making all child-rearing decisions on her own. She is called upon to perform the job of two parents at a time when her own emotional capacity is likely to be diminished and her children's emotional demands and behavior problems are likely to be multiplied. Also, she is apt to be the recipient of more of her children's anger while they treat their infrequently seen father as a favorite uncle.

## What Women Like about Joint Custody

With this portrait of mother custody, it is easy to appreciate the appeal of joint custody. Joint legal custody promises mothers relief from the burden of bearing sole responsibility for major decisions affecting their children. "The doctor thinks that Patricia should have tubes put in her ears sometime in the next few months. Should we have it done now, get a second opinion, or wait another six months and hope her ear infections clear up?" "Do we start Abie in kindergarten this fall or postpone it a year to give him an advantage?" "Is football too dangerous for Eli?" "Should we send Zira to a girls' prep school?" These are the types of decisions that married

couples struggle with throughout their children's lives. Parents with joint legal custody continue to make such decisions together.

Joint physical custody promises the mother assistance with the day-to-day task of raising her children. Her former husband shares the chauffeuring, disciplining, soothing, shopping, and supervising that go with raising children. She gets a chance to step off the treadmill of full-time parenting. When the children return to her home, she has more energy for them and is better able to provide the high-quality attention that most nurtures the developing child.

Joint custody promises the mother, in short, the help with raising her children that she has a right to expect from the person jointly responsible for the children's existence. During marriage, a man is equally responsible for the health, education, and welfare of his offspring. Advocates of joint custody believe that divorce should not relieve fathers of these duties.

For the most part, joint custody delivers on its promises to women. Men who share either legal or physical custody *are* more involved with their children. They are more apt to honor their child-support obligations and less likely to move away from their children. One such father, an accountant in Dallas, turned down four job offers in other cities in order to live close enough for his daughter to spend weeknights with him.

Women with joint physical custody enjoy greater, often equal, sharing of child-rearing tasks. They are much less overwhelmed by the amount of time and energy their children require. "I'm a better mother because I'm not a mother all the time," says one woman, summing up the benefits of joint custody. "And I never feel alone the way many single mothers do. I know my kids have a father; and I can call him in a crisis."

Joint custody has other benefits. Following divorce, many women decide to return to college in order to pursue further study and upgrade their job qualifications. Joint physical custody gives them the extra time needed to prepare for exams and write term papers. A woman who is on fairly good terms with her former husband can even work out flexible custody agreements so that the children spend more time with their father during Mom's exam time and more time with her when college is not in session. (The very concept of flexible custody is usually ignored in discussions of custody; in the next chapter, I describe in some detail how parents can use this concept to fashion tailor-made living arrangements for their family.) Joint physical custody is particularly convenient for women who often go out of town on business. Also, it lets single mothers enjoy a more spontaneous social life without having to worry about the effects on their children of bringing a date home or staying out late at night.

## What Women Don't Like about Joint Custody

The benefits of joint custody do not come without a price, and it is a price that not every woman is willing to pay. So it is essential that parents understand the downside of joint custody before making this choice. A woman needs to know what she is getting into, and a man needs to know what he is asking of his ex-wife. Just what does a woman give up when she agrees to joint custody?

First and foremost, she gives up *power*. Power to select unilaterally her child's school, pediatrician, religious affiliation. Power to move wherever and whenever she wishes. Power to make all the decisions concerning her children that arise on a daily basis: what her children eat, whom they play with, how often they bathe, when they go to sleep. Even the mother who retains legal custody and shares only physical custody gives up authority over her children during the times they are not in her possession.

"In joint custody, what happens is you really lose a lot of control concerning your children," says Regina, a New Jersey homemaker who agreed to joint custody in order to avoid a court battle. "That's hard to take. Can you imagine having someone else control your children? Here I'm having to live with, not only their father—and I happen to disagree with almost everything he does—but whomever he's cohabitating with at the time having a voice in my children's lives. And there's nothing I can do. There's nothing. Can I call him and say, 'I don't like what you're doing and I want you to stop it?' Do you think he really cares whether I like it or not? And, in all fairness, I'm not sure I want any input from him in regards to my household. It's my home, and I have the right to run it the way I choose."

Guided by the desire to retain power, a woman may request sole custody but have the full intention of allowing extensive contact between her children and her ex-husband. She merely wants to ensure that the father's involvement is at *her* discretion and that her word is law in this realm.

The first problem with this approach is that legal restrictions often lead to psychological restrictions. The systematic stripping of his legal authority as a parent threatens and sometimes diminishes the father's sense of parental identity. In the eyes of the law, he is treated more like a favored uncle than a father, and there is the danger that his feelings will change subtly to fit the new role. If this occurs, his children run the risk of losing a father. (And their mother may lose her child-support payments. It is no accident that men with joint custody honor their child-support obligations to a much greater extent than those who are restricted to two visits per month. I must emphasize that not having more access to your child does not justify reneging on your financial obligations. But if a father feels closed out of his child's life, it is perhaps understandable that he may feel some reluctance to sign the child-support checks. And the converse is true: When a man handles his child-support obligations irresponsibly, his ex-wife may be less eager to facilitate his visits with the children.)

The second problem with the mother keeping complete control is that it engenders a lot of anger in most fathers. We cannot expect a man to react with pleasure when he is publicly reduced to the status of a second-class citizen in his own family. The anger that accompanies this loss of power often fans the flames of conflict between parents. If the children are exposed to this conflict, then it is their loss as well.

Sharing child-rearing authority is more difficult for some women than others. A woman who does not work outside the home will want to protect her prerogatives as a full-time mother. The desire to "hold on to what you've got" will be especially acute for this woman if she neither wants nor is prepared for the divorce. As one woman put it, "If he wants to walk out on me, well, there's nothing I can do about it. But if he thinks he's taking the kids with him, he doesn't have a prayer in heaven. I'm going to need the kids now more than ever. What would I do without them? My husband and my children have been my entire life. Now the kids are all I've got."

Indeed, the issue is not just one of power and control, but of identity. Whereas some women welcome joint custody as an opportunity to expand their roles in life, this woman believes it will shrink the one role that is central to her—that of being a mother. Having lost her status as wife, she depends on her children for her sense of who she is and of her place in the world. Raising the children nourishes her self-esteem and provides the central focus around which she organizes her daily life.

A full-time mother whose children are not with her full-time must find alternative sources of fulfillment and meaning in life. Most women in her position would find it difficult to appreciate the advantages of joint custody. If, for the sake of the children, she and her husband were to elect joint custody, they would need to pay careful attention to the issue of timing.

Take, for example, a woman who does not want to be divorced and is not used to working outside the home. At the time of the initial separation, she will want, as much as possible, to keep her life intact and minimize any further feelings of loss. This means maintaining her usual level of involvement with the children. Once she begins a new job, though—the vast majority of divorced women must seek employment to support themselves and their children—and once she starts dating, she may then see the appeal of joint custody. At that time, the advantages of the father's assistance may outweigh the loss of power that accompanies joint custody. With this type of family, in which there has been the traditional division of labor between husband/breadwinner and wife/homemaker, it may work out better for both parents if they ease into a joint-custody arrangement by gradually increasing the father's time with his children rather than attempt an abrupt shift to equal father involvement at the outset of the breakup. This can make the transition easier for the mother, which in turn will benefit the entire family. Joint custody has a much better chance for success when both parents' legitimate needs are taken into consideration. (The next chapter takes up in greater detail the importance of flexibility when timing the custody decision.)

Some women regard the restriction on their geographical mobility as a major drawback of joint custody. It is true that with joint physical custody both parents must remain in fairly close proximity to each other if the arrangement is to benefit the children. School-age children must remain in the same school, and it is better not to separate preschoolers from either parent for long periods of time. Therefore, it is more convenient if the parents live close enough to each other to enable the easy transfer of the children between their homes. Some joint-custody parents live within bicycling distance of each other. Many divorced parents, however, prefer to live in separate communities, so that they do not frequently meet each other at the grocery store, dry cleaner, etc. The key consideration is that each parent live close enough to get the child to school on a regular basis. This makes sharing custody most feasible.

Even when a woman accepts, in principle, the desirability of joint physical custody, she may have several reasons for wanting to keep her options open regarding a future move. She may wish to return to her hometown, or attend school in another state, or take a better job in another city, or marry a man who lives out of town.

She should realize, though, that the supposed freedom to move that comes with sole custody may be more illusory than real. Some divorce decrees specify that, if a mother with sole custody moves far away, custody reverts to the father. Even when this is not in the decree, the father is always free to sue for a modification of custody if the mother is planning a move that will effectively cut off his access to the children. In most jurisdictions, this is considered a valid reason for petitioning the court.

Aside from the problem of legal constraints, a woman must consider the potential emotional impact of a move on her children. We have already reviewed substantial evidence suggesting that most children would be handicapped by such a move. First, it would mean having to adjust to a new school, new neighborhood, and new peer group: Children whose security has already been undermined by divorce do not need further upheaval in their lives. Second, the move would restrict their contact with their fathers.

We have discussed the children's greater access to their fathers as an important benefit of joint custody. But not every divorced woman *wants* this. Reasons vary.

A woman who feels abandoned by her ex-husband may want to punish him. Denying him access to his children, perhaps by moving far away, is her way of retaliating for the suffering he has caused her. Naturally we would hope that this woman would recognize the damage she is doing to her children by using them as pawns to express her anger. The children will certainly become her victims if she sacrifices their interests in order to strike a blow to their father.

Some mothers genuinely believe that their children would be better off not seeing their fathers. They may fear for their children's safety, for example, if the father is likely to abuse or kidnap the children. But these are the exceptions. All too often, a divorced woman's own hurt and anger cloud her assessment of her ex-husband's importance to the children. If she confuses her ex-husband's worth to his children with his worth to her, she may become convinced that her children would be better off without him.

Even a woman who favors extensive contact between her children and their father may change her attitude when she remarries. She may fear that the children's closeness with their father will make it more difficult for their stepfather to establish a good relationship with them. (A father with joint custody who remarries may have similar fears about his children's ability to develop a close relationship with their stepmother.)

This was the case with a family who consulted me recently. The parents had been sharing custody successfully for two years when the mother remarried. She said that a counselor had advised her to restrict her

son's contact with his father in order to allow the youth to "bond properly" with his stepfather. I have no way of knowing if this advice was in
fact given to the mother. It is a view that is widely held, but mistaken. I
told the parents that cutting back on the boy's time with his father could
very well have the opposite effect. If their son perceived the stepfather's
entry into the family as displacing his own father, the boy would probably
resent his stepfather. It would then be more difficult to establish the loving
relationship for which the mother and stepfather had both hoped. Many
children in this circumstance avoid connecting with their stepfathers out
of a sense of loyalty to their fathers.

There does not have to be a conflict between a child's tie to his father
and his tie to his stepfather. The stepfather-child relationship is determined by many factors, such as the personality of the stepfather, the
child's age, and the stepfather's patience in establishing his authority in the
household. If anything, a strong bond between a father and his son, rather
than interfering, will provide the foundation for a close stepfather-child
relationship (unless the father actively discourages this). Children who feel
rejected by their fathers may have a hard time overcoming their expectations of disappointment and trusting other men.

Another reason why some women oppose frequent contact between
their ex-husbands and children is that they miss their children and feel
they don't get to see them enough themselves. A Colorado study found
that "A sizable proportion of mothers with joint legal (15%) and joint
residential (38%) custody complained that their ex-spouse had the children too much of the time." Contrast this with the finding, reported in the
same study, that 50 percent of mothers with sole custody complained
about the father's not visiting enough.

Let us consider this from your child's vantage point. Which is preferable? Having a parent who does not show enough interest in her or having
two parents who complain that they don't get to spend enough time with
her? Knowing that low self-esteem is a key psychological problem for
children after divorce, which is more likely to damage a child's ego? Which
is more likely to bolster a child's feelings of self-worth, to help her feel
wanted, valued, and loved?

Naturally it is best if both parents are satisfied with the living arrangements. But if there is to be dissatisfaction, far better for the mother to
complain that her ex-spouse wants the children too much than to bemoan
his absence from their lives. Although the mother will not like feeling
deprived of time with her child, the paramount consideration in reaching

a custody decision should be the needs of the children, not the parents' wishes. Nevertheless, a mother contemplating joint custody should be aware that one of the predictable drawbacks is that she will miss her children when they are not with her. This is the price that, for years, divorced fathers have paid. With joint custody, the cost is shared.

## The Tie That Binds

For some women, the fear of joint custody is not that the father will have too much contact with his *children* but that he will have too much contact with *her*—that a husband who opposed the divorce might view joint custody as an opportunity to perpetuate the tie to his ex-wife, with the secret hope of achieving a reconciliation.

Many psychologists express the same concern. They look upon parents' request for joint custody with suspicion. In professional vernacular, such a wish indicates that the couple is not completely "emotionally divorced." I could not disagree more.

Rather than assume that a couple who choose to share custody are attempting to avoid the full emotional reality of the divorce, it is more plausible to assume that they are acknowledging and accepting the reality that together they have brought a child into the world, that they are jointly responsible for this child, and that the divorce does not wipe out these facts. Although some parents do indeed cling to ex-spouses and exploit contact with the children as a means to this end, in my clinical experience these parents are in the very small minority. And there is not a shred of evidence from any scientific research to suggest otherwise. Even when this concern is justified, joint-custody agreements can be formulated in such a manner that contact between ex-spouses is limited and circumscribed. In these situations, there can be a neutral site for the transfer of the children from one household to the other, perhaps a relative's home or the school.

Furthermore, we should question the commonly accepted notion that there is something necessarily wrong with a lingering emotional attachment between divorced spouses. Two people fall in love, marry, conceive and raise a child together. Why should we assume that the failure of their marriage will erase entirely the benevolent feelings that existed between the two? The ability to recognize positive feelings in spite of compelling negative ones should be regarded not as abnormal, but as a sign of emotional maturity. A divorced couple who continue to have some positive regard for each other are no less "emotionally divorced" than the couple who claim the total absence of good feelings toward each other. In fact, the opposite is probably true.

## IS JOINT CUSTODY HARMFUL TO CHILDREN?

The most important objections to joint custody concern its impact not on parents, but on children. Despite all the research documenting the psychological damage of separating parents and children, critics claim that joint custody is not the solution. Why not? Why don't more parents, judges, and mental-health professionals endorse joint custody as the life style best suited to the needs of children?

### Only a Pawn in Their Game

To begin with, critics believe that, even if joint custody were a nice idea, it is just not feasible. How can we expect two people who couldn't make a marriage work to cooperate and communicate well enough to share custody? Regina, the New Jersey homemaker who objected to the loss of control that accompanies joint custody, expresses this view: "When I went into joint custody, I really acted from my heart and not from reality. And in my heart what was going to happen was that, whatever problems Marc and I had, those were ours and they were not the children's and that would be it. And that was really immature on my part. Because what would make you think that, if you couldn't get along when you were married, you would get along when you weren't married, especially when it comes to something as important as your children?" A prominent Dallas attorney agrees: "Joint custody requires a great deal of cooperation, communication and understanding after the divorce. [Parents] can't have their feelings easily hurt. I'm pretty negative when it's brought up. I sincerely believe that if they can't communicate enough to stay married, they can't make joint custody work. However, I do believe it is best for the child."

Critics argue not only that parents are incapable of sharing custody but that joint custody increases hostility between them. Even worse, it increases the likelihood that they will enlist the children as pawns in their battle.

Supporters of joint custody claim that it does just the opposite. They believe that joint custody's equal division of parental rights and responsibilities results in less resentment between parents and less motivation to involve children in parental struggles. Certainly the father with joint physical custody does not share the anger and humiliation of the father who has been officially relegated to a peripheral role in his child's life.

Which side is correct? Does joint custody lead to more conflict between divorced parents or less?

The most recent and extensive study to address this question was conducted at the Center for Policy Research in Denver, Colorado. Drs. Jessica Pearson and Nancy Thoennes analyzed data from interviews with over nine hundred parents who had different types of custody (sole maternal, sole paternal, joint physical, and joint legal custody). The parents were tracked for several years following their divorce so that the researchers could learn about the long-term impact of different custody arrangements. The results showed that conflict between divorced parents "did not appear to worsen as a result of the increased demand for interparental cooperation and communication in joint legal or joint residential custody arrangements. To the contrary, *parents with sole maternal custody reported the greatest deterioration in the relationships over time."* (Italics added.) Parents with joint physical custody reported the most cooperation, and this was true even three years after the divorce.

Not only did joint-custody parents get along better, they expressed more satisfaction with their ex-spouses's performance as parents. I thought about this research finding when Brock Henry explained why his shared-custody arrangement has worked so well.

"Allie and I were always friends, respected each other, could talk to one another, and shared certain values, even though our personality clashes and emotional styles made it impossible for us to maintain the intimacy of a marriage. Also, we both love Sarah a great deal, and have a deep commitment to her well-being. The respect and shared values are important—I know that Allie is a good mother to Sarah, and she knows that I'm a good father."

And what about their conflicts? "We each have our foibles and weaknesses, which Sarah is all too eager to relate to the other parent, but we've been able to keep them in perspective. If there's anything that one of us has said or done regarding Sarah that has really disturbed the other, we've been able to talk about it—the deciding factor is always what's good for Sarah, what reduces her stress and anxiety, and since we both are quite close to her, there's never really been an important conflict of attitudes."

When parents are able to maintain their focus on what is best for their child, it is easier for them to cooperate. "Allie and I are both involved in Sarah's school," says Brock. "We both go to the meetings, talk with the teachers, and compare notes. In fact, we compare notes constantly on Sarah's achievements, pleasures, anxieties, struggles, and the process generally reinforces the sense of collaboration and trust. Though the marriage was always emotionally stormy and dissatisfying, we've been able to work out a good, solid, collaborative relationship as parents and extended family members."

Rather than being used as pawns to express their parents' hostility, children in joint custody, like Sarah, witness less tension and more cooperation between their parents than do children in traditional sole-custody arrangements. Of course, this does not mean that having joint custody guarantees a cordial relationship between ex-spouses, or that sharing custody necessarily reduces the strain between parents. Parents who agree to share custody are a select group who, like Brock and Allie, were probably more cooperative in the first place. But their ability to maintain a collaborative relationship for the sake of their children should put to rest the notion that such cooperation between divorced parents is impossible. And it does prove, according to the best scientific evidence currently available, that joint custody *is* feasible. But is it good for the children?

## If It's Tuesday This Must Be . . . Mom's House?

Many prominent judges and lawyers believe that joint physical custody confuses children and undermines their sense of security and stability. Parents echo these concerns. "I don't want my child moving back and forth like a yo-yo," said one mother. "How can he live in two different homes with different rules, different life styles, different expectations?" In essence, critics argue that joint physical custody deprives children of the consistent environment they need, leaves them chronically insecure about where they belong, and makes it impossible for them to maintain a secure relationship with either parent.

Those who favor joint physical custody agree that consistency and stability are important for children. They believe, however, that sole custody creates inconsistency, because it disrupts the relationship between child and noncustodial parent. It is not consistency of the physical environment that is paramount but consistency of relationships. As one mother said, after five years of experience sharing custody of her three children, "To me, joint custody is a continuation of shared parenting."

An advantage of joint physical custody is that it maximizes contact between the child and both parents. This enables the child to avoid the superficial "visiting" relationship that often accompanies sole custody. As we have seen, children who maintain meaningful involvement with both parents have a distinct advantage in coping with divorce. And as for the concern about children being confused by the different rules and expectations of two parents, proponents of joint custody ask, "If children can adjust to the differences between home and school, why can't they adjust to the differences between Mom's house and Dad's house?"

Again psychological research can help us determine which arguments have more merit. Does joint custody hinder or promote security? The truth lies somewhere between these two positions.

Although joint custody does not inevitably promote confusion in all children, some children do have a difficult time adjusting to the shifts in households. In one of the first studies of joint custody, Dr. Susan Steinman found that three out of four children she interviewed had no trouble switching homes. "Their clarity about their schedules and the location of their homes was impressive, particularly since some children switched as frequently as several times a week and had numerous places and people to go to (including school, day care, friends' homes, lessons)."

However, the rest of the children, one out of four, expressed problems with the shifts. Nine-year-old Josh was one of these. Josh alternated months between his mother's home and his father's. This schedule left him confused and worried about losing things. His schoolwork was not up to par and, although he was quite talented, he did not think much of himself. "The big problem with joint custody is that you have to remember where the spoons are," Josh said. His worry about the spoons was just one example of Josh's anxiety about keeping track of things.

Josh's problems are precisely what opponents of joint physical custody fear will be in store for many children who are required to shift between two households. But is this fear justified?

Could Josh's anxiety be a reaction to the divorce itself rather than the result of his particular living arrangements? Perhaps he would experience the same confusion living under the sole custody of his mother and seeing his father every other weekend. Even if Josh's confusion is a consequence of his living arrangements, this does not mean that his family should abandon the idea of joint custody. Alternating months between homes may not be good for Josh, but perhaps another joint-custody schedule would alleviate his confusion. For example, would Josh have an easier time keeping track of things if he shifted between homes more frequently, so that he would not be away from each parent for an entire month?

Dr. Steinman's research, valuable as an early portrait of joint-custody families, unfortunately was not designed to answer such questions. Yet we must have these answers before condemning joint custody as harmful to children. Even if we assume that all the children in this study who were insecure about their living arrangements would prefer the traditional mother-custody arrangement to *any* joint-custody schedule, this would not support a blanket rejection of joint custody. We must remember: For every Josh, there were three other children who adjusted well to their joint-custody arrangements.

But would those children have adjusted better with traditional sole custody? Not according to the latest research. Four independent studies— in Arizona, Pennsylvania, California, and Colorado—asked divorced parents to review a list of psychological problems and check the ones that applied to their own children. When the checklists were tabulated, each study reached the same conclusion. Children in joint custody (legal and physical) had no more emotional or behavioral problems than those in sole custody, but they did not have fewer problems either. According to these studies, the type of custody (joint versus sole) plays a smaller role in determining a child's chances of becoming anxious, depressed, and aggressive than do the five coping factors discussed in chapters 3 and 6—factors such as the quality of the parents' relationships with the child and with each other, the child's regular access to each parent, the parents' own psychological status, the number of changes in the child's life, etc.

The bottom line in the debate over joint custody is that it does not have the negative impact predicted by critics, but it does not automatically result in superior adjustment. The implications of this finding are enormous.

No longer can we cite "the best interests of the child" as a reason for preferring sole custody over joint custody. Parents can now elect joint custody with confidence that this choice will not make life more difficult for their children than the traditional mother-custody arrangement. But we should not harbor the illusion that joint custody is a panacea that will inoculate children against psychological symptoms. Joint custody does not release parents from the obligation to create a positive environment for their children after divorce.

. . .

If our discussion ended here, we might conclude that the ledger is evenly balanced between sole custody and joint custody as far as children's welfare is concerned: Joint custody presents no significant hazards to children, and it offers no special benefits either. This in fact has been the conclusion of many psychologists. For example, an Arizona study comparing children in joint legal custody with those in sole mother custody reports: "The current data do not provide strong support for advocating joint custody *since no difference in psychological symptomatology occurred across custody arrangements.* (Italics added.) In accordance with such reasoning, many psychologists are now expressing reservations about joint custody. As a result, initial public enthusiasm for joint custody may be waning. The joint-custody movement, once considered a promising alternative to the pitfalls of sole custody, is in danger of being grounded shortly after takeoff.

I am troubled by this development, because I believe it stems from an inadequate interpretation of current research. The lukewarm attitude toward joint custody fails to take into account many of the relevant findings of available studies, as well as the considerable limitations of this research. A closer examination reveals a more favorable portrait of joint custody.

## IS JOINT CUSTODY BETTER FOR CHILDREN?

To begin with, "no difference in psychological symptomatology" does not mean "no difference." It means only that joint-custody parents did not differ from sole-custody parents in the number and types of troubling behavior they checked off as typical of their children. Many aspects of the divorce experience are not measured by these behavioral checklists. Also, the absence of differences in psychological symptoms does not imply the complete absence of any emotional differences. Indeed, the very next sentence from the Arizona report reveals, "The only difference in adjustment that occurred favored the children in joint custody." What was this difference? *Self-esteem was higher for children in joint custody.* Although future studies need to corroborate this finding, it makes sense that joint-custody children would feel better about themselves. They know that Daddy is still actively involved in their lives, even though he does not live with Mommy anymore. They do not have to suffer the self-doubt that plagues many children growing up in mother-custody homes, who explain their fathers' relative lack of involvement by blaming themselves. "I must not be a good enough child" is what many children think when their fathers drop out of their lives.

Higher self-esteem was not the only advantage enjoyed by children growing up with joint custody. These youngsters also had more positive attitudes about the impact of the divorce on their lives. Joint-custody boys in particular had fewer negative experiences to report about the divorce and its aftermath than did mother-custody boys. The only other report that compared the *attitudes* of joint-custody children with those in sole custody found the identical result: Joint-custody children were more satisfied with their living arrangements.

That children would be more content with joint custody than sole custody should not be surprising. Parents who share custody generally get along better, and so their children are raised in a more peaceful atmosphere. Equally important, the living arrangements of these children allow them to feel the ongoing presence of both parents in their lives.

As Brock explains, "For Sarah the biggest benefit, above all, has been that she hasn't lost either parent—she still has her daddy, still has her mommy, both very available to her, both very involved with her life." Brock knows that joint custody is no panacea. "She didn't like the separation," he says. "I don't think any child does. And she has had the usual longings for her parents to get back together. Still, though she lost that ideal family unit, she hasn't suffered the trauma of losing one of her parents in the bargain. And she still sees that her mother and father both care about her, and sees them talking to each other and making decisions to take care of her needs."

Brock believes that joint custody has enabled his daughter to develop a close relationship with both her parents. "Since Sarah spends a good deal of time alone with each of her parents, she has a comfortable intimacy with each of us, and a sense of our differences that she values, that doesn't appear in a competitive context. This is an experience that a child doesn't always get, even in the nuclear family. There are some things she will talk about with me but not with her mom, and other things she'll share with her mom."

All four studies on joint custody observed that children in joint custody saw their fathers more often than did children in mother custody, even in cases of joint legal custody where the mother was designated the primary residential parent. We should not overlook the paramount significance of this observation. Children in both mother-custody and father-custody homes are more satisfied when they have more access to the noncustodial parent. And when we take time to listen, these children tell us loudly and clearly that the worst thing about the divorce is that they don't get to see their other parent enough. Of course, you should not choose joint custody (or any form of custody) merely because your child wants it. After all, children do not always want what is best for them. But in this case we should listen closely to what they tell us. Consider the following.

The Colorado study identified four things parents can do to help their children avoid psychological problems:

**1.** Cooperate with each other.
**2.** Avoid physical violence in the home.
**3.** Maintain children's regular access to each parent.
**4.** Minimize the number of changes in the children's lives (such as moving and changing schools).

The more parents provided these advantages, the better adjusted were their children. This same study also found that parents with joint custody were more likely than parents with sole custody to provide these advantages to their children. Joint-custody children experienced more cooperation between their parents, less violence, more contact with both parents, and more geographical stability. (In 81 percent of joint-physical-custody families and 72 percent of joint-legal-custody families, neither parent had moved during the three-year period after the divorce, compared with only 60 percent of sole-custody families.)

Let me recap. Who had fewer problems? Children with more of the four advantages listed above. Which children had more of these advantages? Joint-custody children.

The logical conclusion is that children in joint custody had fewer problems than those in sole custody. For technical reasons that are not at all clear, though, the results of statistical analyses did not allow the researchers to reach this conclusion. Instead, they reported a finding of "no difference" between children's adjustment in joint custody and sole custody. Nevertheless, regardless of statistical quirks, it should not escape parents' notice that the conditions that most help children cope with divorce are more likely to accompany joint custody than sole custody.

## Split Custody: A Variant of Joint Custody

Some divorced couples share their parenting responsibilities not by dividing their children's time between two homes, but by having each parent provide the primary residence for at least one child. This arrangement, known as "split custody," is usually frowned upon by judges and parents, who feel that siblings should never be separated. The rationale seems to be that children lose more in this situation: They lose regular contact not only with one parent, but with their brother or sister as well.

But for some children, the benefits of split custody outweigh the drawbacks. Therefore, we should not be so quick to dismiss this alternative. Unfortunately, to my knowledge, no systematic research exists to guide parents who are entertaining this option.

Split custody is sometimes considered when parents live far away from each other, making regular travel between the two homes unfeasible. I was once consulted by a family in which the father lived in New York and the mother lived in Los Angeles. Both parents were firmly established in their careers and unwilling to move. A year earlier, they had decided to allow their eleven-year-old son to live with his father and their five-year-old daughter to live with her mother. The parents thought the plan was working out as well as could be expected, but they wanted a professional and objective opinion about their children's emotional status. After getting much criticism from relatives and friends, these parents wanted to be sure they weren't making a big mistake. Of course, no parent can be certain of the wisdom of any custody decision. As near as I could tell, though, both children were doing very well with the arrangement, and there did not seem to be any reason to recommend a change. The children were fond of each other, but they had little in common and had never related very closely to each other.

Generally, the greater the age difference between siblings, the more likely a split-custody arrangement might be to serve their needs. But many other factors need to be taken into account. Some siblings who are far apart in ages are very closely bonded. Other siblings, who are very close in age, have such an intense rivalry that they make each other miserable. In some families, each parent has a much better relationship with one child than with the other. This can reach the extreme where a parent shows excessive partiality to one child while rejecting another. Although such families may benefit from psychological treatment, when the favored child-parent alliance is unyielding, the unfavored child may be better off living apart from the rejecting parent.

The factors that affect the probable outcome of split custody are complex, and it is easy for parents to fool themselves into thinking that a split-custody arrangement is best for the children when it may really be a poor compromise between unyielding parents. Thus I recommend that parents who are considering split custody first obtain consultation from a mental-health professional with expertise in child development and custody matters.

## MORE QUESTIONS—AND A PROPOSAL

Many questions remain unanswered. We know that children in joint-custody families have more self-esteem, more positive attitudes about their parents' divorce, and no more behavior problems than children in sole custody. But how does joint custody affect children's psychological development in areas not tapped by behavioral checklists, such as the quality of their relationships with parents and peers? How does joint custody shape a child's image of marriage and divorce? Does joint custody have any effect on children's feelings of being abandoned after divorce? What characteristics of children can help us predict who will do best in which type of joint-custody arrangement? How can parents share custody of children of different ages who have different needs? For instance, the average ten-year-old can tolerate longer separations from each parent than her three-year-old sibling. What is the best way to handle custody when parents live in different cities? Should children spend part of their lives with each parent (e.g., three years with mother, three years with father), or is the discontinuity in school and peer relations not worth the increased contact with the second parent?

We can hope that future research efforts will shed light on these issues, but we cannot wait for such studies before making custody decisions. Each week in the United States, the custody of over twenty thousand children is decided by their parents and by courts. We must take a stand: Should the current system favoring sole custody be continued, should a preference be established for joint custody, or should there be no preference at all?

Throughout this book, I have tried to keep my recommendations closely tied to scientific research. But in this area, that is not possible.

Joint-custody research is at such an early stage that any policy suggestions necessarily must go beyond research findings. True, we know that sole-custody arrangements have many problems that have been extensively documented. We also know that joint custody dramatically reduces the risk of a child's losing contact with a parent after divorce. However, current research leaves open the question of whether the average child will be happier and better adjusted with joint custody or with sole custody. With this caveat, I contend that most families would profit if a cultural and legal presumption favoring joint custody replaced the current presumption favoring sole mother custody.

A presumption of joint custody would institutionalize the expectation that both parents will continue to maintain responsibility for the children they have chosen to bring into the world. Cultural expectations such as this exert enormous influence on our attitudes and behavior. A generation ago, expectant fathers paced the hospital waiting room while their children were being born. All it took was a change in social norms to bring fathers into the delivery room; what was once virtually unheard of is now routine.

As we have seen, the cultural presumption in favor of sole mother custody is so powerful that 90 percent of divorced families abide by it. Women who don't, face social condemnation and guilt. Most divorcing couples assume that the father will have to forgo his closeness to his children and that this is a natural and normal consequence of divorce, not an artifact of social convention.

Sole custody is considered necessary, in part, because we have been led to believe that divorced parents are not able or willing to share responsibility for their children. Yet consider the following: If on the day before their separation a couple must decide whether to send their son to camp, and they don't agree on this, what do they do? They work it out—somehow. They do not go to court and ask a judge to decide. That doesn't occur to them. No one does that. And because there is no social sanction for that course of action, they do not retreat to it. But the moment they become legally separated, there is a temporary custody order, and the parent granted custody (usually the mother) unilaterally makes the decision. It does not occur to her to involve the father; there is little social sanction for *that* course of action.

A presumption of joint custody would change our view of what is "normal" after divorce. Cultural sanctions would then favor parents who continue their role as *coparents* after divorce.

A presumption of joint custody does not mean that all couples will share custody. Some parents do not want custody; others are psychologically unfit for it. Some couples are unable to communicate, cooperate, and compromise enough to make the mutual decisions required by joint legal custody. Other couples live too far apart, or have work schedules and commitments that do not enable them to share physical custody. Under a presumption of joint custody, these families would be regarded as departures from the norm. People who now censure the divorced mother who "gives up her children" would instead criticize the mother who deprives her children of a meaningful relationship with their father (and vice versa). Instead of operating in a climate that views them with suspicion, joint-custody families will occupy the moral high ground. Such support is indispensable if joint custody is to have the best chance of succeeding.

Will a presumption of joint custody lock all divorced families into the same type of rigid "one-size-fits-all" life style that now occurs with the mother-custody presumption? Not at all. Joint custody means that parents continue to raise their children together but in separate households. The manner in which parents share child-rearing responsibilities is as varied in joint-custody families as it is in intact homes. Indeed, an important advantage of joint custody is that it allows for more variation than sole custody. Not every joint-custody family has the same living arrangements or shares authority along the same lines. One agreement may require all major decisions to be mutual, another might divide the spheres of authority so that, for instance, the mother chooses schools, the father chooses religious affiliation, and both choose doctors.

Many proponents of joint custody draw the line at advocating this arrangement for parents in great conflict. They believe that parents entrenched in a custody dispute cannot make joint custody work and that their children will be better off in sole custody. Only one study has addressed this question. Although the study found "no clear evidence that children are better adjusted in either custody type," the considerable limitations of this research preclude our drawing any definitive conclusions from it.

A presumption of joint custody does hold the possibility of removing the issue of custody from parental warfare. Parents will be less eager to sue for custody if they know that the court will probably declare neither parent the "winner" and instead expect the parents to cooperate enough to share custody. This will spare families the trauma of custody litigation, which, as we will see in the following chapter, is virtually guaranteed to result in the deterioration of the psychological health and well-being of children and their parents. With a highly structured time-sharing agreement that reduces the need for frequent contact and negotiation between parents, even parents with little trust in each other can achieve a minimal level of cooperation.

When an attenuation of conflict does not occur, joint custody may still prove its worth by enabling children to maintain a relationship with each parent. The study of couples entrenched in custody disputes found that fewer than 1 percent of parents who were assigned joint custody dropped out of their children's lives; by contrast, 18 percent of parents in sole-custody dispositions, almost one out of five, ceased contact with their children altogether. When children miss out on so much because their parents do not provide a secure and harmonious environment, it seems prudent at least to spare these children the loss of a parent as well.

At a time in life when your children's trust in the permanence of love and commitment is undermined, they need all the reassurance possible that the loss of love between their parents does not extend to them. Keeping both parents involved is the single most important thing you can do to provide this reassurance.

Sharing custody is not easy. It is difficult to get started, and it is difficult to maintain. "It was not easy to work out the arrangement the way we did," Brock said. "Though we had a basic understanding, we were both feeling loss and anger at the breakup of our marriage, and these feelings would often impinge on our discussions about specific issues. We had some real face-offs. Fortunately, once we signed the separation agreement, most of the tension evaporated, and we settled into a routine."

While describing her experiences with joint custody, Regina choked back tears as she recalled some difficult times: "We went through periods at night when Jerry would cry, 'Why did there have to be a divorce? I wish it wasn't this way.' Those were really hard to handle, because I felt that, regardless of what I feel for my ex-husband, that may not be what my children feel, and so I shouldn't try to make them feel the way I did. And that wasn't always easy. Because the most natural reaction was to simply attack him verbally. It was really difficult to see my children so emotionally upset, and yet I had to be impartial. That's really hard. It's almost impossible at times to be impartial. What I would try to tell them was, 'You should love your father. It's okay to love your father. You don't have to choose. You don't have to like me more than him.' And that was really hard to say about someone I didn't like."

# THE BEST AND WORST OF JOINT CUSTODY

Although we have a lot to learn about predicting the outcome of joint custody, experts agree that certain conditions accompany successful joint custody arrangements.

## Joint Custody Works Best When . . .

• each parent believes the other parent is important to the children;
• each parent believes the other parent is a good enough parent;
• the parents live close to each other;
• the children prefer joint custody;
• both parents favor joint custody;
• the responsible parent makes child-support payments regularly;
• parents cooperate well with each other;
• parents are flexible;
• parents communicate well with each other;
• parents protect children from interparental conflict.

## Joint Custody Is Most Apt to Fail When . . .

• one parent is unable to care for the children adequately;
• one parent is adamantly opposed to the arrangement;
• parents live far apart from each other;
• parents maintain high levels of hostility toward each other despite attempts at mediation;
• parents enlist the children as pawns in a war against each other.

Ultimately, the rationale for joint custody is a humane one. There is something just plain decent about divorced parents cooperating for the sake of their children and shielding the children from adult conflicts. I am convinced that many children would benefit if this were to become the ethos that guides parents during and after divorce. Though not for everyone, joint custody is the proper arrangement for the vast majority of divorced parents.

Regina might take comfort in this exchange from *Miss Manners' Guide to Rearing Perfect Children:*

> Dear Miss Manners:
> *Does joint custody mean I always have to be polite to someone I can't stand?*
> Gentle Reader:
> *Yes. But think of the benefits. You will set an unparalleled example of civilized behavior to your children and impress your admirers as one to be trusted even under adversity.*

# 10
## JUDGMENT
## DAY

The custody revolution will be fought on two fronts. First, we need to expand the divorced father's role in the life of his children. I have laid the groundwork for that battle in earlier chapters. Second, we need to make fundamental changes in the way custody decisions are handled. At least as important as *what* parents decide about custody is *how, when,* and *why* they make their decisions. It is time now to address this second front.

## HOW TO DECIDE CUSTODY

Custody decisions can be reached by one of three paths. Both parents may agree on the arrangement. One parent may unilaterally decide to leave the children with the other parent, forcing that parent to assume custody by default. Or there may be a threatened or actual court battle for custody. Each of these routes to custody produces a different outcome for the family.

Parents who agree on custody begin life after divorce with a distinct advantage, and so do their children. These parents are more likely to support each other in decisions concerning the children. The parent who keeps custody generally feels more confident and better prepared to cope with the role of the single parent. Research has shown, for example, that a man who keeps custody by mutual agreement with his former spouse is

more prepared to assume household and child-care responsibilities and adjusts more easily to the divorce. By contrast, a man who has custody thrust upon him when his wife decides to leave the children with him is less prepared for his new life situation. Moreover, he resents having to assume responsibilities that he neither wanted nor sought. Both the father and his children have a harder time coping under these circumstances.

Bob Zimmerman found himself in this situation. He came to see me after his son's preschool teacher expressed concern about the boy's out-of-control behavior. Nine months earlier, Bob's wife had moved out of the house, leaving Bob, in his mid-forties, to care for their two children. Since then, Bob had lost his job, and was unemployed when we began our work together.

During therapy, Bob complained bitterly about the problems that beset most fathers with custody. Chiefly, he could not find a day-care center that had extended hours, or a job that allowed him to take off early enough to pick up his children from day care. His elderly mother took care of the children during the day, but they were really too much for her to handle.

As Bob described his problems, he sounded more angry than depressed about his situation. I began to suspect that he was wallowing in his anger and not doing all that he could to help himself and his children, and so I asked him to tell me more about how it felt to be a single father. Bob told a story that made things a lot clearer to me.

Before marrying, Bob and his wife had agreed that they would not have children. He already had a daughter from a previous marriage, and he was sure he did not want any more children. After seven years of marriage, however, Bob's wife began pressing her desire for children, and Bob reluctantly agreed. Now the children were four and six years old, and Bob was left with full responsibility for their care. To make matters worse, Bob's wife refused to discuss her reasons for leaving and was only minimally involved with the children after the separation.

Now I could understand the source of Bob's anger. Finding a job and day care was difficult, but for Bob the real problem was coming to terms with the fact that, regardless of his wishes, he was now solely responsible for his two children. He was furious about this, and could not vent his anger at his wife, since she was not around. Bob didn't want his children to know how he felt; he knew it would be awful for them to feel unwanted by their father when they had already been abandoned by their mother. So he expressed his anger unconsciously by making the worst of a bad situation. By trying only halfheartedly to cope, he magnified the problems, as if to say, "See how bad this is? I didn't want to be a single parent, so why should I try to adjust? I refuse to accept this situation that you have thrust upon me."

Although the unconscious intent was to get back at his wife by failing to cope with the unwelcome situation in which she had left him, it was not his wife who was harmed by this strategy, but he and his children. This strategy of dealing with anger is more popularly known as "cutting off one's nose to spite one's face." Once Bob became aware that this was, in fact, what he was doing, he was able to acknowledge his fury at his wife openly and begin getting his life back on track. It is no coincidence that his son's behavior began to improve right around this time. Until we show that we can manage life's challenges, we cannot expect our children to do any better.

## Casualties of War: The Effects of Custody Litigation

Even worse than the situation in which one parent unilaterally decides to leave the children with the other is when both parents fight over custody in court. I cannot think of a worse way to decide custody. In fact, the most important advice I can offer parents reading this book—and I cannot stress this enough—is to *avoid custody litigation at all costs!*\*

No aspect of my work is more disheartening than to witness the psychological deterioration of children whose parents are steeped in a battle for custody. School performance drops, aggressive behavior becomes more frequent and drives away friends, sleep problems increase, and chronic tension and unhappiness become the norm. Ironically, embattled parents are often so preoccupied with trying to prove they are good parents that they fail to notice their children's suffering. And if they do notice, their first impulse is not to relieve it, as parents normally would want to do, but to check with their attorneys to see if they can use their children's troubles as ammunition in court: "See, Your Honor, how much the visits with his father hurt my son?" Not only do parents use their children's distress in this manner, but some parents go out of their way to create distress.

---

\*In very rare cases, a child's welfare is severely threatened by contact with one parent. In such a case, the other parent may have no reasonable alternative but to engage in a custody battle. Nevertheless, this should be done only with full awareness of the risks involved.

"I'll have to play rough; and if I play rough, you can bet they will, too."
This was the warning given to Ted Kramer by his attorney in the Academy Award–winning motion picture *Kramer vs. Kramer*. As I watched the
film's emotionally wrenching courtroom scenes, I comforted myself with
the notion that this was only fiction. A real-life custody battle could not
be that horrible. I was wrong. A real custody battle is a lot worse. My first
taste of how much worse came when a Dallas family-court judge asked me
to evaluate a family for the purpose of assisting her in reaching a custody
decision.

Mr. and Mrs. Harvey met in college and fell in love. He loved her
spontaneity and her action-oriented life style. She loved his tenderness;
she thought he would make a good husband and father. They were
married for nine years and had three children before they decided to
divorce. She accused him of being a poor provider: He was unemployed
for a short period of time, and when his father died he signed his inheri-
tance over to his mother even though his own family was in financial
difficulty. He was disappointed in her care of the house and children: He
claimed that he returned once from a business trip and found that the
house was crawling with roaches and the children had impetigo. Both
believed that their relationship suffered from poor communication and
mutual distrust.

They agreed on a joint-custody arrangement in which the children
alternated residences on a weekly basis. This worked well for about four
years. Then Mrs. Harvey met and fell in love with a divorced man, Mr.
Maxwell, and moved in with him. Mr. Harvey, meanwhile, married a
woman with two teenagers. Five months after Mr. Harvey's remarriage,
something happened that brought the cooperative sharing of custody to an
abrupt halt. According to Mr. Harvey, when it was time for the children
to be returned to their mother, his six-year-old daughter, Donna, got
scared and begged him not to make her go. When he asked "Why?" she
said that Mr. Maxwell came in her room at night and "put his thing in my
mouth." Mr. Harvey, enraged, reported this to the appropriate authorities.
The social worker assigned to the case could neither confirm nor disprove
the allegations, but recommended that the girl be evaluated by a clinical
psychologist. Mr. Harvey took Donna to one psychologist who tested her,
and another psychologist who interviewed her. Both psychologists agreed
that Donna was frightened to spend the night at her mother's home.
Donna told the second doctor that her mother's friend tried to put his

"thingamajig" in her mouth. The doctor asked what that was, and Donna said, "Oh, you know; it's his d-i-c-k."

Mr. Harvey went back to court to get sole custody and to ensure that his daughter need have no more contact with Mr. Maxwell. In custody cases, a preliminary hearing is usually held, at which time a judge issues temporary orders that remain in effect until the final trial. In this case, the judge decreed that the children should live with their father while the case was being prepared for trial. Because the judge had good reason to believe that all three children were suffering from emotional problems, he ordered the parents to take them to a psychiatrist for ongoing psychotherapy. The judge also appointed an attorney, known as a "guardian *ad litem*," to represent the children's interests in the case. Finally, the judge ordered the entire family to undergo complete psychological evaluations. This is where I came in.

I met first with the mother and father together, to avoid any appearance of bias that might result from my meeting with one parent before the other. I asked them to tell me why they wanted custody. Mr. Harvey spoke first. He said he could provide a stable and positive environment for his children. His house was in a good school district, and the children had already adjusted well to their new school. He added, "I love my children very much. Living in my home with my wife and stepchildren would give the kids a chance to have a normal life style." I noted that Mr. Harvey did not bring up the sexual-abuse allegation and said nothing critical of his former spouse.

Then it was Mrs. Harvey's turn. "I love the children very, very much. I'm aware that they have problems. Phil can't see; once his learning disabilities are solved, he will grow like crazy. Donna's problems are more profound. I think her father doesn't appreciate the extent of Donna's problems. Sam is the saddest child I know." Mrs. Harvey said she intended to put Phil in a special school for children with learning disabilities, and criticized his current school for not taking more notice of his handicap. Mr. Harvey explained that Phil was not blind; he had a mild visual impairment.

I learned, to my dismay, that the children had already seen *ten* mental-health professionals—counselors, social workers, psychiatrists, and psychologists. By the end of the trial, three more would be added to the list, including me. How, I wondered, after so many false starts, could we ever expect these children to place their trust in a psychotherapist? Based on their experiences, they probably thought either that their parents didn't have enough confidence in any of the therapists to continue the work begun, or that none of the therapists cared enough about them (the children) to continue the work.

After ten letdowns, what would you do when the eleventh person offers help? Would you pour out your heart and entrust your secrets to him? Or would you be suspicious and keep your distance? For the children's sake, I knew I would have to be very clear about what they could expect from their contacts with me; I did not want to become one more therapist who raised false hopes.

All told, the evaluation took six months to complete and more than fifty hours of my time, not counting the many hours I thought about the case when I was not "on duty" (at dinner parties, while driving, while falling asleep, etc.). Because I was comparing the relative advantages and disadvantages to the children of their mother's home versus their father's home, I had to do more than evaluate just the two parents and their three children. I assessed the emotional atmosphere in both homes. I evaluated Mr. Maxwell with special attention to the accusation of sexual abuse. I evaluated the stepmother and her children. And I spoke by telephone with other psychologists who had seen the children, three schoolteachers, the school counselor, Mr. Maxwell's former wife, and two former employers of Mr. Harvey's current wife. In individual sessions I conducted interviews and psychological testing, and in joint sessions with parents and children I assessed the quality of their relationships.

This is not the place for a complete account of this case, but I do want to mention some of the "highlights" of the evaluation in order to give parents an idea of what they can expect if they decide to launch a custody battle.

In one interview, the mother accused the father of coaching his daughter to make the sexual-abuse allegations. In another interview, she said that, if sexual abuse had occurred, it was probably her daughter's teenage stepbrother who was the perpetrator.

Less than two months after the evaluation began, Mrs. Harvey married the man who was accused of sexually molesting her daughter. She claimed that on their wedding night her car was stolen and the thieves stole her diary and urinated in the car. Although lacking any proof, she was convinced that the teenage stepbrother and his "trashy" friends were responsible. She had also been receiving obscene phone calls, which she attributed to the teenage stepsister. The stepbrother and stepsister, of course, denied any wrongdoing.

Because of the sexual-abuse allegation, I had to explore Mr. Maxwell's sexual history and sexual adjustment thoroughly. Embarrassing details of his sexual life were revealed (and subsequently brought up in court), such as past homosexual liaisons. When I inquired about any unusual sexual practices, his face turned red with anger. He thought that I had been fed information by the father, information that he assumed was obtained during a break-in at his condominium that had occurred two months earlier. Apparently he and Mrs. Harvey had returned home one night to find the door lock broken and things in disarray. Lying on the floor were ropes that were kept on a closet shelf—ropes that he and Mrs. Harvey used for bondage during sex. The identity of the trespasser was never discovered.

When I asked about unusual sex practices, a routine question in sexual-abuse investigations, he leapt to the conclusion that I already knew about the bondage practices and that it was Mr. Harvey who had broken into his condominium, discovered the ropes, and told me about them. I explained that, prior to this interview, I had known nothing about the ropes. But he was not convinced. Paranoid thoughts are typical when people are involved in a public battle to defend their fitness as parents and demonstrate the flaws of the enemy.

Mrs. Maxwell (the former Mrs. Harvey) accused the new Mrs. Harvey of being an alcoholic. To investigate this allegation, I called the woman's former employers. They reported a clean work history with no evidence of any drinking problem. Mr. Harvey countered with the accusation that his former wife was heavily involved in mysticism and called herself a witch. She denied the "witch" label, but did admit that she was a "reader"—one who read Tarot cards for spiritual guidance. In a subsequent interview, when I asked the mother what was the best thing she had done for her nine-year-old son, she said, "Opening his mind up to metaphysical concepts."

There were many more allegations, coming mainly from Mrs. Maxwell: The children's stepmother sent them to school in rags; the stepmother called the children "little bastards"; the stepbrother was a juvenile delinquent; the stepsister had become pregnant out of wedlock and had an abortion; the father had a volatile temper; the father had slept with Donna. The case was taking on all the dimensions of a soap opera. And the guardian *ad litem* grew increasingly concerned about the children's welfare.

Upon completing my evaluations, I submitted a fifteen-page report to

212

the judge. A week later, at ten o'clock one Friday night, I was at home when my doorbell rang. I opened the door and was served a subpoena by an officer of the court, ordering me to deliver all my records on the Harvey case to Mrs. Maxwell's attorney. Four days later, the case came to trial. On day four of the trial, I was called to the stand by the children's attorney. My direct testimony took about forty-five minutes; the cross-examination took fifteen hours!

My notes were reviewed by the mother's current psychotherapist. Apparently he had convinced the mother that he could assist her case if she paid him to testify in court. She did hire him for this purpose; he did appear in court; and I learned later that his testimony wound up doing more harm than good for the mother's cause.

In the end, after a two-week trial, the judge awarded custody of the three children to the father. For both parents and both stepparents, the humiliation at having their every vice paraded in a public hearing would not be easily forgotten. For the children, it would be a long time, if ever, before they would have the pleasure of witnessing a cordial interaction between their parents.

One year later, Mrs. Maxwell filed for bankruptcy. A few years later, when I was addressing a group of lawyers on child abuse, I noticed Mr. Harvey's attorney in the audience. During the lunch break, I sat with him and asked about the Harveys. I learned that both couples had filed for divorce within two years of the trial. Somehow I was not surprised. A custody battle is one of the most stressful experiences a person can go through. Very few remarriages can survive the ordeal. This is one reason why I tell my patients that in a custody battle no one "wins."

A "psychological meat grinder . . . vicious, inhumane, and in the long run, pointless." This is how one veteran of a custody battle, Persia Woolley, describes the experience. In *The Custody Handbook*, Woolley, who is convinced that her custody battle "irreparably warped" her family's relationships, beseeches parents to find another way to settle their differences. She learned the hard way that "a custody battle severely victimizes the children involved, creates lifelong hostilities and distrust between parents and children, as well as between the two adults, and squanders the mental, emotional, and financial resources of the family."

Statistics indicate that parents fight over custody in only about one in ten divorces. But this means that each year over a hundred thousand children are involved in a custody battle, an appalling number when one considers the psychological devastation. As Woolley observes, this "adds up to a lot of heartbreak and pain." We hear about some of these cases through the media. When the rich and famous do battle, the tabloids are on hand to bring us every piece of dirty linen. The humiliation at hearing their parents' divorce discussed on television is something these children will never forget.

The outlandish excesses of, say, a Pulitzer custody fight, with its allegations of drug abuse and atypical sexual practices, are not the unique province of the rich and famous. As I learned from the Harvey case, the poor and unknown sling the mud with the best of them. And with the costs of a custody battle running in the tens of thousands of dollars, many are left poor in the end. Money set aside for medical emergencies and college tuition is diverted into the pockets of attorneys, private investigators, psychologists, and expert witnesses.

Still not convinced that it is lunacy to engage in a custody battle? Think about this. When you go to court, you relinquish the power to decide what is best for your own children. You subject yourself and the welfare of your children to the whims of a total stranger—a judge scheduled by the luck of the draw to hear your case. If you don't like your judge, if you think he is biased, there is nothing you can do about it. In the courtroom, the judge has absolute authority. Will your judge be reasonable and patient, or will he be capricious and eager to get your case over with as soon as possible? Will the judge take a dislike to you or your attorney? Will the judge have a fight with his wife on the morning of your hearing? Could these things affect his handling of your case and his ultimate decision? And what does the judge know about children in general and your children in particular?

**If You Must Fight in Court, Use an "Impartial" Expert, But Beware of the Risks.** If you are unfortunate enough to find yourself in the position of litigating for custody, the least you should do is request that the judge receive assistance from a mental-health professional. Under the judge's orders, this person will take the time to get to know your family and make a recommendation regarding the best living arrangements for your children. This was my role in the Harvey case, conducting a type of examination called a "custody evaluation" or a "social study." The examiner is seen as an "impartial" expert because of his neutral status at the outset. Most professionals prefer to function in this capacity rather than as an advocate—or "hired gun"—for one parent. With access to both parents, we have much more information to rely on in making a recommendation. Often all that is accomplished when both parents hire their own experts is that the professionals get richer, the parents get poorer, and the conflicting testimonies of the two professionals cancel each other out. In the meantime, there is no objective assessment of the needs of the children.

For the psychologist (or social worker or psychiatrist), a custody evaluation can be a stimulating professional challenge and an opportunity to contribute meaningfully to the best interests of the children caught in the cross fire of their parents' war. But the rewards of the challenge are soon outweighed by the mental anguish, the threats, the schedule disruptions necessitated by being on call to give testimony, and the unpaid bills that are part and parcel of this work. As a result, many competent psychologists I know who are in private practice have ceased doing court-ordered custody evaluations. I have reason to believe that this is true across the country.

Parents and courts should take notice of this. It means that the odds of finding a gifted psychologist to conduct a custody evaluation are growing slimmer. If the psychologist is new to the work, he is handicapped by lack of experience. And if he has been doing these evaluations for years, you have another worry. Is the professional doing this because he enjoys custody evaluations and is good at them, or does he have no alternative because he has been unable to earn a good living treating patients in private practice? Such evaluations are very lucrative for professionals, and therefore very costly to the families paying for them: You should expect to pay a fee in the range of $2,000 to $8,000.

The cost of a custody evaluation can be multiplied if the examiner administers unnecessary tests. For example, I consulted on one case in which the examiner gave lengthy IQ tests to three adults and one child involved in the dispute. My sense was that the examiner included the IQ test as a standard part of all her examinations. She might argue that these tests provided valuable information about the participants' problem-solving abilities, which would shed light on the parents' capacities to make good child-care judgments. (This doesn't explain the child's IQ test.) But such information can be assessed much more directly and efficiently. The extra tests certainly earned more money for the psychologist, in what was an unnecessary expenditure of time and money for the litigants. Their intelligence was not in question, and had nothing to do with which custody arrangement would best serve this child's needs.

In the selection of an impartial evaluator, I believe it is preferable to find a psychologist who allocates at least a portion of his professional time to seeing children in psychotherapy. This psychologist is apt to have a deeper knowledge and understanding of child development and of the needs of children from divorced homes. Professionals who lack this experience often take the theories they learned in graduate school and apply them in a haphazard and incorrect manner. In the words of my brother, Alan, they suffer from being "only book smart." This was certainly true of the psychiatrist mentioned in chapter 1; you may recall that she recommended giving custody to a mother who practiced satanic sexually abusive rituals on her four-year-old son!

I would like to say that incompetent custody evaluations are rare, but experience has shown otherwise. I have had the opportunity to review evaluations conducted by professionals throughout the United States. In many cases, I have had access to the actual test data that served as the basis for their conclusions and recommendations. You would be horrified at what passes for an adequate evaluation. Obvious biases are disguised as pronouncements of established scientific fact. Psychological test data are misinterpreted to support the examiner's conclusions. Alternative explanations of the data are ignored.

A blatant example of this came to my attention when I was asked by a mother's attorney to review the report of a custody evaluation. A family counselor in Los Angeles had conducted the evaluation on orders from the judge. During an interview, the counselor asked the six-year-old girl a hypothetical question: "If you were going to take a rocket to the moon, and there was only room for one parent to go with you, who would you choose?" Without skipping a beat the girl said, "Daddy." On the basis of this response, the examiner leapt to the conclusion that the little girl had a stronger relationship with her father than with her mother!

I'm sure that most readers can think of other explanations that do not support this inference. Could she have chosen her father for the make-believe trip to compensate for seeing so little of him in the past several weeks? Could she associate her father more with scientific or mechanical matters and therefore think he would make a better copilot on her journey into space? Could she have answered "Daddy" because *he* brought her to the interview and was most on her mind at the time? Even granting the assumption that her response indicates a general preference for her father over her mother (although this is not a valid assumption), what is the basis for her preference? Is it because Daddy buys her lots of gifts? Because he lets her stay up later at night? Because he doesn't make her do her homework?

Examiners rarely conduct follow-up studies to assess the accuracy and outcome of their recommendations. So it is possible for an examiner to make poor recommendations consistently without ever learning what he is doing wrong.

A custody evaluation, properly conducted, is a complex undertaking that relies on expertise in many areas. A competent evaluator must have a thorough understanding of the psychological development of children. He must be proficient at assessing the personalities of children *and* adults, and he must have a sophisticated understanding of these personalities. He must strive to get at the truth about each parent's role in the life of the children and about each parent's capacity to deal with the responsibilities of custody. This is one of the toughest aspects of the custody evaluation, because invariably each spouse minimizes his own liabilities and exaggerates those of the other parent. The examiner's conclusions need to be well reasoned and supported by objective data. And he must be trained to recognize his own biases and keep these from influencing his handling of the case. Psychological evaluations are no place for Ouija-board tactics.

The inadequacy of many custody evaluations is one more reason why you should avoid custody litigation: It is not easy for a judge to get a reliable feel for a child's best interests in the time allotted for a typical divorce hearing.

In some cases, an evaluation is so shoddy and inferior that I am willing to lend my services to the attorneys in the case, as I did in the Los Angeles case mentioned above. I identify the flaws of the evaluation and help the attorneys prepare a cross-examination of the professional to ensure that those flaws are exposed in court. It is my hope that, if more psychologists were subjected to such cross-examinations, they would exercise more diligence and care in their evaluations, reports, and recommendations to the court. When the happiness and well-being of families hang in the balance, there is simply no excuse for professionals to take such a cavalier approach to their work.

Fortunately, in many cases the situation is more positive. In Dallas, for example, the courts employ family-court counselors to conduct custody evaluations. These counselors have earned a well-deserved reputation for conducting thorough and accurate social studies. The existence of competent evaluators notwithstanding, a parent should be aware that having an "impartial" evaluator assigned to his or her case, although better than relying on a hired gun, still offers no guarantee that the court will accurately assess the best interests of the child.

## Desperation

Each year, in thousands of cases, the frustrations and hostilities surrounding a custody battle erupt into violence, the abduction of a child, or both. This occurred in Dallas one night in October 1988. Dallas police were dispatched to the home of Shirley Mercer. When they arrived on the scene, they found Mrs. Mercer's estranged husband, Harold Mercer, holding his two-year-old daughter, Robin, on his lap—and a knife at her mother's throat.

The twenty-eight-year-old man had recently lost custody of his two children, and now he threatened to harm both his wife and his daughter if he was not allowed to see his children. After a two-hour standoff and then a violent struggle, police arrested Mercer. One month later, family-court Judge Carolyn Wright heard testimony that Mercer had threatened to abduct his children and flee. Judge Wright denied him visitation rights until he had received a psychological evaluation and treatment.

The next day, also in Dallas, Jody Clay Slater attempted to abduct his twenty-one-month-old daughter outside her day-care center. When his former wife and her boyfriend, a sheriff's deputy, tried to stop him, Slater shot and killed the couple. Slater apparently was disturbed about losing visitation rights; he was on probation for kidnapping his daughter earlier that year. Acquaintances of his said he had threatened to kill "everyone involved" in taking away custody, including the judge.

Though murder and kidnapping are rare in custody cases, threats and assaults are not. "Frequently, people have lawyers who report to the judges that they have a client coming down here to kill the other side," said Judge Wright. Clearly, the child who witnesses such violence and threats carries a much heavier burden than the child whose parents find less drastic and less traumatic means to settle their differences.

Kidnapping (or "child-snatching," as it is sometimes called) is never a viable solution to a custody dispute; it is misguided at best, brutal at worst, and always tragic. It compounds the trauma to the child, leaving a legacy of terror and pervasive insecurity from which most children never fully recover. That so many distraught parents even seriously entertain the thought of snatching their own children gives further evidence of the poverty of our current system and the desperate need for a custody revolution.

## Mediation

On their own, or with their lawyers' assistance, most couples are able to reach an agreement about custody without resorting to a battle. Fortunately, couples who can't agree have another option before taking their dispute to court; they can take their dispute to a *mediator*.

A custody mediator is a neutral person who attempts to help parents resolve their disputes in a cooperative and peaceful manner. The process of mediation emphasizes parents' own responsibility for making the decisions that affect their children. The mediator's job is to facilitate communication, keep the focus on present issues and not past grievances, and thereby prevent discussions from degenerating into a series of unproductive accusations, criticisms, and name-calling. As often as necessary, the mediator reminds parents of the benefits of an amicable resolution.

Most child-custody mediators act as advocates for the children. They keep the children's welfare at the center of the deliberations by educating parents about the psychological development of their children, by clarifying misconceptions about what children from divorced homes do and do not need, and by refusing to sanction any proposed agreements that would be destructive to the children.

The mediator does everything possible to help parents find a mutually acceptable solution to their dispute—a solution in which no one "loses." He or she may offer alternative plans that have not occurred to the parents, and even make recommendations. Because of the mediator's neutrality, his or her recommendations are more apt to be received nondefensively by parents.

Every time Lou and Glenda Nichols tried to discuss the issue of custody, they became embroiled in a heated argument that ended in threats to take each other to court. Glenda felt that Lou had a poorer understanding of their son's needs, and she objected to the various proposals Lou made regarding future living arrangements. Lou felt that Glenda's objections were merely her attempt to control him—just as he felt she had done in their marriage. Thus, he dismissed her arguments without giving them any careful consideration. He seemed to be operating on the principle that, if Glenda said it, it must be wrong.

Fortunately, their attorneys were less inclined to litigate custody disputes (attorneys vary in the extent to which they advocate peaceful resolutions versus knock-down, drag-out courtroom battles). The lawyers agreed that their clients should seek mediation.

The mediator began the first session with a monologue about the importance of keeping the focus on Michael, the couple's three-year-old son. Before either parent had a chance to voice beliefs and preferences, the mediator clearly established his neutrality. He would evaluate any and all proposals from the standpoint of Michael's needs, regardless of who offered the proposal.

Having been told by the lawyers that Lou wanted an arrangement in which Michael would shift residences every three months, the mediator included in his monologue several statements about a young child's inability to tolerate long separations from his parents. This gave him an advantage when Lou ultimately voiced his plan for sharing custody. Before Glenda could jump in with her usual objections, the mediator said that Michael was lucky that his father wanted to be so involved with him. This made Lou more receptive to what the mediator had to say next. The mediator referred back to his opening statements about a three-year-old child's sense of time and difficulty with long absences and challenged Lou to think of another schedule that would be more in tune with Michael's needs.

Had the mediator first allowed Glenda to voice her objections (which were substantially the same as his), and then agreed with her, this would have undermined his credibility with Lou. As it stood, Lou could back down from his proposal without losing face or feeling he was capitulating to Glenda. Ultimately, the mediator was able to make specific recommendations that helped this couple fashion an acceptable agreement that served Michael's needs well.

Despite a mediator's contributions, the power to make the final decisions is left in the hands of the parents. The mediator only assists; the parents decide.

Mediation spares parents the sense of impotence that comes from being coerced, under penalty of law, to abide by a decision handed down by a total stranger—a decision regarding their own access to their own children! It spares parents the infantilizing experience of pleading to a higher authority to intervene in their conflict, like fighting siblings running to their mother. It spares parents the indignity that comes from displaying their dirty linen in a public court hearing, and the escalation of hostility that is the invariable byproduct of this display.

Instead, successful mediation enhances the self-esteem of the participants. Parents emerge with renewed confidence in their ability to cooperate with each other in order best to meet their children's needs. And

# HOW TO SELECT A CUSTODY MEDIATOR

**1.** Although many attorneys now mediate or arbitrate divorce settlements, I recommend that disputes over the living arrangements of the children be referred to a professional with a background in child psychology. It is often helpful for the mediator to become acquainted with your children and evaluate their needs before you begin discussing alternative custody plans. Also, you may want the mediator to assist in monitoring your children's progress after you begin implementing your agreement. If the children are not doing well, the mediator with expertise in children's psychological problems will be able to help you determine what type of changes or interventions may be necessary.

**2.** It is preferable to consult with a mediator in private practice who is well established in your community. If your family develops a good relationship with the mediator, you may want to use his or her services in the future. It is frustrating to begin with a different professional each time an issue arises over which it might be beneficial to consult with a mediator.

**3.** Beware of credentials. People have advertised their services as divorce mediators with no more training than brief participation in a weekend course. They have had no supervised experience and often have a very limited background in child development. I believe the best custody mediators have experience in conducting psychological evaluations and psychotherapy. They can be psychologists, psychiatric social workers, or psychiatrists.

**4.** The mediator you select will have a crucial impact on the long-term psychological well-being of you and your family. This is not the time to rely on advertisements in the Yellow Pages or elsewhere. Ask someone you trust for a referral. It can be another parent who has used the services of a mediator, your child's pediatrician, or your attorney. Also, you may check with your local professional society of mediators. Be aware, though, that membership in such an organization may guarantee only a minimum level of training with few, if any, checks on competence.

| MEDIATION VERSUS LITIGATION | | |
| --- | --- | --- |
| | Mediation | Litigation |
| Allows parents to retain control over decisions affecting their children | YES | NO |
| Enhances parents' self-esteem and dignity | YES | NO |
| Promotes communication and cooperation between parents | YES | NO |
| Reduces hostility between parents | YES | NO |
| Increases both parents' commitment to the custody decision | YES | NO |
| Allows for "trial" living arrangements before making a final decision | YES | NO |
| Expands the range of options for custody and visitation | YES | NO |
| Allows for flexibility of living arrangements in response to changing needs of the family | YES | NO |
| Keeps personal and family matters private | YES | NO |
| Minimizes government interference in family life | YES | NO |
| Results in financial savings to parents and to the public | YES | NO |

self-respect grows when they resolve their difficult conflicts with humanity, dignity, and autonomy. Because the decision is their own, and not imposed by an outside authority, both parents are more apt to abide by their agreement. This should be viewed as a significant advantage of mediation over the current system, in which only a minority of divorced fathers comply with court-imposed child-support provisions.

An added attraction of mediation is that parents are spared the financial expense of a trial. Society, too, reaps the benefits of mediation: Overburdened court schedules are alleviated, thereby resulting in a significant savings in public funds. One expert estimates a savings of over $180 million per year if all custody cases were mediated. Finally, in an age when people all over the world are seeking to curtail government intrusion into their personal lives, mediation achieves a separation of family and state in an area where government intervention not only is unnecessary but actually impedes the family's adjustment to divorce.

By now it should be evident that I enthusiastically endorse mediation. Although research is still at an early stage, I am convinced that mediation benefits children. The children are exposed to less conflict between their parents, and the parents themselves escape the psychological problems caused by custody battles. I believe that mediation is so vastly superior to custody litigation that in coming years it will replace litigation as the primary means of resolving custody disputes.

Mediation is the wave of the future, and it is a major battlefront of the custody revolution.

## Consultation

When people decide to get a divorce, generally the first thing they think of is seeing a lawyer. I would like to suggest another step: Obtain the services of a custody consultant. A custody consultant is a mental-health professional with expertise in child development and custody matters. This specialist directs parents' attention to issues that are relevant in formulating an optimal custody plan. He or she assists parents in identifying reasonable alternatives and helps parents evaluate children's reactions to different plans. Even parents who work out their own custody agreement can benefit from having an experienced consultant review their proposed living arrangements. Not only are parents inexperienced in these matters, but their objectivity is apt to be compromised by the emotional turmoil of the marital separation. In the next section, you will meet the Coopers, a family who sought my services as a custody consultant. Their story illustrates how parents can be helped to reach judicious living arrangements for their children.

## WHEN TO DECIDE CUSTODY

Whether you agree on custody, mediate a dispute, or litigate, custody can be decided anytime from the moment you first decide to separate to the day your last child goes off to college. Your children will benefit, though, if an agreement about custody has been reached—however tentative—by the time the separation plans are announced to them. Children are anxious enough just learning about the impending separation. Not telling the children where they are going to live and when they are going to see each parent can only compound their distress.

### Postponing the Final Decision

The initial living arrangements do not necessarily have to be permanent. Indeed, parents may wish to defer their final decision until they have had the opportunity to live for a while with the proposed arrangements. They can then determine through experience, rather than guesswork, whether this plan suits their family. For example, many single parents admit that, if they had known how hard it was to raise children alone, they would have pursued joint custody with more vigor. When the initial custody plan is not satisfactory, a couple who are handling their decision in a nonadversarial manner have the luxury of trying alternative plans until they find the one that works best. This is another advantage of mediation. Such trial arrangements are virtually unheard of in our family courts.

Dale and Audrey Cooper and their three-and-a-half-year-old daughter, Laura, reaped the benefits of such flexibility. The Coopers consulted me because Laura was so unhappy each time her father said goodbye after his every-other Sunday visit; she would wander listlessly from room to room. Dale had begun to think that his visits were doing more harm than good. Although the thought of not seeing his daughter pained him, he wondered if he should forgo the visits for Laura's sake.

I met with Laura in my office playroom. She had large blue eyes and wispy blond hair framing a round face. Her parents had told her that I was a "worry doctor" who would try to help her with her sad feelings. Laura seemed to accept this, and when she met me she wasted no time with small talk but got right down to business, playing with a family of little plastic dolls. Over and over again, she enacted the same drama. The little girl's father took her shopping, and then they played hide-and-seek to-gether. When the father hid, the girl looked everywhere for him but couldn't find him. She looked in the bedroom, she looked in the bath-room, she looked in the kitchen. She looked in front of the house, behind the house, and on the roof. I asked Laura what was happening.

Laura said, "She can't find her daddy."

"Where did he go?" I asked.

"I don't know."

"Will he come back?"

"Maybe, in a long, long, long, long time."

Then, with a triumphant smile on her face, she quickly brought the daddy out from hiding and waved him in the air.

Clearly, Laura had re-created her inner turmoil in her play. She missed her daddy terribly and felt abandoned by him. After each visit, it was as though he had dropped off the face of the earth. Laura had never even seen his new home. His absences seemed interminably long, and she couldn't predict when he would return. We could now understand Laura's listless wandering after each visit. She was hoping to find her father in one of the rooms, and perhaps needed to convince herself that he was not really somewhere in the house. (An advantage of working with young children is that they usually do little to disguise the meaning of their play, thereby making it easier for the therapist to recognize their inner feelings.)

With this understanding, I advised the Coopers to shorten the time between visits. To a child Laura's age, a two-week absence seemed more like two months. Rather than bow out of Laura's life, Dale needed to become more involved. And Laura needed to see where he lived, so that she could be reassured that "out of sight" did not have to mean out of existence.

With my assistance, Dale and Audrey formulated a shared-custody plan in which Laura would spend every Monday and Tuesday with her father and every Wednesday, Thursday, and Friday with her mother. Weekends would be alternated between the two. Under this plan, Laura would never be apart from either parent for more than five days. When we evaluated the plan a month later, both parents agreed that things were better, but both had the same observation: Laura did better when she was with each parent for the longer period of time, and had difficulty adjusting to the shorter stays. Just as she got settled into one home, it seemed that it was time to move back to the other. Also, the frequent transfers were harder on the parents. We agreed to try alternating full weeks, though I was concerned that Laura might not tolerate well such a long absence from her mother. Next month, both parents reported that the arrangement had worked out much better, and they assured me that Laura showed no signs of distress about it. Dale and Audrey decided to incorporate this plan, along with open telephone access to each parent, in their final divorce agreement.

The Coopers tried three different plans before they settled on the one that suited them best. Had they left the decision to a judge, and suffered the hostility, polarization, and communications breakdown that accompany custody litigation, in all likelihood they would have been locked permanently into a custody disposition that was detrimental to Laura's welfare.

Postponing the final custody decision can assist couples who are working in a cooperative manner to determine the best among several alternatives. However, when cases are postponed in litigation, the delays occur for different reasons and usually do more harm than good.

If the judge has ordered a custody evaluation, the constraints of the psychologist's schedule may cause the evaluation to take a few months. Attorneys will use tactics to postpone litigation if they think it will assist their case. For example, the attorney representing the parent who has temporary custody usually believes that the judge is less likely to alter this situation the longer it goes on, so the attorney requests numerous postponements and drags his feet whenever possible. (Some dissatisfied parents have accused attorneys of prolonging their case in order to charge higher fees.)

Even when both sides are ready for the hearing, they must wait for an opening in the court schedule. This may not occur for many months, because of the backlog of cases. Be forewarned that it is not unusual for the resolution of a custody case to take from one to three years. In the meantime, of course, the emotional health of the entire family deteriorates in the "battlefield" atmosphere.

If you have to litigate, for your sake and your children's urge your attorney to move as quickly as possible. It is my hope that, as more couples choose mediation instead of litigation, the court backlog will be relieved. Then couples who have to resort to litigation will be able to have their cases resolved more expeditiously. In the meantime, judges need to realize that, no matter how wise a custody decision, if it is delivered after prolonged litigation, the children have suffered needlessly.

## Flexible Custody

Even when reached after careful consideration and experience with different plans, custody arrangements are often modified during the course of a child's life. Changes in the family and within the child can trigger such modifications. The arrangement that worked best when the parents were single may not be optimal when one or both remarry. What worked well when a child was four may not be so appropriate when she is ten—or fifteen.

After two years of alternating weeks with Laura, Dale and Audrey Cooper had some good reasons for revising their daughter's living arrangements. Dale had remarried, and about this time Audrey returned to graduate school. Laura got along well with her stepmother, and it made sense for her to begin spending more time in her father's home, particularly around Audrey's exam period. On the other hand, Laura spent more time with her mother in the summer and when Audrey was between semesters.

The most frequent reasons for shifts in custody are: the child's behavior becomes unmanageable or unacceptable (usually a boy in the custody of his mother); the child feels a strong urge to experience life with the other parent; a parent moves; a parent remarries; or any combination of the above.

No matter what their reason, parents often feel that something is drastically wrong if they change custody, that they have somehow "failed." They have the sense that in "normal" families (that is, normal *divorced* families) the same custody arrangements remain in place until the child leaves home for good. Since so little is written about changing custody, their attitude is understandable. Nevertheless, I believe the practice is so common that it deserves its own label. I call it "flexible custody." This denotes a living arrangement that is responsive to changing family needs and circumstances. Rather than look down on parents who change custody arrangements, I believe we should give these families our respect and support. The alternative is to stick rigidly to the original plan despite significant changes that make it no longer optimal. This is clearly a disservice to the children.

The need to shift custody may grow out of a normal psychological need whose gratification is thwarted by the very structure of traditional sole-custody arrangements. Growing up with both parents in the home, a child may shift the strength of his affections numerous times through the course of his life. The child loves and feels a strong bond with both parents. But during certain phases, the child may be closer to her mother; during other phases, she seeks out the company of her father more.

At times, this process is obvious to members and acquaintances of the family. They may say, "She's her father's daughter." Or "Lately his father can't do anything right." Other times, the process is so subtle that it is only years later, in retrospect, that the family becomes aware of the pattern that existed earlier. These fluctuations can even occur more rapidly in response to parents' shifting moods. For example, when one parent is preoccupied with personal worries or problems on the job, the other parent may be more readily available to the children.

Children growing up in the custody of one parent do not have this advantage. If they begin feeling a need to get closer to their noncustodial parent, the only way they may be able to do so is to move in with that parent. This is particularly true if the parents live far apart from each other.

As with the original decision, the custody shifts can come about through mutual agreement between the parents (with or without a consultant's or mediator's assistance) or through courtroom litigation. Naturally mediation is easier and faster, less expensive, and less traumatic for the entire family. Even when parents agree between themselves on a proposed change, I recommend they consult with a psychotherapist experienced in custody matters. This professional can help the family clarify the reasons for the change and assess the wisdom of the move.

A change of custody requires a major adjustment on the part of each parent and the child. It should not be decided impulsively or treated casually. It should not be regarded as an automatic solution to conflict between the custodial parent and child. A better course of action would be first to understand the reasons for the conflict. If the problems can be resolved without a change in custody, this may be preferable. In some cases, changing custody merely transfers the problems from one household to the other.

On the other hand, as we saw in our discussion of psychological minefields, sometimes what appears as conflict between a son and his mother may really be a sign of the boy's excessive closeness to his mother and his attempt to gain some psychological distance. In these cases, a shift to more active father involvement, whether in the form of father custody or joint custody, may be the most effective course of action. It is because of the complexity of the decision that I think it is important for a family to consult with a professional before modifying custody.

228

Parents who try to modify custody by returning to court should be aware that the custody battle could last until their child is legally an adult. The conflict exacerbated by litigation generally does not diminish when the judge's decision is handed down. Parents may seize any excuse to return to court and prolong the hostilities.

Children who are subjected to this type of ongoing litigation throughout most of their childhood can rarely escape being severely traumatized. A good portion of their lives is spent, not only in witnessing the most vicious sort of conflict between their parents, but in a constant state of uncertainty about where and with whom they are going to live. If you really care about your children, you will not do this to them. Instead, you will make every attempt to resolve your custody dispute in a timely fashion.

## THE BASIS FOR A GOOD CUSTODY DECISION

For the custody decision to have the best impact on children, it is not enough for it to be reached peaceably, by mutual agreement, and be well timed. It must also be chosen for the right reasons.

The best situation occurs when both parents, after careful consideration, work out a custom-tailored living arrangement that takes into account their own circumstances and abilities and their children's needs. If one parent retains sole custody, it should be because that parent is more capable of meeting the children's needs on a daily basis. As reasonable as it sounds, too many custody decisions ignore this principle.

Many divorcing couples are not even aware that a wide range of alternatives exists. Instead, the shadow of the motherhood mystique obscures all but the traditional option, in which the mother retains sole custody and the father visits with his children a few days each month. As we have seen, this arrangement often results in emotional hardship and dissatisfaction for the mother, father, and child. "Because everyone else does it" is not a good rationale for a custody decision—not, at least, if your goal is to maximize your child's chances of coping with your divorce.

Unfortunately, when couples do entertain alternatives to the motherhood mystique, they rarely rely on calm, objective, informed judgment about their children's psychological needs. Often they are caught up in an atmosphere that is endemic to couples breaking up—bruised egos, vengeful passions, overwhelming anxiety, and crippling depression. Under the sway of such powerful feelings, parents may seek custody, or give it up, for the wrong reasons.

Extracting a better financial settlement or avoiding child-support payments are not good reasons to seek custody. Forcing your spouse to remain in the marriage is not a good reason to seek custody. Punishing your spouse is not a good reason to seek custody. Nor are proving your worth to the world, alleviating your guilt, or relieving your loneliness.

Parents sometimes *relinquish* custody for the wrong reasons. Men who have been rejected by their wives might expect that their children, too, will no longer want them. In most cases, this is a big mistake. A depressed woman who feels inadequate as a mother might conclude, like Joanna Kramer in the film *Kramer vs. Kramer,* that her child would be better off without her. This is also a mistake. The solution to such problems is psychotherapy. Abandoning your child will only contribute further to your low self-esteem.

Some parents develop an irresistible desire to escape from family responsibilities. This is more likely to occur in people who had children at a young age. They may have the illusion that they can turn back the hands of time by walking out on their families. Women who believe that their identities have been stifled in suffocating marriages may be anxious to establish a substantial geographical distance between themselves and their ex-husbands. By casting off the roles of wife and full-time mother, they hope to flourish as individuals. Instead of the hoped-for sense of autonomy and relief, however, parents who act on this motive often experience an increase in shame, guilt, loneliness, and low self-esteem. As I indicated earlier, the family that is abandoned in this manner has a harder time coming to terms with the divorce. Any parent considering such a rash move should first try to clarify what it is he or she really wants. Some parents expect that a separate sense of identity will automatically accompany a physical separation. Psychotherapy can help them realize that true autonomy consists not of changing one's state, but of changing one's state of mind. They may then find that their psychological needs can be met without abandoning their children.

Parents are sometimes pressured by others to agree to a particular custody disposition. If you let yourself be thus influenced, the result may well be a decision not in your child's best interests. This is what happened to Cheryl Schwartz. When she told her mother of her plan to share custody equally with her former spouse, Cheryl's mother was horrified. She told Cheryl that she was shirking her responsibilities as a mother and abandoning her child. Feeling guilty about the divorce already, Cheryl eventually succumbed to her mother's criticism. She kept sole custody. Her former husband moved out of town a year later, and Cheryl was left with the burden of raising her daughter on her own. She couldn't be sure, but Cheryl thought her ex-husband probably would not have moved if he had been more involved with his child.

Pressure to make a certain custody decision can come from your spouse, relatives, friends, attorneys, and psychotherapists. It can even come from your children.

## Should We Ask the Children
## Where They Want to Live?

Parents often ask me, "How much input should our children have in the custody decision?" I believe children should be consulted to determine their thoughts and feelings about various proposed arrangements. Sometimes it is even better if they have an opportunity to try out different plans. Their reactions can then provide additional information for parents to consider before reaching a final decision.

In some cases, a child's wishes will have a strong influence on the final outcome. Generally, as mentioned earlier, the older the child, the more useful the parents find this information. However, it is not a good idea for parents (or the consultant, mediator, evaluator, or judge) to ask children which parent they prefer to live with. Even when children volunteer a preference, divorcing parents should make clear to them that the living arrangements will be decided by the parents or a judge—*never* by the children. The reason for this is that children often feel guilty for having a preference, even when they don't tell anyone about it. Absolving them of responsibility for the custody decision helps alleviate this guilt.

Here is a good rule of thumb to follow: *Don't let your child make decisions after the divorce that he would not have been allowed to make when you were married.* Children don't decide where the family lives when the parents are together; there is no reason why they should decide where they live when their parents are apart.

## The Primary-Caretaker Guideline:
## A Flawed Proposal

By serving as a ready-made answer to the question of what to do with the children after divorce, the motherhood mystique at least spared parents

# HOW TO TELL THE CHILDREN ABOUT YOUR CUSTODY DECISION

Once the custody decision is made, parents face the task of telling their children and preparing them for the changes. It is surprising how often parents fail to tell their children why they are divorcing or to explain the family's new living arrangements. When parents do not talk openly about such matters, the children are less likely to voice their own concerns. Instead, the children will develop a variety of fantasies to explain the divorce and the custody situation, none of which may correspond in the least with reality.

**1.** Parents should be together when they tell children about their impending separation. This offers the children a reassuring demonstration that the parents can continue to function cooperatively in meeting the needs of their children.

**2.** The new living arrangements should be carefully explained. Parents should tell children why they have decided on these particular living arrangements.

**3.** If, for any reason, the children are going to see little of one parent after the separation, it is imperative that they understand that this is no reflection of their own worth. For example, if a mother, seeking autonomy and escape from the demands of family life, moves far away from the children, she needs to explain that her decision reflects her own needs and is not a reaction to anything the children did. Unfortunately, this is a very difficult concept for children to grasp. Children who see little of the noncustodial parent invariably suffer a loss of self-esteem. Nevertheless, parents should try their best to explain that their absence is no reflection on the children. The children should then be encouraged to seek substitute relationships (by spending more time with friends, grandparents, aunts and uncles, etc.).

**4.** Children should be encouraged to talk about their reactions and feelings and to ask any questions on their minds. Children sometimes need to ask the same question repeatedly. Although this gets tedious for parents, they should understand that the questions are not intended to "bug" them. Rather, such questions are a sign that the children have still not fully understood or accepted the answers. Try to be patient with these questions and repeat your answers. When your children no longer need to ask questions, they will stop on their own. If you order them to stop asking questions, they will not stop thinking about the issues; they will merely exclude you from their inner thoughts.

**5.** Although it doesn't help for parents to "fall to pieces" when announcing the divorce, it is certainly expected that they will experience and communicate strong feelings. It does not hurt the children to see their parents cry. Breaking up *is* hard to do, and when parents are open about expressing their own sadness at the failure of the marriage, this gives children permission to acknowledge and communicate their own sadness. The more children communicate their feelings, the easier it is for parents to provide needed reassurance and guidance.

**6.** Be aware that your own attitude about the divorce may color the way you respond to your children's feelings. Generally, the parent who wants the divorce is inclined to emphasize the positive aspects for the children (e.g., less parental fighting, two birthday parties, more Christmas or Hanukkah presents). To assuage guilt, this parent may overlook or minimize the children's distress. The parent less in favor of the divorce does the opposite. This parent is ever on the lookout for children's stress reactions and uses them as evidence to oppose the divorce.

Parents should try to separate their own feelings from their children's. Children need their feelings recognized and validated as normal and understandable. If children feel that a parent does not want to hear anything negative about the divorce, the bad feelings will not go away. They merely go underground, where they do more damage and are less accessible to parents' reassurances. On the other hand, it does not help children to magnify the crisis and burden them with a rejected parent's own sense of hopelessness.

and judges the ordeal of making a difficult decision. Parents "knew" that children belonged with their mothers and that child-rearing was not a job for which men were particularly well suited. In the unusual situations in which a father wanted custody, the court's task was relatively simple: Determine whether the mother was grossly unfit. If she was, the father could have the children; if she was not, she kept the children.

With the collapse of the motherhood mystique so imminent, some experts propose to fill the vacuum with a new standard to guide custody decisions—a presumption in favor of "the primary caretaker." Under this guideline, custody would be awarded to whoever is designated the "primary" parent.

The wish for an easy formula to simplify custody decisions is understandable. Upon close examination, though, we find that this formula is not so easy to apply. What does it mean to be the primary parent, and how do we decide this? The usual answer—that it is the parent who devotes the most time to raising the child—rests on a false premise. It assumes that, the more time a person spends with a child, the greater that person's contribution is to the child's well-being and the more important that person is to the child. If this were true, it would mean that in some wealthy families custody should be given to the child's nanny!

I do not believe it makes any sense to equate the amount of time a person spends with a child with that person's importance in the child's life. Research indicates that we cannot even assume that, the more time a parent interacts with a child, the better their relationship will be. In fact, we all know of parents who are *too* involved with their children, so-called smothering parents, who squelch any signs of their child's independence.

If extent of contact is not the basis for distinguishing primary from secondary parents, what is? Is the primary caretaker the parent who does the most to foster the child's sense of security, the person to whom the child turns in time of stress—the role most often associated with mothers? Or is it the parent who does the most to promote the child's ability to meet the demands of the world outside the family and to make independent judgments—the role most often associated with fathers? We really have no basis for preferring one contribution over the other. Both are necessary for healthy psychological functioning.

We can say that both parents contribute *distinctively* to their child's welfare. And at different developmental stages a child may relate better to one parent than the other, or rely on one parent more than the other. But over the course of a child's life, both parents are important, and we have absolutely no grounds for labeling one parent "primary" and the other parent "secondary."

## Enlightened Custody

The challenge facing parents is to create a custody plan that accomplishes three objectives. First, it should suit the child's current age and be responsive to the future needs of the child. It should not automatically entrench one parent in the permanent role of sole custodian. Second, rather than ignore the different roles parents play, it must reflect and capitalize on these differences. And third, a good custody plan should maintain the child's meaningful involvement with *both* parents. Let us see how these guidelines can help parents plan wise living arrangements for their children.

In the first year of life, babies form strong attachments to both their parents. For their sense of security, though, they are more emotionally dependent on whoever takes care of their daily needs—feeding, changing diapers, bathing, putting to sleep, holding, soothing, etc. When these needs are met adequately, a foundation is laid for the development of trust in others and self-esteem. When these needs are not met in a satisfactory and consistent manner, there is a greater likelihood that the child will have difficulty relating well to others and feeling good about himself.

Because of this link between basic child care and psychological health, experts advise parents to maintain the continuity of basic care to which their babies are accustomed. If the mother has assumed major responsibility for nurturing her baby, which is the usual case in our society, she should continue to do so after the divorce. The father's relationship with his child is still important, and this should be maintained on a regular basis with frequent contact. In fact, if an infant or a toddler undergoes an extended separation from either parent, his or her relationship with that parent will suffer and the child will feel rejected or abandoned.

Unfortunately, some parents and judges do not understand the damaging impact of extended separations between parents and young children. I once received a call from a desperate mother who was seeking to modify her custody arrangement. The judge in her case thought he was being "progressive" when he awarded the parents joint custody of their eight-month-old son. The divorce decree specified that the child would alternate residences every three months. Because the father lived in another state, this meant that mother and son would be separated for three months twice each year. Until the divorce this child had been cared for by his mother. Recognizing the importance of maintaining consistency in the care of infants, I was concerned that the arrangement did not promote the best interests of the child. Under this custody plan, the boy would experience prolonged absences from *each* parent. In the long run, the father would regret having insisted on the arrangement. Research indicates that his son would be more likely to suffer psychological problems and would be a more difficult child to raise.

Note that I am not advocating an automatic preference for the mother. If the father has provided most of the early child care, then he certainly should maintain this role after the divorce. In families where the parents have more or less shared the basic care-giving, they should continue to do so after the divorce. What I am suggesting is that, contrary to tradition, the important consideration is not the sex of the parent but the continuity of the child's care and relationships.

Children of preschool age have different needs and capabilities, and custody arrangements should reflect these changes. The preschooler is no longer so dependent on the parent who provides the basic care, and he can tolerate longer absences from each parent. Divorced parents of preschoolers should therefore try to have the child spend significant blocks of time with each parent. Always, though, parents need to monitor their child's reactions to the living arrangements, and let their observations guide them in fine-tuning the plan.

Brock and Allie are sensitive to their daughter's needs and use her emotional well-being as the gauge by which they calibrate their custody plan. From the time of the separation, Sarah spent three days a week with one parent and four days with the other. "She was three at the time, and clearly not happy with the split," says her father. "She would be missing the other parent a great deal, but just when it seemed unbearable for her, she would get to see the one she was missing. I never tried to deny that she missed her mommy. I would comfort her, and say, 'Of course you miss Mommy, and you'll see her tomorrow,' and we would call Mommy on the phone if possible. The same thing seemed to go on at Allie's house. After a time, though, Sarah did seem to understand that she hadn't lost anyone, and she began to develop the trust that she *would* be with Mommy or Daddy in a few days at the most.

"Allie was always trying to suggest that Sarah not switch so often, that it would be better to spend a week with each parent. She seemed to feel that she developed more intimacy with Sarah over the longer period of time. I didn't have that experience, and also found it difficult professionally and socially to be the sole caretaker for a whole week at a time, since I didn't have the resources for babysitters that Allie did. Once, at Allie's insistence, we did try the week-to-week schedule, but Sarah didn't like it at all—she was just missing the other parent too much, and it turned out the parent missed her too much as well. As she gets older, however, I could imagine that this might change."

By elementary-school age, as we have seen, the average child in a sole-custody family adjusts better in the custody of the same-sex parent. Thus, if parents are not able to share custody, they should try to ensure that a boy spends much time with his father and a girl spends much time with her mother. Parents and courts should exercise caution before choosing a living arrangement that would keep a boy from meaningful involvement with his father or a girl from meaningful involvement with her mother. Even for children of this age, however, we cannot reduce the custody decision to a simple formula. Suppose the mother is an airline flight attendant whose work keeps her frequently out of town, and the father is a writer who works at home. Wouldn't it make more sense for their seven-year-old daughter to come home to her father rather than attend an after-school day-care center? Of course it would. But this type of thinking is foreign to a system enshrouded by the motherhood mystique, a system that believes all children belong in the sole custody of their mothers.

Throughout this book, I have stressed the importance of basing the custody decision on multiple factors. Certainly the sex of the child and of the parent need to be considered, but not to the exclusion of the child's age, personality, special needs, and relationship with each parent, as well as the personality, child-rearing practices, circumstances, and availability of each parent.

In families with children of widely differing ages, the task of formulating optimal living arrangements becomes even more complicated. When discussing flexible custody, I made the point that a child's needs change with the passing years and that these changes may necessitate adjustments in the living arrangements. The plan that works for a three-year-old boy may not be best for him when he is thirteen. By the same token, the plan that works best for a young child may not be the best plan for his older sibling.

Conventional custody dispositions keep all siblings together: They visit Dad as a group, and return to Mom as a group. As we have seen, this practice disregards the need of all children to have time alone with each parent, special time that fosters the individual bond between parent and child. It also ignores the reality that different-aged children respond differently to leaving their home base. Infants and toddlers do not do well with long separations from the parent who does most of the care-giving. Adolescents can tolerate long separations from their parents, but they usually connect strongly to their peer group and are less willing to spend entire weekends away from friends.

When every child in the family has the same living arrangements, the visit is apt to stress some more than others and may not be optimal for any of the children. Parents who take an enlightened approach to custody instead try to individualize their children's living arrangements. It is usually desirable to keep siblings together part of the time, while providing each child with opportunities to receive individual attention from each parent.

Take the case of a family with three children: four-year-old Callie, ten-year old Shaun, and fourteen-year-old Aaron. Aaron is very closely identified with his father. He shares his dad's interests in computers and fishing. He resents his mother's attempts to discredit the father and cannot accept his mother's new boyfriend as a member of the family. Aaron expresses a strong desire to live with his father.

Little Callie, by her father's own admission, is more closely bonded with her mother. Although she enjoys spending time with her father, she gets homesick for her mother after a few days' absence.

The middle child, Shaun, feels close ties with both parents and expresses a desire to live with both of them.

Both parents love their children and have much to offer all of them. The challenge for the parents was to create a residential plan that did the following: accommodated the changing developmental needs of each child, allowed each child to have time alone with each parent, allowed each parent to have time off from parenting, and satisfied the parents' desire to have significant input in their children's lives.

This family settled on the following plan. Aaron lived primarily with his father and spent every other week from Thursday afternoon to Monday morning with his mother. Shaun alternated weeks (from Thursday afternoon through the next Thursday morning) between his two homes. (Note that children who have liberal access to both parents think of themselves as having two homes rather than being a visitor in one.) Callie lived primarily with her mother and spent every other week from Thursday afternoon to Monday morning with her father.

This may sound complicated. Indeed, it took the family a while to get used to the schedule. One thing that helped the family keep track of it was a set of calendars that indicated where each child would spend every night. A copy of each calendar was posted on the refrigerator in both homes. The calendars that were most useful to the parents are reproduced below. If you study the calendars, you will see that this plan accomplished three of the four desired objectives.

It accommodated the different needs of each child. It gave each parent eight days off per month from full-time parenting. And both parents continued to have an active involvement in their children's lives. All this was accomplished without the children's making any more transitions between homes than children in standard sole-custody situations. Shaun's arrangement gave him an equal amount of time with each parent. Callie spent twice as many nights with her father (and Aaron twice as many nights with his mother) as do children with conventional every-other-weekend visits.

The one goal not met by this schedule is that it does not provide Shaun and Callie time alone with their father, or Shaun and Aaron time alone

## FATHER'S SCHEDULE

| Mon. | Tues. | Wed. | Thurs. | Fri. | Sat. | Sun. |
|---|---|---|---|---|---|---|
| Aaron | Aaron | Aaron | Aaron Shaun Callie | Aaron Shaun Callie | Aaron Shaun Callie | Aaron Shaun Callie |
| Aaron Shaun | Aaron Shaun | Aaron Shaun | | | | |
| Aaron | Aaron | Aaron | Aaron Shaun Callie | Aaron Shaun Callie | Aaron Shaun Callie | Aaron Shaun Callie |
| Aaron Shaun | Aaron Shaun | Aaron Shaun | | | | |

| MOTHER'S SCHEDULE | | | | | | |
|---|---|---|---|---|---|---|
| Mon. | Tues. | Wed. | Thurs. | Fri. | Sat. | Sun. |
| Shaun Callie | Shaun Callie | Shaun Callie | | | | |
| Callie | Callie | Callie | Aaron Shaun Callie | Aaron Shaun Callie | Aaron Shaun Callie | Aaron Shaun Callie |
| Shaun Callie | Shaun Callie | Shaun Callie | | | | |
| Callie | Callie | Callie | Aaron Shaun Callie | Aaron Shaun Callie | Aaron Shaun Callie | Aaron Shaun Callie |

with their mother. Instead of formally scheduling such times, the parents decided to arrange them on a flexible basis, with the intent of spending at least one day a month alone with each child. As things turned out, it was not difficult for the father to find time alone with Callie. Her older brothers spent a lot of time with friends on Saturday and Sunday and occasionally spent a weekend night at a friend's home. Aaron resisted scheduling time alone with his mother, which of course is not unusual for a fourteen-year-old. However, with brief shopping excursions, chauffeuring to various activities, and a later bedtime than his siblings, Aaron and his mother found time to be together. Both parents, however, had to make more of a deliberate effort to plan time alone with Shaun.

This family thought the advantages of their arrangement more than made up for the extra effort it took to keep track of and implement the schedule. The parents paid close attention to their children's emotional status and found that the children were adjusting well. The children thought it was neat that their parents went to such lengths to maintain contact with them, although Aaron didn't really want to spend so much time with his mother.

Custom-made residential plans, like custom-made suits, may eventually have to be altered. Two years later, this family's plan changed and became less complicated. Callie could now tolerate longer absences from her mother, so her schedule overlapped much more with Shaun's, but with slightly more time in her mother's care. Aaron was sixteen and very involved with his peer group and school activities. As in many families with teenagers, neither parent saw much of him, although he tended to sleep more nights in his father's home.

I present this account as an illustration of how one family solved the problem of accommodating the different needs of their children. Certainly there were some drawbacks—no custody plan is perfect—but by and large the plan worked well and suited both parents and children. I do not wish to suggest, however, that parents use this schedule as a model for their own living arrangements.

The lesson I *would* like parents to take from this discussion is the desirability of fashioning their own plans that take into account the particular needs of their own families. I am aware that custom-tailored plans are not an easy way to decide custody. But history has taught us that simple approaches to custody, based on the parent's sex alone, result in simple-minded decisions that sacrifice the well-being of divorced families. The triumph and legacy of the custody revolution will be, not the substitution of a new mystique for the old, but the removal of custody decisions from the realm of stereotypes and myths.

Judgment day for your family can come in court, in a mediator's office, or in your living room.

It can come when you first separate, when your divorce becomes official, or years later.

It can come with vengeance, violence, manipulation, or desperation. Or it can come with reason, compassion, and understanding.

It can come with shame or guilt or fury or despair or resignation or indifference. Or it can come with inner satisfaction, hope, and sometimes pride. You can count on its coming with trepidation; life's toughest decisions are made without certainty or guarantees.

It can come quickly, with little consideration given to alternatives. Or it can come with hours of deliberation and forethought. But it won't come easily.

It can be rigid and permanent, unyielding to changes in your family's needs, or it can be flexible and responsive, accommodating the currents of change as your children pass through life's stages.

. . .

When you divorce, there is no escaping judgment day. A custody decision must be made. How, when, and why it is made will all have lasting effects on your family. Grandparents, other relatives, and friends have a stake in the outcome. But, primarily, judgment day is for you and your children. Handling this decision with responsibility, wisdom, sanity, and sensitivity is the single most important thing you can do to help your children cope with the crisis of divorce.

## Epilogue

# WHAT SHALL WE DO WITH THE CHILD?

**E**very Thursday evening for the past year, I had met with the same group of teenage boys for therapy. And every Thursday evening, Paul read a comic book or *Mad* magazine while waiting for group to begin. Except this Thursday. When I entered my waiting room, I found Paul sitting without his usual props and looking troubled. And though he usually tried to avoid talking about "serious" things, this evening Paul began the discussion. He announced he had just learned that his parents were getting a divorce.

Paul's announcement provoked an immediate reaction from Ronny and Bruce, who were eager to share their own experiences and offer advice. Both were veterans of divorce: Ronny lived with his father, Bruce with his mother. I suggested that the group first give Paul a chance to explore his own feelings. After allowing time for this, I invited the others to contribute. The first thing both boys spoke about, their clear priority and paramount concern, was custody.

"Don't drift away from the parent you don't live with," counseled Ronny. "I don't live with my mother, and now, when I visit her, it's like she's more like a friend than a real mom. I don't know her so well." (Ronny subsequently moved in with his mother and was fortunately able to establish the deeper relationship with her that he sought.)

"It would have been better for me to live with my dad," Bruce said. "I haven't learned to discipline myself, 'cause I can con my mom. I get by with too much. You know, sometimes it's not easy being a free spirit."

Bruce had become aware that the lack of limits in his life had made it harder for him to cope with the demands of adolescence.

Several weeks later, Paul reported that his parents had worked out a joint-custody arrangement. He would alternate between homes every two months. Two months and one week later, the group heard Paul complain about his difficulties adjusting to the move from Dad's house to Mom's. Getting used to the change was taking longer than he'd anticipated.

From discussions such as these, the boys in my group learned two valuable lessons that every divorcing parent should grasp. First, there is no perfect custody disposition. Every arrangement has its advantages and disadvantages. Second, there is no universally optimal custody disposition. What suits one family may not be best for another.

The discussion among this group of teenagers showed more wisdom than the verbal exchange that took place one morning on a television talk show. The two guests were a female psychologist and the president of a fathers'-rights organization. The interviewer asked each guest what standard he or she thought should guide custody decisions. The psychologist argued that, since women are more involved in primary caretaking, they *deserved* custody. The fathers'-rights advocate agreed that our society assigns child-rearing responsibilities to mothers and therefore most fathers are less involved with their children. But, he added, when a man has been doing what he is supposed to according to society's prescriptions, it is not fair to penalize him for his reduced involvement with his children by denying him custody. Instead, we should reward him with joint custody. At this point, the interviewer turned to the psychologist and said, "He's got a good point there."

But he really did *not* have a good point. In fact, neither guest's reasoning made much sense. In my view, the interviewer missed a golden opportunity to point out to both guests that they were overlooking the most relevant consideration. Both were blinded by the same basic premise, an idea reminiscent of pre-nineteenth-century thinking about children: namely, that children are property to be "awarded" to the rightful owner. The point both guests missed is that the only proper basis for a custody decision is the needs of the child. Loving parents do not place their sense of entitlement above their wish to achieve the best possible circumstances for their children.

For the past seventy years, under the aegis of the motherhood mystique, we have assumed that sole mother custody is the best situation for children after their parents' divorce. I hope I have succeeded in demonstrating that this assumption is unwarranted and that we will all benefit from a fundamental change in the way custody decisions are made. Let me summarize the observations that lead to this conclusion and form the intellectual foundation of the custody revolution.

- The development of the preference for mother custody had nothing to do with the best interests of children. Rather, it was based on a stereotypic view of the nature of women, a view that emerged in response to economic pressures and was supported by unproven psychological theories.
- Research has established that fathers are just as important to their children's psychological development as mothers.
- The traditional sole-mother-custody disposition produces numerous problems for all members of the family, including a deterioration in parent-child relationships.
- Divorced men can rear and nurture their children competently and are equally capable of managing the responsibilities of custody.
- Research comparing children in father-custody homes and mother-custody homes shows no difference in the adjustment of the average child.
- On the average, children in the sole custody of the parent of the same sex cope better with divorce than children in the custody of the parent of the opposite sex.
- Children who maintain meaningful involvement with both parents have a distinct advantage in coping with divorce.
- One of the best predictors of good adjustment in children after divorce is low conflict between the parents. Reliance on joint custody and mediation of custody disputes can reduce postdivorce conflict.

These observations make it clear that we need a major overhaul in how we handle custody decisions. The current system—a preference for sole mother custody and a reliance on the adversary system to resolve disputes—is bankrupt. To replace it, we need to implement the following proposals:

- Stop discriminating against fathers in custody matters and against divorced mothers who want their ex-husbands involved in raising the children.
- Tailor custody to fit the circumstances and needs of each individual family rather than force every family into the same mold.

• As much as possible, maintain the child's meaningful involvement with both parents. Although not suitable for every family, the norm in our society should be for divorced parents to have some form of joint custody.

• Arrange for siblings to have time alone with each parent, rather than requiring all children in the family to conform to the same arrangements.

• Maximize the time a child spends with the parent of the same sex unless other factors militate against this.

• Keep living arrangements flexible and open-ended—rather than fixed for the life of the child—in order to accommodate changes in the family.

• Replace the adversary system with professional consultation and mediation as the primary means of resolving custody disputes.

As we enter the final lap of this century, I believe that the goals of the custody revolution are within reach. I see several encouraging signs. Divorced mothers, in growing numbers, are objecting to an unfair system that requires them to do the job of two parents while struggling to earn a living. This has always been too much to expect; but in the past, women kept their grievances private, unaware that their problems were shared by millions. Now that research has uncovered the widespread dissatisfaction with our current system, women feel freer to make their complaints public, and they are doing so.

Divorced fathers, too, are becoming increasingly vocal in rejecting their role as second-class citizens in the lives of their children. In a logical but delayed reaction to feminism's campaign against traditional sex-stereotyped division of roles, men are insisting that they are perfectly capable of raising their children. And they have the evidence to back them up.

I am encouraged that joint custody and mediation are capturing the attention of state legislatures and courts. Unfortunately, there is a nascent backlash against joint custody. It is my hope that books such as this will help to quiet the backlash: Joint custody is a good idea and should be given a fair chance to prove itself.

Ironically, the increase in custody litigation may also forecast the imminent success of the custody revolution. When mothers were virtually assured of winning custody, very few fathers gave any thought to bucking the system. We can assume that the increase in contested custody means that the motherhood mystique is losing its hold. The turmoil accompanying this increase in custody litigation can be likened to the social unrest that precedes a political revolution. Both are unstable situations that inevitably lead either to a return and strengthening of the old order or to the establishment of a new system.

The time is ripe for fundamental change. For the sake of our children, let us hope that this change moves us forward rather than backward, that we will not let eighteenth-century ideas guide twenty-first-century custody decisions. Too many children have suffered too much already. As I bring this book to a close, I am thinking about one such child, a young boy for whom the custody revolution is too late. His suffering epitomizes what is wrong with our current system of deciding custody and why we need a radical change in our beliefs and practices.

When I first met Dick, he was not what you would call warm and engaging. He kept his emotional distance and hid his deep sense of inadequacy behind a mask of belligerence and bravado. Dick was a victim of a particularly vicious custody battle. Like many children exposed to excessive parental conflict, he chose the toy soldiers in the playroom to enact his personal tragedy symbolically, and thereby help me understand it.

Dick placed a little soldier in the middle of a battlefield. Missiles and bombs were dropping everywhere around the soldier. There was no place to run for cover. Eventually the soldier was struck by mortar that split him right down the middle. "He is coming apart," Dick said.

After he lay in two pieces on the battlefield, someone finally noticed the soldier and took him to a hospital where, Dick told me, "They find a doctor who can weld him back together again."

These are not easy times for our children. Family life has deteriorated. A sense of community has all but disappeared from most neighborhoods. Stress has mushroomed. Relatives are spread far and wide, which reduces the opportunities for children to receive the additional nurturing that instills hope and compassion. Our schools no longer serve as a refuge from domestic turmoil, as they once did. In fact, the social and academic pressures of school often exacerbate children's inner turmoil.

Violence is more prevalent and more immediate, courtesy of television and videotapes. The old warning "Don't talk to strangers" has grown into an hours-long seminar in which young children are led to believe they are responsible for protecting themselves from sexual abuse. And the media let no one forget that unspeakable cruelties lurk around many corners. And then, of course, we all live under the threat of instant annihilation.

For our children, the intact family is the last bastion of familiarity, security, and solace. So we can forgive them their difficulty understanding and accepting the necessity for divorce. We can show them how to handle difficult times with wisdom, strength, and compassion. We can create a family structure that assures children that *they* have not been divorced, a structure that safeguards their birthright to *two* parents. And we can hope for society's support in this endeavor.

Perhaps then there will be fewer little soldiers in need of welding.

# APPENDIX

This book draws on numerous research studies conducted by social scientists throughout the country, concerning thousands of families. To provide an example of one type of intensive study, this appendix describes the basic design of the initial studies of the Texas Custody Research Project. It does not include a description of our subsequent studies of stepfamilies (in which eighty-one families participated), or a study of noncustodial mothers conducted under the supervision of John Santrock and me (in which sixty women participated).

Divorce researchers must decide which of two strategies to follow in designing a study.

One strategy is to survey a very large group of people, usually by mailing them questionnaires. This approach increases our confidence in the general applicability of the findings to a wide range of people. But it does not provide an in-depth portrait of the participants or allow us to observe and test the subjects directly in order to verify the accuracy of their responses to the questionnaire.

The second strategy is to focus on a smaller group of people who can be studied intensively and observed directly. The advantage of this approach is that we glean a much richer and deeper understanding of the functioning of these families. The drawback is that we must be more cautious in applying the results to other groups of people until independent studies support our conclusions. The latter strategy was followed by most of the studies cited in this book, with the exceptions noted in the text, and it is the strategy we followed in our Texas project. As mentioned earlier, our confidence in our conclusions has been buttressed by corroborating evidence from many independent research projects.

## SAMPLE

The subjects of our studies are sixty-four white, predominantly middle-class families in which the children range in age from six to eleven years. Half the children are boys and half are girls. Approximately one-third of the children come from families in which the father was awarded custody following divorce, one-third come from families in which the mother was awarded custody, and one-third live in parentally intact families with no history of marital separation. The three types of families were individually matched for age of the children, family size, and socioeconomic status. Socioeconomic status was determined by the Hollingshead Two-Factor Index of Social Position. The two custody groups also were matched for the child's sibling status and for the child's age at the time of the parents' separation.

Matching groups of subjects on different factors, such as family size, ensures that the groups are equivalent with respect to those factors. This allows us to rule out the possibility that the matching factor is responsible for any group differences we find. Take, for example, the factor of family size. If we study groups that are equivalent in family size, then a finding that single mothers have more trouble controlling their children than single fathers is definitely not related to the mothers' having more children to supervise. This leaves us free to explore other explanations.

A separation period of ten months, on the average, preceded the final decree. In matching our groups, we chose the child's age at the time of separation, rather than at the time of legal dissolution, because we believed the former age was the psychologically more significant event for children. The children's average age at separation was five years, and at the time of the study eight years and four months. Thus, an average of three years and four months had elapsed since the breakup of the marriage.

Because we were conducting an intensive study of each family, which required a large time commitment and much disclosure of personal information, our participants were volunteers recruited from the community. For most of the divorced fathers and mothers, custody was uncontested; ex-spouses relinquished custody because they either did not want custody or had no conscious preference. All families in which there was a history of remarriage or modification of custody were excluded from the studies, as were children who were previously identified as having an emotional or behavioral disorder.

# APPENDIX

## MEASURES AND PROCEDURES

A multimethod approach to studying child development was followed. Parents and children were videotaped interacting in the university laboratory, given a battery of personality tests, and interviewed separately. In addition, the children and their parents responded to projective-story tasks, and teachers reported their perceptions of the children on two different rating forms.

Each child was videotaped with his or her custodial parent, interacting in structured laboratory situations, and the videotapes were rated on dimensions such as (but not limited to) the child's maturity, warmth, independence, and self-esteem and the parent's use of authoritarian, permissive, and authoritative styles of interaction.

The videotaping of the family interaction was followed by a short break, and then the child was interviewed, using a structured interview schedule with open-ended and multiple-choice-format questions. The entire interview was audiotaped, and the first part of the interview, lasting ten minutes, was also videotaped.

Part one of the interview consisted of twenty-three highly structured questions that were specifically worded so as to avoid eliciting any cues about family structure that might influence subsequent raters of the videotape. Examples include: "What school do you go to?" and "What is your favorite TV show?"

Subsequent questions were designed to assess children's perceptions of parental roles (stereotyped versus nonstereotyped), their relationship with each parent, their feelings about separation from parents, their understanding of divorce, and predictions about their own future marital status. To control for order effects, questions about the mother were arranged in a separate block from questions about the father, and the order of administration of the blocks was counterbalanced within groups. In other words, half the children in each group answered questions about the mother first, and the other children were questioned about the father first. Supplemental questions for children from divorced homes addressed their perspectives on the divorce and its effect on the family, and their attitudes toward their parents' possible remarriage.

Children's behavior during the interview was rated on such dimensions as cooperativeness, anxiety, and self-esteem. Sex of the interviewer was counterbalanced within groups, so that half the girls and half the boys from each family structure were interviewed by men and half by women.

During the interview, all children were shown a series of seven illustrations and asked to create original stories in response to the pictures. These projective stories (see page 144) were rated in eight categories: (1) attribution of blame for the divorce, (2) belief in parental reconciliation, (3) wish for parental reconciliation, (4) feelings about the father's possible remarriage, (5) feelings about the mother's possible remarriage, (6) custody arrangements, (7) custody preferences, and (8) whether or not the child in the story was given a choice about custody.

Custodial parents were interviewed in their homes, using a structured interview schedule with open-ended and multiple-choice-format questions. They were asked about their child-rearing practices, their own and their children's social and emotional functioning, and their relationship with their children and their spouses (or ex-spouses). Supplemental questions for divorced parents addressed the reasons for the divorce and custody assignment, the children's acute reactions to the separation and longer-term adjustment since the divorce, the children's visits with the noncustodial parents, and the parents' adjustment to divorce including the use of support systems. All interviews were audiotaped.

The following personality tests and scales were administered to all children: Children's Nowicki-Strickland Internal-External Control Scale, Child's Personal Attributes Questionnaire, Child's Trait Stereotype Questionnaire, Dickstein Self-Esteem Scale, General Anxiety Scale for Children, Toy Preference Questionnaire, and Adaptive Behavior Inventory for Children. The last inventory seeks information from the parent about the child. The personality scales administered to parents were: Adjective Check List, Adult Nowicki-Strickland Internal-External Control Scale, Personal Attributes Questionnaire, Socialization scale of the California Psychological Inventory, and a projective task. In addition, each child's teacher completed forms that rated the child on many different dimensions.

We used state-of-the-art procedures for ensuring high reliability, validity, and independence of ratings. Also, to eliminate the possibility that rater bias might contaminate the results, wherever possible raters were kept naïve about the family structure of the children. Approximately seven contact hours were spent with each family, and another ten hours per family were devoted to scoring, rating, and analyzing the data.

Further information, details, and references regarding these studies can be obtained by writing to the author at: 16970 Dallas Parkway, Suite 202, Dallas, TX 75248.

# NOTES

## INTRODUCTION—CUSTODY CASUALTIES

PAGE

19    Ayn Rand, *Atlas Shrugged* (New York: Random House, 1957).

      Betty Friedan, *The Feminine Mystique* (New York: W. W. Norton, 1963).

22    Ann Snitow, "Motherhood: Reclaiming the Demon Texts," *Ms.: The World of Women*, vol. I, no. 6 (May–June 1991), pp. 34–37.

## CHAPTER 1—THE BIRTH OF THE MOTHERHOOD MYSTIQUE

28    Abigail Adams and William Blackstone quoted in Joan Kennedy Taylor, "Remember the Ladies," *Reason*, vol. 19, no. 1 (May 1987), p. 33.

31    *Freeland v. Freeland*, 92 Wash. 482, 483–84, 159 P. 698, 699 (1916).

      *Random v. Random*, 41 N.D. 163, 165, 170 N.W. 313, 314 (1918).

      *Hines v. Hines*, 192 Iowa 659, 572, 185 N.W. 91, 92 (1921).

      *Jenkins v. Jenkins*, 173 Wis. 592, 181 N.W. 826 (1921).

      *Tuter v. Tuter*, 120 S.W. 2d 203, 205 (Mo. App. 1938).

# CHAPTER 2—THE FATHER FACTOR

PAGE

35   Sigmund Freud, *An Outline of Psycho-Analysis*, ed. and trans. James Strachey, 1940 (New York: W. W. Norton, 1969, paperback), p. 45.

John Bowlby, *Maternal Care and Mental Health* (Geneva: World Health Organization, 1951).

36   Bowlby acknowledged: John Bowlby, *A Secure Base* (New York: Basic Books, 1988).

37   Michael Lamb wrote an influential article: Michael E. Lamb, "Fathers: Forgotten Contributors to Child Development," *Human Development*, vol. 18 (1975), pp. 245-62.

Some of the books about fathers are: Henry Biller and James Meredith, *Father Power* (New York: David McKay, 1974); Phyllis Bronstein and Carolyn Pape Cowen, eds., *Fatherhood Today* (New York: John Wiley & Sons, 1988); Michael E. Lamb, ed., *The Role of the Father in Child Development* (New York: John Wiley & Sons, 1976); Michael Lamb, ed., *Fatherhood and Family Policy* (Hillsdale, N.J.: Lawrence Erlbaum Associates, 1983); Ross Parke, *Fathers* (Cambridge, Mass.: Harvard University Press, 1981); Kyle Pruett, *The Nurturing Father* (New York: Warner Books, 1987).

Among the numerous studies on father-child attachment are: Michael Lamb, "The Role of the Father: An Overview," in Lamb, *Role of the Father*, pp. 1-63; Michael Lamb, "Father-Infant and Mother-Infant Interaction in the First Year of Life," *Child Development*, vol. 48 (1977), pp. 167-81.

Ross Parke and Douglas Sawin, "The Father's Role in Infancy: A Re-Evaluation," *Family Coordinator*, vol. 25 (1976), pp. 365-71.

38   Another series of studies: A. M. Frodi, M. E. Lamb, L. A. Leavitt, W. L. Donovan, C. Neff, and D. Sherry, "Fathers' and Mothers' Responses to the Faces and Cries of Normal and Premature Infants," *Developmental Psychology*, vol. 13 (1978), pp. 490-98. For further discussion of mens' child-care skills, see Parke, *Fathers*.

Bill Gale, "Men Who Love Babies," *Parade*, December 24, 1989, pp. 4-7.

Pruett, *Nurturing Father*, p. 30.

40   Henry Biller and Margery Salter, "Father Loss, Cognitive and Personality Functioning," in David R. Dietrich and Peter Shabad, eds., *The Problem of Loss in Mourning: Psychoanalytic Perspectives* (Madison, Conn.: International Universities Press, 1989), p. 347.

Frank A. Pedersen, Judy L. Rubinstein, and Leon J. Yarrow, "Infant Development in Father-absent Families," *Journal of Genetic Psychology*, vol. 135 (1979), pp. 51-61.

PAGE

40     Kathleen A. Clarke-Stewart, "And Daddy Makes Three: The Father's Impact on Mother and Young Child," *Child Development*, vol. 49 (1978), pp. 466–78.

41     Norma Radin, "The Role of the Father in Cognitive, Academic, and Intellectual Development," in Lamb, ed., *Role of the Father*, pp. 237–76.

       Robert W. Blanchard and Henry B. Biller, "Father Availability and Academic Performance Among Third-Grade Boys," *Developmental Psychology*, vol. 4 (1971), pp. 301–5.

42     Second-, third-, and fourth-grade girls: V. J. Crandall, R. Dewey, W. Katovsky, and A. Preston, "Parents' Attitudes and Behaviors, and Grade-School Children's Academic Achievements," *Journal of Genetic Psychology*, vol. 104 (1964), pp. 53–66.

       Outstanding female mathematicians: E. H. Plank and R. Plank, "Emotional Components in Arithmetic Learning as Seen Through Autobiographies," *The Psychoanalytic Study of the Child*, vol. 9 (1954), pp. 274–93.

       College women with strong analytical ability: J. Bieri, "Paternal Identification, Acceptability and Authority, and Within Sex-Differences in Cognitive Behavior," *Journal of Abnormal and Social Psychology*, vol. 60 (1960), pp. 76–79.

       Biller and Salter, "Father Loss," p. 351.

       Pedersen, Rubinstein, and Yarrow, "Infant Development."

       Milton Kotelchuck, "The Infant's Relationship to the Father: Experimental Evidence," in Lamb, ed., *Role of the Father*, pp. 329–44.

44     Biller and Salter, "Father Loss," p. 362.

45     Leonard Shengold, *Soul Murder* (New Haven: Yale University Press, 1989).

       Alice Miller, *Thou Shalt Not Be Aware: Society's Betrayal of the Child* (New York: Meridian, 1986).

       Judith Herman, *Father-Daughter Incest* (Cambridge, Mass.: Harvard University Press, 1981).

       Stephen Sondheim, *West Side Story* (New York: Random House, 1957), p. 114.

46     Richard Koestner, Carol Franz, and J. Weinberger, "The Family Origins of Empathic Concern: A 26-year Longitudinal Study," *Journal of Personality and Social Psychology*, vol. 58 (1990), pp. 709–17.

       Marion Radke-Yarrow quoted in Daniel Goleman, "Surprisingly, Fathers Are Key to Empathy in Kids," *Dallas Morning News*, July 14, 1990, p. 2C.

       John Santrock, "Father Absence, Perceived Maternal Behavior, and Moral Development in Boys," *Child Development*, vol. 43 (1975), pp. 455–69.

47     Martin Hoffman, "Father Absence and Conscience Development," *Developmental Psychology*, vol. 4 (1971), pp. 400–406.

       Another study: Martin Hoffman, "Identification and Conscience Development," *Child Development*, vol. 42, (1971), pp. 1071–82.

PAGE
47    Henry Biller, *Paternal Deprivation: Family, School, Sexuality and Society* (Lexington, Mass.: Lexington Books, 1974); Henry Biller and R. S. Solomon, *Child Maltreatment and Paternal Deprivation: A Manifesto for Research, Treatment and Prevention* (Lexington, Mass.: Lexington Books, 1986).

48    Excellent reviews of the research on father-son relationships and juvenile delinquency can be found in Henry Biller, "The Father and Personality Development: Paternal Deprivation and Sex-Role Development," and Esther B. Greif, "Fathers, Children, and Moral Development," both in Lamb, ed., *Role of the Father*, pp. 89–156, 219–36.

49    Michael Lewis and Marsha Weinraub, "The Father's Role in the Child's Social Network," in Lamb, ed., *Role of the Father*, pp. 173–78.

# CHAPTER 3—CONVENTIONAL CUSTODY

51    University of Virginia study: E. Mavis Hetherington, Martha Cox, and Roger Cox, "The Aftermath of Divorce," in J. H. Stevens, Jr., and Marilyn Matthews, eds., *Mother/Child, Father/Child Relationships* (Washington, D.C.: NAEYC, 1977), p. 174.

54    The California study quoted is Judith S. Wallerstein and Joan B. Kelly, *Surviving the Breakup* (New York: Basic Books, 1980), pp. 305–6.

55    "soul murder": I first saw this term in Leonard Shengold, *Soul Murder* (New Haven: Yale University Press, 1989).

60    E. Mavis Hetherington, "Effects of Father Absence on Personality Development in Adolescent Daughters," *Developmental Psychology*, vol. 7 (1972), pp. 313–26.

       Dr. Hetherington's follow-up study: E. Mavis Hetherington and Ross D. Parke, *Child Psychology: A Contemporary Viewpoint* (New York: McGraw-Hill, 1986).

       Ten years after their parents' separation: Judith S. Wallerstein and Sandra Blakeslee, *Second Chances* (New York: Ticknor and Fields, 1989).

61    Ethel S. Person, *Dreams of Love and Fateful Encounters* (New York: Penguin, 1989), p. 44.

       Wallerstein and Blakeslee, *Second Chances*, p. 70.

       Statistics indicate: H. Pope and C. W. Mueller, "The Intergenerational Transmission of Marital Instability: Comparisons by Race and Sex," *Journal of Social Issues*, vol. 32, no. 1 (1976), pp. 49–66.

62    Men who prior to the age of twelve suffered the death of their fathers: G. Jacobson and R. G. Ryder, "Parental Loss and Some Characteristics of the Early Marriage Relationship," *American Journal of Orthopsychiatry*, vol. 39 (1969), pp. 779–87.

PAGE

64    Several studies have demonstrated: A thorough review can be found in Robert E. Emery, "Interparental Conflict and the Children of Discord and Divorce," *Psychological Bulletin*, vol. 92 (1982), pp. 310–30. See also Kathleen A. Camara and Gary Resnick, "Interparental Conflict and Cooperation: Factors Moderating Children's Post-Divorce Adjustment," in E. Mavis Hetherington and Josephine D. Arasteh, eds., *Impact of Divorce, Single Parenting, and Stepparenting on Children* (Hillsdale, N.J.: Lawrence Erlbaum Associates, 1988).

65    For a good description of how to recognize depression in children of divorce, see Neil Kalter, *Growing Up with Divorce* (New York: Free Press, 1990; New York: Fawcett Columbine, 1991).

69    Kalter, *Growing Up with Divorce*, p. 14.

70    E. Mavis Hetherington, Martha Cox, and Roger Cox, "Long-Term Effects of Divorce and Remarriage on the Adjustment of Children," *Journal of the American Academy of Child Psychiatry*, vol. 24 (1985), pp. 518–30.

Nationwide study of 699 children: John Guidubaldi and Joseph D. Perry, "Divorce and Mental Health Sequelae for Children: A Two-Year Follow-up of a Nationwide Sample," *Journal of the American Academy of Child Psychiatry*, vol. 24 (1985), pp. 531–37.

74    The statistics on children who rarely see their fathers are found in Frank F. Furstenberg, S. Phillip Morgan, and Paul D. Allison, "Paternal Participation and Children's Well-Being After Marital Dissolution," *American Sociological Review*, vol. 52 (1987), pp. 695–701.

75    Wallerstein and Blakeslee, *Second Chances*, p. 7.

Hetherington, Cox, and Cox, "The Aftermath of Divorce," pp. 169–70.

76    The statistics on divorced fathers' contact with their children come from Nicholas Zill, "Behavior, Achievement, and Health Problems Among Children in Stepfamilies: Findings from a National Survey of Child Health," in Hetherington and Arasteh, eds., *Impact of Divorce*, p. 336. These figures do not differentiate the circumstances resulting in single-parent status. Thus, some of the single mothers may never have married. Families in which the father had died or it was not known whether he was living were, however, excluded from this analysis. A more recent study by the National Commission on Children found that one in five children in mother-custody homes had not seen his or her father in more than five years (reported in the *Dallas Morning News*, November 22, 1991, p. 1).

The statistics on phone contact, and on children's view of their fathers' homes as their own, come from Frank F. Furstenberg, Jr., "Child Care After Divorce and Remarriage," in Hetherington and Arasteh, eds., *Impact of Divorce*, pp. 251–52. This study also reported that close to half of all children living with single parents had not seen their other parents during the preceding twelve months.

77    "coming around the corner . . .": Bob St. John, "Home Holds Painful Memories for Divorced Father," *Dallas Morning News*, September 23, 1984, p. 37A.

PAGE

78 "... children belong with their families ...": James W. Sullivan, "A Father's View of Divorce," *Dallas Morning News*, November 12, 1985, p. 17A.

79 A recent study: Sanford H. Braver, Sharlene A. Wolchik, Irwin N. Sandler, B. S. Fogas, and D. Zventina, "Frequency of Visitation by Divorced Fathers: Differences in Reports by Fathers and Mothers," *American Journal of Orthopsychiychiatry*, vol. 61 (1991), pp. 448–54.

John W. Jacobs, "Involuntary Child Absence Syndrome: An Affliction of Divorcing Fathers," in John W. Jacobs, ed., *Divorce and Fatherhood: The Struggle for Parental Identity* (Washington, D.C.: American Psychiatric Press, 1986).

80 One cannot easily predict postdivorce parent-child relationships: Wallerstein and Kelly, *Surviving the Breakup.*

82 For research on authoritative parenting, see Diana Baumrind, "Current Patterns of Parental Authority," *Developmental Psychology Monographs*, vol. 4, no. 1, pt. 2 (1971), pp. 1–103; E. Mavis Hetherington, Martha Cox, and Roger Cox, "Effects of Divorce on Parents and Children," in Michael Lamb, ed., *Nontraditional Families* (Hillsdale, N.J.: Erlbaum, 1982); John W. Santrock and Richard A. Warshak, "Father Custody and Social Development in Boys and Girls," *Journal of Social Issues*, vol. 35, no. 4 (1979), pp. 112–35.

# CHAPTER 4—PIONEER FATHERS

87 The information in this chapter is distilled from over thirty research studies published in professional journals and books in addition to the author's own research studies. For a complete bibliography, write the author at: 16970 Dallas Parkway, Suite 202, Dallas, TX 75248.

91 "What is your real basic motive ...": Karen W. Bartz and Wayne C. Witcher, "When Fathers Get Custody," *Children Today*, September–October 1978, p. 35.

"I had to take out a loan . . .": Deborah Anna Leupnitz, *Child Custody* (Lexington, Mass.: D. C. Heath, 1982), p. 25.

95 "There's lots of times . . .": C. A. Richards and I. Goldenberg, "Fathers with Joint Physical Custody of Young Children," *American Journal of Family Therapy*, vol. 14 (1986), p. 157.

In one study: Leupnitz, *Child Custody*, p. 167.

96 "You asked me what it was like . . .": Leupnitz, *Child Custody*, p. 124.

"It is difficult to have a romantic dinner . . .": Geoffrey Greif quoted in Dennis Meredith, "Dad and the Kids," *Psychology Today*, June 1985, p. 67.

97 Nathaniel Branden, *Honoring the Self* (Los Angeles: Jeremy Tarcher, 1983).

PAGE

99    "I predicted at the outset . . .": Leupnitz, *Child Custody*, p. 99.

The quote from the father of two teenagers comes from Leupnitz, *Child Custody*, p. 102.

100   "It was not the case . . .": Leupnitz, *Child Custody*, p. 108.

"Technological innovations . . .": Leupnitz, *Child Custody*, p. 110.

102   Michael E. Lamb, "The Changing Roles of Fathers," in Michael E. Lamb, ed., *The Father's Role: Applied Perspectives* (New York: John Wiley & Sons, 1986), p. 11.

104   Custodial fathers are even more satisfied with custody: A. M. Ambert, "Differences in Children's Behavior Toward Custodial Mothers and Custodial Fathers," *Journal of Marriage and the Family*, vol. 44 (1982), pp. 73–86; J. M. Fricke, "Coping as Divorced Fathers and Mothers: A Nationwide Study of Sole, Joint, and Split Custody," unpublished master's thesis, University of Nebraska, 1982; Leupnitz, *Child Custody*.

"A high level of self-confidence . . .": Branden, *Honoring the Self*, p. 14.


# CHAPTER 5—MAVERICK MOTHERS


106   "the tragic equation": Patricia Paskowicz, *Absentee Mothers* (New York: Universe Books, 1982).

Ann Landers, "The Matter of Custody Is Personal," *Dallas Morning News*, October 13, 1988, p. 8C.

107   Maria Constantatos, "Non-custodial Versus Custodial Divorced Mothers: Antecedents and Consequences of Custody Choice," unpublished doctoral dissertation, University of Texas Health Science Center at Dallas, 1984. Other studies of noncustodial mothers include: Judith L. Fischer and Jane M. Cardea, "Mothers Living Apart from Their Children: A Study in Stress and Coping," *Alternative Lifestyles*, vol. 4 (1981), pp. 218–27; Judith L. Fischer and Jane M. Cardea, "Mother-Child Relationships of Mothers Living Apart from Their Children," *Alternative Lifestyles*, vol. 5 (1982), pp. 42–53; Geoffrey L. Greif and Mary S. Pabst, *Mothers Without Custody* (Lexington, Mass.: Lexington Books, 1988); M. Isenhart, "Divorced Women: A Comparison of Two Groups Who Have Retained or Relinquished Custody of Their Children," *Dissertation Abstracts International*, vol. 40 (1979), 5628-A (University Microfilms No. 8004334); F. O. Keller, "The Childless Mother: An Evaluation of Deviancy as a Concept in Contemporary Culture," *Dissertation Abstracts International*, vol. 36 (1975), B-6, 4164-B (University Microfilms No. 76-4541); Patricia Paskowicz, *Absentee Mothers*; D. L. Polson, "Runaway Wives: A Comparison of Marital Status, Feminism, and Self-Actualization," unpublished master's thesis, United States International University,

PAGE

San Diego, California, 1977; Anna Sklar, *Runaway Wives* (New York: Coward, McCann and Geoghegan, 1976); R. Todres, "Runaway Wives: An Increasing North American Phenomenon," *Family Coordinator*, vol. 27 (1978), pp. 17–21.

109     "I found motherhood an enormously oppressive task . . .": Rita Rooney, "When Dad Is Given Custody," *Parade*, February 24, 1980, p. 5.

110     "Noncustodial mothers are maligned . . .": Greif and Pabst, *Mothers Without Custody*, p. 149.

        Constantatos, "Non-custodial Versus Custodial Divorced Mothers," p. 128.

114     "There is a great yearning and emptiness . . .": Paskowicz, *Absentee Mothers*, p. 207.

        According to a nationwide survey: Greif and Pabst, *Mothers Without Custody*, p. 162.

116     Constantatos, "Non-custodial Versus Custodial Divorced Mothers," p. 129.

123     For more information about Mothers Without Custody, write to P.O. Box 27418, Houston, TX 77227-7418, and enclose three stamps.

# CHAPTER 6—FATHER CUSTODY VERSUS MOTHER CUSTODY

129     In Iowa and Missouri: Karen W. Bartz and Wayne C. Witcher, "When Fathers Get Custody," *Children Today*, September–October 1978, p. 35.

133     Nine scientific studies: (1) Kathleen A. Camara and Gary Resnick, "Interparental Conflict and Cooperation: Factors Moderating Children's Post-Divorce Adjustment," in E. Mavis Hetherington and Josephine D. Arasteh, eds., *Impact of Divorce, Single Parenting, and Stepparenting on Children* (Hillsdale, N.J.: Lawrence Erlbaum Associates, 1988), pp. 169–95; (2) Ian Gregory, "Anterospective Data Following Childhood Loss of a Parent: I. Delinquency and High School Dropout," *Archives of General Psychiatry*, vol. 13 (1965), pp. 99–109; (3) J. S. Lowenstein and E. J. Koopman, "A Comparison of Self-Esteem Between Boys Living with Single-Parent Mothers and Single-Parent Fathers," *Journal of Divorce*, vol. 2, no. 2 (1978), pp. 195–208; (4) Deborah Anna Leupnitz, *Child Custody* (Lexington, Mass.: D. C. Heath, 1982); (5) J. L. Peterson and Nicholas Zill, "Marital Disruption, Parent-Child Relationships, and Behavior Problems in Children," *Journal of Marriage and the Family*, vol. 48 (1986), pp. 295–307; (6) W. S. Rholes, T. L. Clark, and R. Morgan, "The Effects of Single Father Families on Personality Development," unpublished manuscript, Texas A&M University, College Station, Texas, 1982; (7) Rhona Rosen, "Children of Divorce: What They Feel About Access and Other Aspects of the Divorce Experience," *Journal of*

PAGE

*Clinical Child Psychology*, vol. 6, Summer (1977), pp. 24–27, and "Children of Divorce: An Evaluation of Two Common Assumptions," *Canadian Journal of Family Law*, vol. 2 (1979), pp. 403–15; (8) R. Schnayer and R. R. Orr, "A Comparison of Children Living in Single-Mother and Single-Father Families," *Journal of Divorce*, vol. 12, nos. 2/3 (1988/1989), pp. 171–84; (9) Richard A. Warshak and John W. Santrock, "Children of Divorce: Impact of Custody Disposition on Social Development," in E. J. Callahan and K. A. McCluskey, eds., *Life-Span Developmental Psychology* (New York: Academic Press, 1983), pp. 241–63.

# CHAPTER 7—THE GENDER CONNECTION

140    Roxanne Pulitzer with Kathleen Maxa, *The Prize Pulitzer* (New York: Ballantine Books, 1989), p. 208.

141    Four independent investigations: (1) Kathleen A. Camara and Gary Resnick, "Interparental Conflict and Cooperation: Factors Moderating Children's Post-Divorce Adjustment," in E. Mavis Hetherington and Josephine D. Arasteh, eds., *Impact of Divorce, Single Parenting, and Stepparenting on Children* (Hillsdale, N.J.: Lawrence Erlbaum Associates, 1988), pp. 169–95; (2) Ian Gregory, "Anterospective Data Following Childhood Loss of a Parent: I. Delinquency and High School Dropout," *Archives of General Psychiatry*, vol. 13 (1965), pp. 99–109; (3) J. L. Peterson and Nicholas Zill, "Marital Disruption, Parent-Child Relationships, and Behavior Problems in Children," *Journal of Marriage and the Family*, vol. 48 (1986), pp. 295–307; (4) W. S. Rholes, T. L. Clark, and R. Morgan, "The Effects of Single Father Families on Personality Development," unpublished manuscript, Texas A&M University, College Station, Texas, 1982.

Marla Beth Isaacs and Irene Raskow Levin, "Who's in My Family?: A Longitudinal Study of Drawings of Children of Divorce," *Journal of Divorce*, vol. 7, no. 4 (1984), pp. 1–21.

145    Camara and Resnick, "Interparental Conflict and Cooperation," p. 192.

Judith S. Wallerstein and Sandra Blakeslee, *Second Chances* (New York: Ticknor and Fields, 1989).

146    Survey of eleven thousand Minnesota high-school students: Gregory, "Anterospective Data."

Nationwide study: Peterson and Zill, "Marital Disruption."

Female college students raised by single fathers: Rholes, Clark, and Morgan, "Effects of Single Father Families."

147    Ross A. Thompson, "Fathers and the Child's 'Best Interests': Judicial Decision Making in Custody Disputes," in Michael E. Lamb, ed., *The Father's Role: Applied Perspectives* (New York: John Wiley & Sons, 1986), p. 88.

PAGE

147    The report from the National Academy of Sciences: Martha J. Zaslow, "Sex Differences in Children's Response to Parental Divorce: 2. Samples, Variables, Ages, and Sources," *American Journal of Orthopsychiatry*, vol. 59 (1989), pp. 118–41; quote from p. 136.


# CHAPTER 8—PSYCHOLOGICAL MINEFIELDS: COPING WITH THE GENDER CONNECTION


154    Robert S. Weiss, "Growing Up a Little Faster: The Experience of Growing Up in a Single-Parent Household," *Journal of Social Issues*, vol. 35, no. 4 (1979), pp. 97–111.

159    A psychiatrist reported: Richard A. Gardner, *The Psychotherapeutic Techniques of Richard A. Gardner* (Cresskill, N.J.: Creative Therapeutics, 1986), pp. 393–97.

162    Neil Kalter, "Long-Term Effects of Divorce on Children: A Developmental Vulnerability Model," *American Journal of Orthopsychiatry*, vol. 57 (1987), p. 595.

167    William H. Sack, "Gender Identity Conflict in Young Boys Following Divorce," *Journal of Divorce*, vol. 9, no. 1 (1985), pp. 47–59.

170    "I had to swallow hard . . .": Paul Levine, "Can a Man Raise a Child All by Himself?," *Parade*, April 1, 1990, p. 9.

       Seymour Fisher and Rhoda L. Fisher, *What We Really Know About Childrearing* (Northvale, N.J.: Jason Aronson, 1986), pp. 105–6.


# CHAPTER 9—JOINT CUSTODY: PANACEA OR PANDEMONIUM?


184    "I'm a better mother . . .": Susan Crain Bakos, "Separate-But-Equal Parenting," *American Way*, December 1981, p. 84.

189    Colorado study: Jessica Pearson and Nancy Thoennes, "Custody After Divorce: Demographic and Attitudinal Patterns," *American Journal of Orthopsychiatry*, vol. 60 (1990), pp. 233–49; quote from p. 242.

191    A prominent Dallas attorney agrees: Glenna Whitley, "One Dad, One Mom, Two Homes," *Dallas Morning News*, January 8, 1984, pp. 1F, 8F.

PAGE

192       Pearson and Thoennes, "Custody After Divorce," p. 238.

193       More cooperative in the first place: A California study of 149 divorced parents reached the same conclusion (W. S. Coysh, Janet R. Johnston, Jeanne M. Tschann, Judith S. Wallerstein, and Marsha Kline, "Parental Post-Divorce Adjustment in Joint and Sole Physical Custody Families," unpublished manuscript, Center for the Family in Transition, Corte Madera, California, 1988).

194       Susan Steinman, "The Experience of Children in a Joint Custody Arrangement: A Report of a Study," *American Journal of Orthopsychiatry*, vol. 51 (1981), pp. 403–14.

195       Four independent studies: (1) Marsha Kline, Jeanne M. Tschann, Janet R. Johnston, and Judith S. Wallerstein, "Children's Adjustment in Joint and Sole Physical Custody Families," *Developmental Psychology*, vol. 25 (1989), pp. 430–38; (2) Deborah Anna Leupnitz, *Child Custody* (Lexington, Mass.: D. C. Heath, 1982); (3) Pearson and Thoennes, "Custody After Divorce"; (4) Sharlene A. Wolchik, Sanford L. Braver, and Irwin N. Sandler, "Maternal Versus Joint Custody: Children's Postseparation Experiences and Adjustment," *Journal of Clinical Child Psychology*, vol. 14, no. 1 (1985), pp. 5–10.

196       Arizona study: Wolchik, Braver, and Sandler, "Maternal Versus Joint Custody," p. 8.

197       Joint-custody children were more satisfied: Leupnitz, *Child Custody*.

198       Children tell us loudly and clearly: See Rhona Rosen, "Children of Divorce: What They Feel About Access and Other Aspects of the Divorce Experience," *Journal of Clinical Child Psychology*, vol. 6, Summer (1977), pp. 24–27; Richard A. Warshak and John W. Santrock, "The Impact of Divorce in Father-Custody and Mother-Custody Homes: The Child's Perspective," in Lawrence A. Kurdek, ed., *Children and Divorce* (San Francisco: Jossey-Bass, 1983), pp. 29–46.

         The Colorado study: Pearson and Thoennes, "Custody After Divorce." Financial stress and sex of child were also linked to child adjustment.

202       "no clear evidence . . .": Janet R. Johnston, Marsha Kline, and Jeanne M. Tschann, "Ongoing Postdivorce Conflict: Effects on Children of Joint Custody and Frequent Access," *American Journal of Orthopsychiatry*, vol. 59 (1989), pp. 576–92.

205       Judith Martin, *Miss Manners' Guide to Rearing Perfect Children* (New York: Atheneum, 1984), p. 27.

# CHAPTER 10—JUDGMENT DAY

213       Persia Woolley, *The Custody Handbook* (New York: Summit Books, 1979).

# INDEX

# INDEX

# INDEX